SEXUAL EXPLOITATION OF PATIENTS BY HEALTH PROFESSIONALS

Sexual Medicine, Volume 4
HAROLD I. LIEF, M.D., SERIES EDITOR

VOLUMES IN THE SERIES

Lief and Hoch: **International Research in Sexology, 1984**
Selected Papers from the Fifth World Congress

Segraves and Haeberle: **Emerging Dimensions of Sexology, 1984**
Selected Papers from the Sixth World Congress

Burgess and Hartman: **Sexual Exploitation of Patients by Health Professionals, 1986**

Persky: **Psychoendocrinology of Human Sexual Behavior, 1986**

Ross: **Psychovenereology, 1986**

Pope and Bouhoutsos: **Sexual Intimacy between Therapists and Patients, 1986**

SEXUAL EXPLOITATION OF PATIENTS BY HEALTH PROFESSIONALS

Edited by
Ann W. Burgess, R.N., D.N.Sc., and
Carol R. Hartman, R.N., D.N.Sc.

FEB 2 5 1987

PRAEGER

New York
Westport, Connecticut
London

Library of Congress Cataloging-in-Publication Data

Sexual exploitation of patients by health professionals.
   (Sexual medicine; v. 4)
   Includes index.
   1. Medical personnel and patient. 2. Medical
personnel—Sexual behavior. 3. Sexually abused
patients. I. Burgess, Ann Wolbert. II. Hartman,
Carol R. III. Series. [DNLM: 1. Professional-Patient
Relations. 2. Sex Offenses. W1 SE99F v.4 / HQ 71 S5183]
R727.3.S473   1986   362.2   86-9318
ISBN 0-275-92171-9 (alk. paper)

Library of Congress Catalog Card Number 86-9318
ISBN: 0-275-92171-9

First published in 1986

Praeger Publishers, 521 Fifth Avenue, New York, NY 10175
A division of Greenwood Press, Inc.

Printed in the United States of America

The paper used in this book complies with the Permanent
Paper Standard issued by the National Information Standards
Organization (Z39.48-1984).

10   9   8   7   6   5   4   3   2   1

We dedicate this book to all victims who have suffered
sexual exploitation by health professionals.

Contents

Foreword by Harold I. Lief, M.D.   xiii

PART 1: INTRODUCTION TO THE PROBLEM   1

1   Roles of the Health Professional in Cases Involving
    Sexual Exploitation of Patients   5
    S. Michael Plaut and Barbara Hull Foster
        Intimacy and Exploitation in the Professional Setting   7
        Options for Redress   12
        The Processing of a Complaint   15
        Guidelines for the Health Professional   18
        Preventive and Long-Term Measures   20
        Notes   23

PART 2: THE PATIENT'S PERSPECTIVE   27

2   The Good Deed Undone   29
        The Molestation Disclosed   30
        Response to Disclosure   31
        The Molestation Reported   31
        Hospital Reaction   32
        Earlier Incidents   32
        The Charges Filed   33
        Pretrial Maneuvers   33
        The Trial   34
        The Aftermath   36

3   Trying to Forget   37
        The Victim's Account   37
        The Lawyer's Follow-Up Statements   40
        Epilogue   41

PART 3: THE CONSULTANT'S PERSPECTIVE   43

4   Observations on a Case of Patient Sexual Abuse   45
    Frederic E. Oder
        Background   45
        Treatment Issues   46
        Questions for the Profession   48

5   Sexual Malpractice Litigation   49
Daniel Burnstein
     Overview of Cases   49
     Interview, Investigation, Negotiation, and Trial   56
     Special Issues   58
     Notes   59

6   Sexual Abuse of Anesthetized Patients   61
Audrey W. Mertz
     Community Response   61
     Official Response   63
     Consequences to the Anesthesiologist   63
     Civil Suits   63
     Patient Response   64
     Aftermath   65
     Note   65

7   Gynecologist-Patient Sexual Abuse: I. A Medical Board's
View   66
Marylin Beck and Lori Long
     Case History   66
     Case Investigation   69
     Settlement Negotiations   71

8   Gynecologist-Patient Sexual Abuse: II. An Evaluation
of Victims   74
Ann Wolbert Burgess
     Patients' Backgrounds   74
     The Abusive Incident   75
     Decisions after the Incident   76
     Medical Board Decision and Community Response   79
     Patients' Reactions   79
     Observations   82
     References   83

9   The Rape Crisis Center View   84
B. Joyce Dale
     The Victims   85
     The Victimizations   86
     Victim Reactions during the Assault   87
     Victim Reactions Immediately Following the Assault   88
     Long-Term Impact of the Assault   89
     Response of the Criminal Justice System   90
     Response of Helping Professionals   90
     Official Response of the Medical Community   91

10   Workshops on Patient-Therapist Sexual Relationships   93
Marjorie Braude
    Defining the Problem   93
    Dealing with the Problem   94
    Questionnaire Responses   94
    Note   96

PART 4: THE SOCIAL CONTEXT   97

11   When the Pediatrician Is a Pedophile   99
Carolyn Moore Newberger and Eli H. Newberger
    Whose Interests Are Served? The Case of the
    Pediatrician Pedophile   100
    A Moral Analysis of the Case of Dr. Smith   102
    Toward Responsibility in the Case of Dr. Smith   105
    References   106

12   Sexual Exploitation by Health Professionals in Cartoons
of a Popular Magazine   107
*Judith A. Reisman, Deborah F. Reisman, and
Barry S. Elman*
    Background   107
    Methods   108
    Results   109
    Discussion   117
    References   118

13   Institutional Resistance to Self-Study: A Case Report   120
Nanette K. Gartrell, Silvia Olarte, and Judith L. Herman
    Phase One: June 1982–March 1983   120
    Phase Two: May 1983–May 1984   123
    Phase Three: June 1984–December 1984   125
    Conclusions   127
    Notes   127

PART 5: TREATMENT ISSUES   129

14   Post-Traumatic Stress Disorder and Child Molestation   133
Calvin J. Frederick
    The Post-Traumatic Stress Disorder Classification   133
    Psychological Assessment   134
    The Perpetrators   136
    Criteria for Post-Traumatic Stress Disorder   137
    Signs of Child Molestation   138
    Diagnostic Dilemmas   139
    Treatment Recommendations   139
    References   141

15   Sexualized Therapy: Causes and Consequences   143
Roberta J. Apfel and Bennett Simon
        Causes of Patient-Therapist Sexual Contact   143
        Consequences of Therapist-Patient Sexual Contact   146
        Consultation and Evaluation   148
        Notes   150

16   A Walk-In Counseling Center Approach to Therapist
Sexual Misconduct   152
Gary R. Schoener and Jeanette Hofstee Milgrom
        Initial Meeting with Victims   152
        Therapeutic Responses to Victims   153
        Mediation through a Processing Session   154
        The Aftermath   155
        Secondary Victims   156
        The Therapist as Offender   157
        Victim Advocacy Resources   158
        References   158
        Appendix A: Selected Items from the Supervisor/
        Counselor Volunteer Application of the Walk-In
        Counseling Center   159
        Appendix B: Checklist of Administrative Safeguards   161

17   Time-Limited Treatment Groups for Patients Sexually
Exploited by Psychotherapists   163
Ellen Thompson Luepker and Carol Retsch-Bogart
        Intake Interviews   164
        Presenting Problems at Intake   165
        Goals at Intake   165
        Observations of Therapists' Roles at Intake   166
        Group Themes   166
        Outcome   171
        Disposition at Termination   171
        Conclusions   172
        Notes   172

18   Open-Ended Group Therapy for Victims of Therapist
Sexual Misconduct   173
Phyllis A. Kaufman and Elizabeth Harrison
        Group Description   173
        Group Goals   174
        Group Issues   175
        The Group Process   175
        Impacting Events   177
        References   177

19   Dynamics of Treatment Groups for Victims of Therapist
      Sexual Misconduct   178
      Debra S. Borys, C. Buf Meyer, Roberta L. Falke, and
      Janet L. Sonne
           Impact of Patient Problem Areas on Group Sessions   179
           Benefits and Limitations of the Group Approach   181
           Countertransference   182
           Conclusions   184
           References   184

Index   185

List of Contributors   191

Foreword

Explicit sexual contact between health professional and patient is frequent. It is difficult to obtain accurate estimates of its occurrence because of the clandestine nature of these encounters, the obvious reluctance of the involved professional to admit his or her unethical behavior, and the victim's shame-induced need to deny or hide participation. Despite the hindrances to accuracy, a general consensus of surveys is that 5–10 percent of health professionals, primarily, but not exclusively, physicians and mental health professionals, have engaged in what Burgess and Hartman call "sexual exploitation." Acts of sexual exploitation are generally repeated with multiple patients, hence the overwhelming and frightening recognition that many thousands of patients are exploited sexually every year.

Yet, relatively speaking, only a handful of complaints are made annually. One of the major contributions of this book is to describe, through detailed case histories, the anguish of victims and their families (often multiplied if they take action against their professional oppressors), the inertia (and often actual cover-up) of the medical-health community in helping victims seek redress, and the enormous obstacles to fair judgments and decisions created by an adversarial legal system and the bureaucratic quicksand of hospital, professional society, and state review boards.

Despite the psychic trauma involved, courageous patients, mostly women, persist in bringing complaints against offending professionals, and their case histories are set forth here. Some of these are very painful to read, painful and shocking; yet they are illuminating. Several cases of pediatrician pedophiles exploiting boys and girls in their care, combining sexual exploitation with child sexual abuse, will anger and disturb many readers, perhaps even more so than gynecologists who pervert the pelvic examination. It is ironic that one licensing board tried to solve this kind of problem by mandating that an offending gynecologist confine his practice to anesthesiology, when one of the most horrendous cases in this book describes an anesthesiologist who would arrange to have his unconscious female patients passively fellate him. In that instance, a few courageous nurses fighting the active resistance of physicians forced the hospital over a two year period to disclose the facts.

Lest the reader think this book is only a collection of cases, let me correct that misperception. Burgess and Hartman, leading experts themselves, have gathered together contributors who speak to the multiple issues involved. A general review of the subject in the opening chapter is succeeded by chapters on the patient's perspective, the consultant's (medical and legal) perspective, the effects of sexual abuse on the victims, and the special vantage points of the rape crisis center and other treatment and counseling approaches. A number of group methods of treating patients, some of whom could be suffering from post-traumatic stress disorder, are also described.

The subject is so vast and important that it should occasion no surprise that this monograph is the second one dealing with sexual abuse and exploitation of patients and clients in our series on Sexual Medicine. It should find a responsive audience among health professionals and concerned patients.

Harold I. Lief, M.D.

PART 1

Introduction to the Problem

This book is about health professionals who sexually exploit their patients. Although several books address the topic of sexual assault, this book examines situations that many people find difficult to believe—situations in which professional roles are used to gain sexual access to victims.

Sexual victimizations in which one person exerts force over another person—legally defined as rape—have been well documented in crime statistics and national surveys as well as in studies of rapist motivational intent and of victim trauma response. Rape research has aided in refuting the myth that women enjoy rape, has increased our understanding of human sexuality, and has provided argument against examinations of victims in sex offense cases.

However, sexual victimizations characterized by one person exerting sexual dominance over a person of unequal power status have been less adequately addressed. The clinical literature on the subject deals primarily with family member sexual assault (incest) and the child sex industry (child sexual abuse); both these situations involve child-adult sexual activity—behavior proscribed by federal and state statutes. Sexual situations in which an adult in an authority position uses sex to take advantage of another person with less power may be termed sexual exploitation. The victim is used primarily for individual gratification, profit, or other selfish reasons.

Such sexual exploitation is the focus of this book. Data from patients who disclosed sexual misconduct by a health professional, most frequently a physician or psychotherapist, are examined. Although the term "sexual misconduct" often triggers debate over the precise type of sexual activity, in this book it is used specifically to denote a health professional's intention to misuse the clinical setting for sexual contact.

Although there is a professed stringent ethical code among health professionals against sexual encounters with patients, it is acknowledged by health practitioners that these sexual encounters are increasing in number. Social awareness of this practice is also increasing. In criminal cases, stronger distinctions are being made among characteristics of sexual exploitation; these characteristics range from charges of rape to indecent assault and battery. For example, on the basis of these distinctions several cases were adjudicated in Massachusetts in 1984–85.

Recognition of the problem of sexual exploitation by health professionals has brought certain results. In Minnesota, the 1984 state legislature mandated the forming of the Task Force on Sexual Exploitation by Counselors and Therapists. Approximately 60 health professionals and lay citizens worked directly on the project, and testimony about the problem was provided by 40 people at a public hearing covered extensively in the news media. The task force determined that sexual exploitation of patients was a widespread problem among counseling professionals, and recommendations were made to address the problem. These included (1) a statewide plan for educating mental health professionals who work with the problem, (2) a plan for educating the public on the problem of sexual exploitation of clients, and (3) proposals for changes in criminal, civil, and administrative law.

Safeguards against sexual involvement with patients is generally built into the training programs of health practitioners. For example, in most mental health programs students are taught that sexual feelings can and do develop in people seeking psychological help as well as in professionals treating the patients. Psychoanalytically based theories are taught to help explain this reality, and supervision of trainees is designed to reduce acting-out impulses toward patients.

Why, then, do some health practitioners sexually exploit patients? Several explanations for such behavior have been articulated. At one extreme is the rationalization that therapy is enhanced through the sexual encounter. Another explanation suggests that the intensity of the intimate therapeutic relationship has strong potential to mislead the participants. A third suggestion is that critical periods or events in the life of the health professional may predispose the individual to initiating a sexual relationship.

Although these reasons may seem plausible and possible, research has not shown them to be factors in the patterns of sexual exploitation. The accounts in this book, derived from information from victims, may indeed represent the more deviant and traumatizing patterns of sexual exploitation by professionals. Nevertheless, they strongly suggest that the cause of the sexual exploitation rests heavily within the character of the abusing professional. In our experience, transgressions are not associated primarily with young, inexperienced health professionals. Instead, older, experienced health practitioners who often have had sexual contact with more than one patient are implicated. In addition, sexual exploitation occurs under a variety of conditions that convincingly point to the disturbance of the professional. Sexual contact has been reported as taking place during physical and dental examinations and even while patients were under anesthesia. Young as well as old patients of varying physical comeliness have been exploited, which contradicts the presumption that patient attractiveness is responsible for seductions and sexual advances. The offender pattern is remarkably similar to that of identified sex offenders. Methods of controlling victims, manners of self-defense when confronted, and the pursuit of further exploitation resemble behaviors of convicted sex offenders.

Nevertheless, society frequently has responded to sexually exploiting health professionals by suggesting that the exploitation is transient and reasonably explainable. Rather than addressing the offense, recommendations for dealing with the problem often focus on career change options for the offender. Some health professions, emphasizing compassion, minimize and confuse issues as well as justify acts of exploitation. They blame the victim and accuse colleagues of hysteria and purient sexual interests. There is a lack of clarity among professionals within the mental health field as to how to identify sexually abusive colleagues. In addition, the privacy of professional practices seldom allows for public scrutiny, thus placing a heavy burden of proof on the victim. Victims recount that their attempts to bring professionals, in particular mental health professionals, to trial for exploitive behavior were often as upsetting as the abuse itself.

The main objective of this book is to present information, written by patients and professionals, about the sexual exploitation of patients. We believe it imperative to increase awareness that sex between patient and health professional is a fundamental betrayal of the sanctioned role of the provider. Second, this book presents case material that highlights the complex strategies used by determined sexual offenders within their professions. These strategies are designed for physical and psychological control and manipulation of victims. A third objective is to provide information regarding therapeutic efforts on behalf of sexually abused patients. Finally, the book highlights professional and legal responses to the problem as well as how these responses are molded by social conditions. Underscoring these objectives is our observation that sexual exploitation by health professionals is nested in a complex relationship with social systems. Although these social systems establish rules that say the exploitation is taboo, they confuse the issue by supporting this very exploitation through their anticipation of its possible occurance and their minimization of its negative impact.

We begin with an overview of the problem of patient sexual exploitation by health practitioners. In Chapter 1, S. Michael Plaut and Barbara Hull Foster examine the extent of the problem, the determination of standards in the professional setting, and the formal mechanisms for case resolution. In their discussion of the resolution of one case, they illustrate how health professionals were involved at various stages of the case investigation. Finally, individual and institutional guidelines for addressing and preventing patient sexual exploitation are proposed.

Roles of the Health Professional in Cases Involving Sexual Exploitation of Patients

S. Michael Plaut and Barbara Hull Foster

The sexual involvement of health professionals with patients and clients has become an area of increasing concern over the past 15 years. Cases reaching courts of appeals have involved members of a number of professions, including medicine [2, 22, 25, 39], psychology [7, 11, 27], chiropractic [33], dentistry [28], and optometry [6]. A report issued by the American Association of State Psychology Boards (January 23, 1985) disclosed that six of ten suspensions or revocations reported by state boards were related to sexual misconduct. Of the 314 ethical complaints considered by the American Psychological Association in 1981 and 1982, 17 percent were related to allegations of "sexual intimacy, dual relationships, exploitation, or sexual harassment" [14]. The same percentage of recent malpractice claims against psychiatrists was related to charges of "undue familiarity" [16]. Some years earlier, the malpractice policy covering psychologists ceased coverage of "licentious, immoral or sexual behaviors intended to lead to or culminating in any sexual act" [38], although there have been recent efforts to provide some level of coverage against such allegations. The American Psychiatric Association has been struggling with the issue of whether dropping such insurance coverage would act as a deterrent or whether it would represent a lack of concern for the victims of sexual misconduct [16].

Concern with this problem has resulted in several surveys and studies that have reported data elicited from either practitioners [3, 5, 17, 20, 29] or patients [4]. In addition, thoughtful discussions of the issue have dealt with the therapeutic impact and ethical implications of sexual involvement with patients in psychotherapy [8, 12, 18, 24, 38, 42].

The primary reason for the sensitivity of this issue has been described by Dahlberg [8]. "The sex act in our culture," he wrote, "is the prototype of the intimate relationship. Like it or not, the act carries that significance; and for that reason the exploitation involved . . . strikes deeper into the core of human personality and therefore is more potentially damaging to the persons involved.''

Despite the gravity of the issue, there has been some reluctance to discuss or investigate sexual misconduct in depth because it is considered clearly unethical, too controversial, and too sensitive out of fear that open discussion will damage the reputation of the profession [8, 20, 26, 38]. Other factors may contribute to the lack of open discussion. First, there is the well-established tendency for most people to consider themselves to be more ethical than their professional colleagues [26]—an assumption that may lead to feelings that a serious ethical concern is someone else's problem. Related to this is the stereotype of male practitioners exploiting female clients. Although this has been true in the majority of cases [3], there are indications that the number of complaints against women practitioners is rapidly increasing, possibly because patients who have been involved in homosexual relationships with female therapists are becoming less reluctant to admit to such relationships [40].

Many professionals may not have given serious thought to connections between their personal values regarding therapeutic relationships and the values espoused by their respective professions. Licensure of professionals involves the granting of certain privileges, by the state, in return for adherence to standards of practice and ethical behavior as determined by the profession. This concept is well stated in the *Ethical Principles of Psychologists*, which points out that "psychologists' moral and ethical standards are a personal matter . . . except as these may compromise the fulfillment of their professional responsibilities, or reduce the public trust in psychology or psychologists" [1].

Finally, patients may be reluctant to disclose sexual involvement with health professionals for several reasons: they may feel guilty for initiating sexual activity, for responding to a sexual overture, or for allowing a sexual situation to continue. Patients may also wish to protect the health professional from a harsh penalty.

The nature of the therapeutic relationship between professional and patient necessitates a certain level of trust, intimacy, and vulnerability, which may at times be awkward and confusing for practitioner and patient alike. It is not unusual for a health professional to feel sexually attracted to a patient. Such feelings need not be of concern if they are acknowledged and if the practitioner continues to relate to the patient in a professional manner. However, when a practitioner yields to the tendency to exploit such a relationship, both the welfare of the patient and the level of trust in the profession are threatened.

The fact that exploitation does occur means that other professionals must become involved in its prevention or resolution, either informally as peers or more formally as supervisors, consultants, or representatives of the profession sitting in judgment of colleagues. It is important, therefore, that health practitioners acknowledge that the problem exists, confront their feelings about the issue, maintain an awareness of relevant community and professional standards of behavior, and assume some level of responsibility for dealing with the issue in a fair and constructive manner [37, 38].

The remainder of this chapter explores what determines standards of sexual behavior in the professional setting and describes formal mechanisms through which cases of alleged sexual exploitation may be resolved, illustrating the various roles that health professionals may play in such cases. It also provides general guidelines for dealing with the issue of sexual involvement and suggests preventive approaches to the problem.

INTIMACY AND EXPLOITATION IN THE PROFESSIONAL SETTING

Several factors come into play in cases of sexual exploitation of patients by health professionals. These factors are presented in Figure 1.1 and will be discussed in greater detail throughout the remainder of this chapter.

The Professional Context

Sexual intimacy between professional and patient carries somewhat different implications in psychotherapeutic and nonpsychotherapeutic settings. The psychotherapeutic relationship puts both therapist and patient at perhaps the greatest level of vulnerability because of the frequently long-term nature of such relationships and the great degree of emotional dependence of the patient on the therapist. At times, sexual contact is initiated by a therapist as a form of therapeutic intervention. However, both the value of such interventions and the ability of the patient to provide informed consent are questionable and controversial [8, 32]. Cases involving sexual intimacy without therapeutic intent have included therapists responding to advances of patients [38] and therapists initiating sexual encounters [13]. Some cases have not involved actual physical contact, but have been based on other forms of sexually exploitive behavior, such as nude swimming parties at the home of a therapist [21] or the description of sexual acts, unrelated to the patients' medical complaints, to patients who were presumably under hypnosis [31].

Serious cases involving practitioners in nonpsychotherapeutic settings have been based on instances of sexual misconduct in the context of patient examination or treatment. Examples include excessive genital manipulation during gynecological examinations [4], breast examination of an adolescent girl by an optometrist [6], inappropriate use of a vibrator by a chiropractor

FIGURE 1.1. Aspects of Patient Sexual Exploitation by Health Professionals

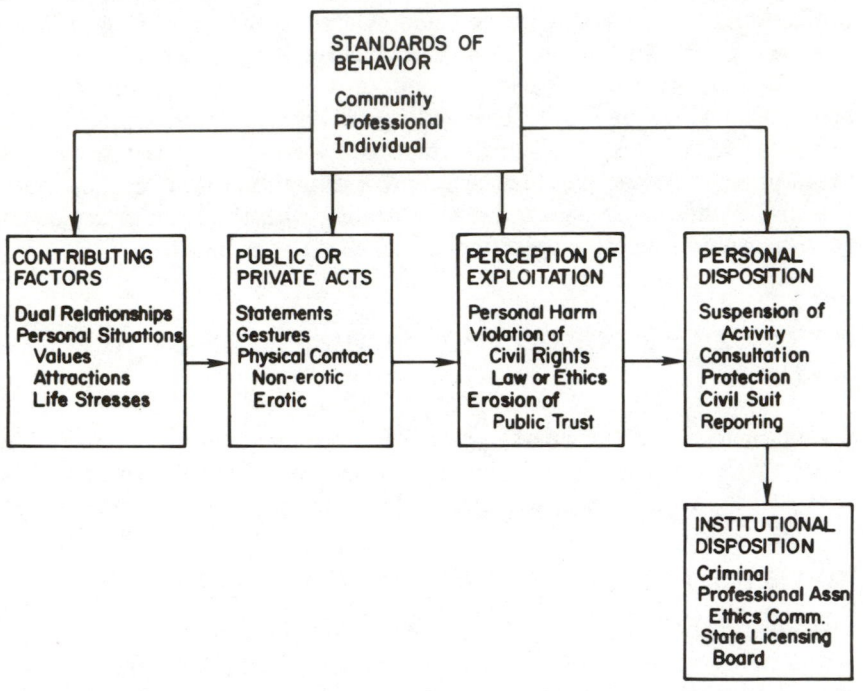

Source: Compiled by the authors.

[33], sexual intercourse by a physician with an anesthetized adolescent girl [22], and fondling of an anesthetized dental patient [28].

Occasionally a professional and a patient may become romantically involved outside the practice setting. However, such relationships are viewed with caution, even when the professional relationship between the two individuals has been ended and the patient has been appropriately referred [8, 12].

Levels of Intimacy

It is useful to consider intimacy in a professional relationship as a graded phenomenon (Figure 1.2). The order of steps along the continuum in Figure 1.2 is not absolute; some individuals may not consider erotic behavior to be the most intimate aspect of a relationship. The three curves in the upper portion of the figure represent the idea that certain types of professional

FIGURE 1.2.   Intimacy Continuum

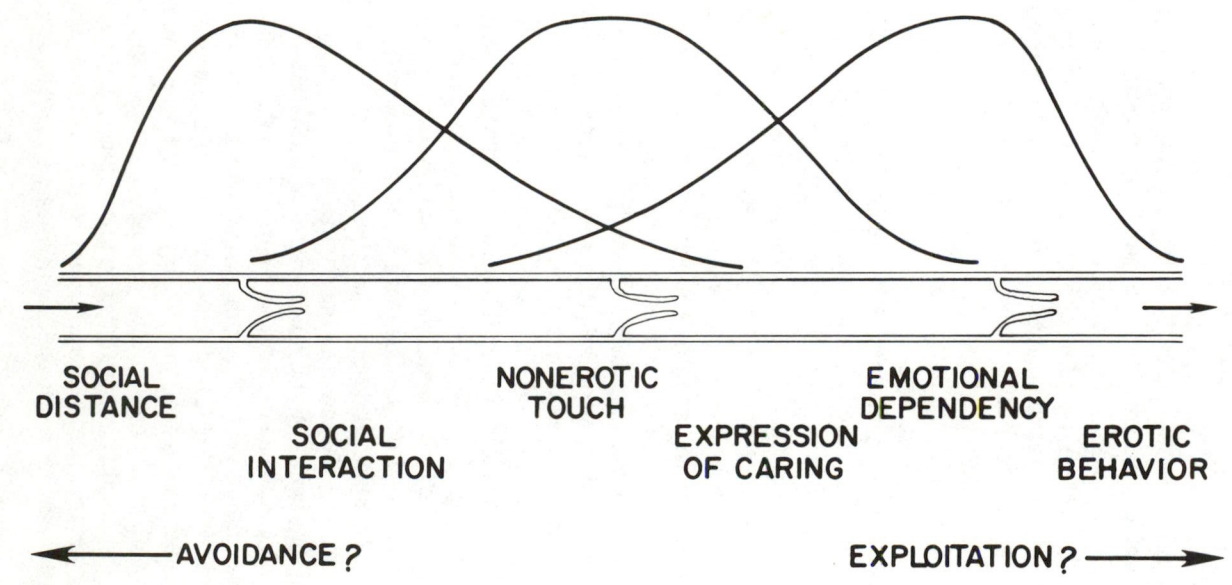

SOCIAL
DISTANCE

SOCIAL
INTERACTION

NONEROTIC
TOUCH

EXPRESSION
OF CARING

EMOTIONAL
DEPENDENCY

EROTIC
BEHAVIOR

←――AVOIDANCE ?

EXPLOITATION ?――→

Source: Compiled by the authors.

relationships may function most effectively at various levels of intimacy. The horizontal tube with its unidirectional valves represents the notion that intimate relationships may, for a given individual, reach a point of no return. Certain aspects of intimate relationships in the professional setting are discussed below.

Intimacy vs. sex. As mentioned earlier, a definition of sexual exploitation need not assume physical contact between professional and patient; actions have been taken against professionals who have encouraged patients to become personally involved with them in various ways. This may include social interaction, travel, domestic employment, or even promises of marriage [12, 21]. A judge in one case cited the inappropriateness of "conduct which confuses the patient as to the therapist's motives and thus undermines the therapeutically necessary feeling of trust in the therapist" [12].

Irreversibility. "Sexual acting out," wrote Dahlberg [8], "cannot be reversed. Once done, it remains a fact between the participants." Even less intense forms of intimacy may result in a feeling of inevitability, depending on the individuals involved. In a survey of psychologists treating patients who had been sexually involved with previous therapists, Bouhoutsos et al. [3] found that 10 percent of the relationships began casually, with "one thing leading to another." After studying sex-related attitudes and behaviors of 460 male physicians, Kardener et al. [19] concluded that the freer a physician is with nonerotic contact with patients (hugging, kissing, affectionate touching), the more likely he would be to engage in erotic practices with them. However, a subsequent study of female physicians did not find such a relationship, even though a greater proportion of 164 female physicians actually engaged in nonerotic contact [29].

Vulnerabilities. Surveys and case studies have strongly suggested that instances of sexual exploitation tend to occur when the practitioner is likely to be experiencing a life crisis [3, 5, 8]. Such a crisis, coupled with the opportunity provided by the clinical setting, may increase the probability that a sexual encounter will occur. Dahlberg [8] studied sexual exploitation involving psychotherapists and noted that therapists often find themselves in the position of being attractive to their patients.

Varying Standards. Studies of general attitudes regarding sexual involvement have yielded a spectrum of feeling and opinion. For example, in a study of psychologists representing various schools of psychotherapy, Holroyd and Brodsky [17] found that 25 percent of humanistically oriented therapists frequently engaged in nonerotic contact with patients, whereas only 5 percent of psychodynamically oriented therapists did so. However, these groups did not differ in extent of erotic contact. This same study also reported that a higher percentage of male (30 percent) than female (12 percent) therapists felt that erotic contact might be beneficial to the treatment of their patients. As mentioned earlier, other studies have reported differences between male and female physicians in attitudes toward physical contact in the clinical setting [19, 29].

Legal and Ethical Standards

Codes of ethics of various professions as well as licensing laws governing specific professions vary in their definitions of sexual misconduct and exploitation. For example, some licensing statutes have proscriptions against "immoral behavior" or "unprofessional conduct," which leave sexual exploitation open to interpretation [11, 31, 34]. In other instances, prohibitions are more specifically defined. The 1979 revision of the *Ethical Principles of Psychologists* added the statement that "sexual intimacies with clients are unethical" [1, 14], and a similar statement appears in the ethical code of the American Psychiatric Association [16]. The psychologists' code of ethics defines sexual harassment in terms of its perception by the individual [1]. This code also cautions against acts that "reduce the public trust" in the profession or that "violate or diminish the legal and civil rights of clients."

The majority of published discussions of sexual misconduct appear in the psychiatric or psychological literature and emphasis tends to be on the impact of sexual interactions on the therapeutic relationship. Such sexual relationships are often considered to be incestuous because of both the extent of the intimacy between therapist and patient and the unequal power relationship between them [24, 38]. Taylor and Wagner [38] conclude that it is "simply not fair" when a therapist turns the therapeutic relationship into a sexual one. Kardener [18] makes a similar point with regard to physicians in general. "The physician," he writes, "as a source of healing, support, and succor, becomes lost to his patient when he changes roles and becomes a lover."

An especially controversial area of discussion involves the use of sexual intimacy as a therapeutic intervention in a psychotherapeutic setting. Many question the therapeutic benefit of such activity [8, 15, 21, 38], yet Riskin [32] says there is insufficient information for drawing this conclusion. However, many authors have stated that a patient cannot give properly informed consent and that the dangers of sexual interactions are substantial [21, 38]. In one case [21], a court ruled that the "relationship between psychiatrist and patient is analogous to the guardian-ward relationship" and that "the guardian cannot claim that a ward is capable of consenting." Some authors [15, 38] have proposed a personal test of one's motivations for utilizing sex as a therapeutic intervention. It is suggested that therapists consider whether they would be willing to provide the same service for the older, obese, or unattractive client who may have the same need for such services as young, attractive patients of the therapist's own sexual orientation.

Community and Social Standards

As one might expect, opinions in the community regarding sexual misconduct by health professionals also vary. One district court of appeals in Florida [33] reviewed a case involving a male chiropractor who, while treating a patient for a back condition, used a vibrator in the patient's pubic area causing her to have orgasm. He then undressed, straddled the patient's legs, and manipulated himself to orgasm. The court held that the original penalty of license revocation was "unreasonable and excessive, in view of [the] chiropractor's 22 years of unblemished service to his profession and patients, affidavits attesting to his good moral character, and other mitigating circumstances . . . ." In the great majority of cases, however, the courts have upheld licensure revocations for sexual offenses, considering that professional boards were best able to set reasonable standards for and to impose appropriate penalties on their colleagues [6, 7, 11].

Although the number of alleged offenses that result in complaints is unknown, it is clear that the increased willingness of patients to make complaints is in part a result of increasing support from fellow victims, spouses, subsequent therapists, and community support groups. In addition, patients have become less reluctant to admit that they became sexually involved with a health professional in whom they had placed their trust [4, 14, 40].

OPTIONS FOR REDRESS

A patient who feels sexually exploited may choose from several avenues for formally resolving the issue. Each serves a different purpose, and effectiveness may vary with the nature of the offense, the jurisdiction in which the offense occurred, the profession of the alleged offender, and the preferences of the patient (these issues have also been discussed by Stone [37]).

Civil Lawsuit

The course of action that usually comes to mind first is civil action, which provides a mechanism through which a complainant can be directly compensated for the actions of a health professional. The patient can sue for breach of contract and/or malpractice and may recover damages for the cost of treatment, subsequent costs of healing, and/or "pain and suffering." These suits, generally between the complainant and the malpractice insurance company of the accused professional, are frequently settled out of court. Stone [37] has pointed out that suits involving sexual misconduct are more likely to be successful when sexual activity has occurred in a therapeutic context than when they are based on sexual affairs outside the practice setting.

Criminal Action

In some jurisdictions, a professional accused of sexual misconduct may be charged with either statutory rape or assault and battery [37, 41], with a conviction possibly resulting in a fine or imprisonment. A conviction also could have implications for the professional's licensure status, again depending on the laws of a particular jurisdiction. Both civil and criminal action are appropriate avenues for redress when the professional involved is not licensed and is practicing under "exemption" provisions of state licensing laws (e.g., nonlicensed marriage and family counselors or sex therapists).

Employer Action

An employer may be in a position to take action against a professional employee [10], especially if the employing institution has its own system of judicial review, as do many universities. This course of action may be especially appropriate when the individual is not licensed. However, if possession of a license is a condition of employment, action against an individual by a state licensing board may result in automatic termination of employment.

Professional Association Review

Most professionals belong to national or state associations, which may provide such benefits as preferred malpractice insurance rates, life or disability insurance, or specialty certification. In cases where a professional is not licensed, membership in a professional association may be an alternative to licensure, depending on state law. Such societies typically have codes of ethics as well as ethics or professional standards review committees, whose adverse judgments can result in suspension or termination of membership.

The value of such an action depends on the value of association membership to the individual concerned. In addition, the investigatory potential of ethics committees is limited by their lack of subpoena power and by their vulnerability to civil action if they do not grant an accused member appropriate due process rights. Ethics committees frequently refer a case to a licensing board, taking action against an individual if and when an adverse decision is handed down by the board.

State Licensing Board Review

If a health professional accused of sexual misconduct is licensed to practice in a given state, the state licensing board can consider taking action under one or more provisions of the licensing statute. Licensure actions have a number of potential advantages over the options outlined above:

1. Such action may be the most powerful from the point of view of the licensee and of the patient, as an adverse decision can either limit or prevent professional practice, thereby protecting other patients against further instances of professional misconduct.
2. License revocations resulting from allegations of sexual misconduct have typically held up in appeals courts, which respect the ability of each profession to set appropriate limits on professional behavior [6, 7, 11].
3. Although statutes of limitations may affect the ability of a patient to bring either a civil or criminal case after a protracted length of time [9], licensure statutes rarely include such limitations. This is especially important in cases of sexual misconduct, as it is not unusual for patients to wait some length of time before bringing charges. Bouhoutsos et al. [3], in a study of sexual involvement between patients and psychologists, found that 14 percent of the patients who took formal action waited three years or more before doing so.
4. In certain cases, action by a licensing board could result in a financial settlement in addition to or in lieu of action against a license, thus eliminating the need for civil action.
5. A licensure action is likely to be much easier for the patient than a procedure involving courtroom appearances, as board procedures are typically less formal, involve less public exposure, and can more easily preserve the patient's confidentiality.
6. An adverse decision by a licensing board can result in further action through one of the redress options described earlier. Action against a licensee can improve chances for success in a civil case and/or pave the way for further action by an employer, a professional association, or another jurisdiction in which the individual may hold a license.

Despite these advantages, there is substantial variability among jurisdictions in how licensing boards operate. They may differ, for example, in the extent and specificity of legal proscriptions against sexual exploitation, the extent to which due process rights are provided, and the nature of actions taken against offenders. In addition, in most jurisdictions a complainant does not have the right to appeal a case dismissed by a licensing board. However, suggestions have been made for improving case handling procedures [35].

THE PROCESSING OF A COMPLAINT

The following case provides a model of procedures followed in the disposition of a sexual complaint and illustrates the roles played by the various health professionals involved. Figure 1.3 illustrates the steps involved in a licensing board case in Maryland (numbers in the text correspond to steps in the figure). The report is based on a case considered by the Maryland State Board of Examiners of Psychologists. Neither dates nor identities are disclosed in order to preserve confidentiality.

Dr. X——, a former clergyman, in his early fifties, had a private practice as a licensed psychologist and was also employed by a mental health clinic. He was married and well regarded as a clinician by his patients and his colleagues.

Six complaints alleging sexual misconduct by Dr. X—— were received by the state board of examiners. Three were from former patients of Dr. X——, and three came from health professionals serving as subsequent therapists of these patients. The patients were women, ranging in age from 18 to 35, who had been patients of the doctor either in his private practice or

FIGURE 1.3. The Processing of a Complaint by a State Licensing Board

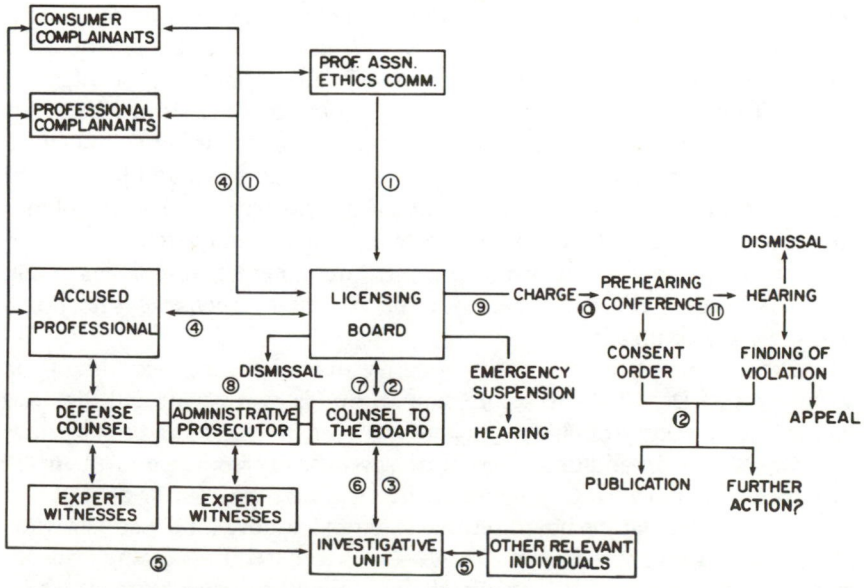

Source: Compiled by the authors.

in the clinic. Complaints had also been brought to the American Psychological Association and the Maryland Psychological Association, both of which informed the state board of the complaints and of their intent to await board action before taking independent action. The matter was also brought to the attention of Dr. X——'s supervisor in the clinic, also a health professional, who declined to consider action against Dr. X—— until the board had considered the case.

As required by the board, the complaints were submitted in writing and included a release of relevant patient records (step 1). The complaints were referred to the Board's counsel (step 2). After determining that the board had jurisdiction, counsel referred the complaints to the investigative unit of the state's department of health and mental hygiene for investigation (step 3). Dr. X—— and the complainants were informed that the case was being investigated and were asked to provide their cooperation (step 4).

The complainants alleged a variety of inappropriate behaviors. These included verbal remarks reflective of Dr. X——'s sexual interest, fondling of breasts and genitals, sexual intercourse, inappropriate disclosure of personal information to a patient, violation of a patient's confidentiality, referral by the doctor of a patient from the clinic practice to his own private practice, and a suicide attempt by one of the patients that was apparently linked to the sexual advances of the psychologist.

Field interviews were conducted with individuals connected with the case (step 5), including Dr. X——, the patients, the professional complainants, and Dr. X——'s clinic supervisor. Appropriate records were subpoenaed by the board. The board decided that Dr. X—— should undergo a psychological evaluation; Dr. X—— agreed, and chose a board-appointed psychologist.

Reflecting a pattern of behavior not uncommon in cases of alleged sexual exploitation, one of the patients attempted to withdraw her complaint. In doing so, she cited the success of her therapy, her personal and professional regard for the therapist, and her concern with the excessive level of punishment likely to result. Her change of heart may have been related to a series of calls from Dr. X——, in which he prevailed upon her not to pursue the matter. The board's chairman met with the patient to encourage her not to withdraw the complaint.

Other issues of concern during the investigation were the continuing unwillingness of Dr. X—— to secure counsel on his own behalf and the initial lack of cooperation from his physician-employer, who appeared to be protecting Dr. X——. In addition, there were several calls from one of the health professional complainants, who was concerned that the board's actions were excessively slow, that the board refused to interview additional patients whose alleged sexual involvement with Dr. X—— was based on hearsay evidence, and that the board did not immediately insist that the doctor cease his professional practice.

During the course of the investigation, the board became concerned that Dr. X—— apparently did not comprehend the gravity of the situation. Therefore, the board considered suspending his license on an emergency basis, which is permissible provided that a hearing on that particular issue is granted within 30 days. This did not turn out to be necessary, as Dr. X—— signed an agreement to limit his practice to male patients and conducted his practice under the frequent supervision of a board-appointed psychologist. Dr. X——'s physician-employer initially refused to enforce the conditions of this agreement within the clinic setting, a situation that was remedied by the board's referring the matter to the state commission on medical discipline.

Once completed, the investigative report was submitted to the board's counsel (step 6), reviewed for probable cause that the licensing statute had been violated, and forwarded to the board for a decision on whether to dismiss the case or to charge the psychologist with one or more violations (step 7). Once the board voted to issue charges against Dr. X——, an administrative prosecutor was appointed by the office of the attorney general (step 8). After reviewing the case, he prepared a charge letter for the signature of the board's chairman (step 9). The letter included the allegations against Dr. X——, the licensing statute violations that the administrative prosecutor agreed were supportable, dates of a hearing and of a prehearing conference, and a strong recommendation that Dr. X—— secure counsel on his behalf.

A licensee accused of violating a licensing statute has a right to a formal hearing (step 11). If the licensee is convinced that no wrongdoing was involved, a hearing may provide the only mechanism for dismissal of the charges. This hearing is typically preceeded by a prehearing conference, attended by the licensee and the defense attorney, a representative of the board, the board's counsel, and the administrative prosecutor (step 10). At the very least, this conference may be used to discuss rules of evidence related to an impending hearing. However, cases are frequently resolved at such a conference by the licensee entering into a negotiated agreement that is subsequently approved by the board.

Although it is often assumed that a consent agreement essentially constitutes plea bargaining, such a resolution has a number of potential advantages over a hearing resolution. For all parties, there is a substantial saving of the time and money involved in what could be a lengthy hearing. In addition, both the licensee and the patient or patients are spared the possibility of public exposure. Although a consent agreement does not include a formal admission of guilt, by participating in such an agreement the licensee accepts the actions of the board and waives all rights to appeal. This eliminates the possibility that a board action resulting from a hearing may be overturned by an appeals court. Finally, the range of possible penalties is not restricted to those specifically stated in the licensing statute (e.g., revocation or suspension of license, reprimand, fine, etc.). The board now has the option of recommending penalties that are creative, flexible, and constructive.

Dr. X—— was willing to agree to a revocation of his license, with the inclusion of the following provisions: that he would not reapply for reinstatement of his license for at least one year; that during that period, he would submit to psychotherapy with a board-approved therapist; that he would submit to supervision by a board-appointed psychologist; that he would see female patients only in the presence of another licensed therapist; that he would maintain the continuing education standards of the board; and that he would function in compliance with the licensing statute in all other respects. In addition, the names of the three patients involved were not revealed in the consent order, which is available to the public under the Maryland Public Information Act. (It is also through such a process that a licensee may agree to provide financial restitution to a complainant).

Licensing boards in Maryland are not required to disclose the consideration of specific complaints until and unless they result either in a consent order or in a final order resulting from a hearing. Thus, the confidentiality of the licensee is protected unless adverse action is taken. At that time, the documents are not only available to the public on request, but also may be distributed by the board in the hope of deterring future violations (step 12). In the case of Dr. X——, notification of the case was sent to the local newspaper, to the two professional societies that had also received complaints, to another jurisdiction in which Dr. X—— was licensed, to the American Association of State Psychology Boards, and to the complainants themselves. As of early 1986, Dr. X—— has been expelled from at least one professional society, has terminated his job with the clinic, and has not yet followed through on the measures that, by his agreement, would be prerequisite to relicensure in Maryland.

GUIDELINES FOR THE HEALTH PROFESSIONAL

A health professional may play any of a number of roles in the processing of a complaint against a colleague. In addition, health professionals might become involved as teachers, clinical supervisors, and representatives of the profession as well as on an informal basis. The following guidelines for dealing with sexual misconduct are suggested for health professionals in these roles.

Standards of Behavior

Regardless of personal values, health practitioners must be sensitive and responsive to the ethical and legal standards of professional behavior and to the relevant mores of the community. Concerns about sex-related behavior may include not only physical acts, but also comments, gestures, or statements that might be perceived as unprofessional.

Our expectation of health professionals is that they do not allow their sexual attitudes, values, and needs to compromise their obligations to patients in the clinical setting. Therefore, those professionals in a position to pass judgment on possible offenders should conduct themselves by the same professional standards. The individual who proposes legislation, regulations, or ethical codes; prosecutes a case; defends an accused professional; sits on a disciplinary board; prepares statements for the profession or for the public; advises a colleague or a client; or reports an alleged wrongdoing bears no less a level of professional responsibility than the individual who may have exploited a patient. Health practitioners must strive to seek an appropriate balance among the need for protection of the public, the welfare and confidentiality of the patient, the level of public trust in the profession, and the rights and welfare of the alleged offender.

Options for Redress

It is useful for health professionals to be aware of the avenues for dealing with cases of alleged sexual misconduct. Options include seeking personal compensation through the civil courts and seeking disciplinary action through the criminal courts, an employer or educational institution, a professional association ethics committee, or a state licensing board or disciplinary commission. Each has advantages and disadvantages based on the profession involved, the jurisdiction, the rigors of proof required, and the specific circumstances of the case.

Assistance to Patients

At times, a health professional may serve as or help refer a sexually abused patient to a subsequent therapist or practitioner. There may also be community resources or self-help groups to which a patient can be referred.

Patients often need assistance in making a decision to file a complaint. In their study of over 500 cases of alleged sexual misconduct, Bouhoutsos et al. [3] found that only 52 percent of the patients knew that their therapist's behavior was either unethical or illegal and only 13 percent of the instances resulted in complaints filed by the patient or by another person on the patient's behalf. As noted in the case of Dr. X—— and in other cases [2], patients often have mixed feelings about filing a complaint and may benefit from sound, unbiased counsel in making an appropriate decision.

Complaint Filing

Codes of ethics may encourage a professional with knowledge of an ethical infraction first to confront the alleged offender directly [1]. However, a health professional whose knowledge of such an offense is based only on hearsay evidence may be subject to defamation action. One often can file a complaint with a licensing board in good faith without the risk of liability, and actions based on such complaints have survived appeal precedures even when a patient has not filed a complaint directly [39]. However, if the information about an alleged offense has been acquired through professional interaction with a patient, the patient's confidentiality must be respected. Stone [36] has discussed this ethical dilemma and has recommended as a possible solution the involvement of a second health professional or an attorney as a neutral consultant to the patient. In this way, the patient has a professional resource available for independent consultation, while the relationship between the patient and the original therapist is preserved.

Sexual Attraction to Patients

It is not unusual for a health practitioner to feel sexually attracted to a patient. Such feelings need not impede the therapeutic relationship if the practitioner acknowledges these feelings, maintains a clear separation between personal feelings and those expressed by the patient, sets appropriate limits for the patient, and refrains from discussing personal problems with the patients [12, 38, 43].

The practitioner should be aware of the tendency to rationalize or deny the presence of intense feelings that may compromise the professional relationship, especially if the patient is being seen in psychotherapy. Consultation with a colleague, superior, or therapist may help the practitioner to deal more objectively with such feelings, while best serving the interests of the patient.

PREVENTIVE AND LONG-TERM MEASURES

While suggestions outlined above can be implemented by the individual health professional, the following recommendations for long-term, preventive measures require institutional support.

Professional Education

If a profession is to expect certain standards of sexual behavior on the part of its members, it must address this issue during the course of professional training [17]. This might be done through courses in professional ethics or human sexuality and would best include a discussion component. "Ethical prescriptions alone are not enough," write Edelwich and Brodsky [12].

"Students need to work through their personal reactions to the sexual questions that will arise for them in practice." One attempt at professional education is the American Psychiatric Association's recently announced plans to develop a videotape of sexual situations that can arise in therapy. The vignettes are intended to increase sensitivity and stimulate discussion among medical students, residents, and psychiatrists [16].

Role Models

Even more important than courses, perhaps, are the role models provided by clinical teachers and supervisors. The often intense relationship between student and mentor bears characteristics of power imbalance and dependency similar to those in the relationship between health professional and patient. It is in this student-teacher relationship that the example for the future may first be set [30]. In addition, licensed practitioners can serve as role models to other professionals and paraprofessionals over whom they have supervisory responsibility. This might even include occasional discussions or in-service training about the sexual aspects of the clinical relationship [23].

Continuing Education

For the graduate professional, continuing education courses can address these same issues. Such courses, seminars, and workshops might best be sponsored by professional societies, with the assistance of resource people familiar with the interpersonal and legal issues involved.

Consumer Education

When consumers are concerned about the behavior of health professionals and wish to inform appropriate authorities, they are likely to call either a professional association or a licensing board. Staff members who receive such inquiries should be adequately prepared to provide appropriate information, support, and referrals. Professional associations can help educate the public by preparing brochures [16] and by sponsoring speakers for community interest groups.

Public Disclosure of Case Findings

The public often assumes that professional members of licensing boards and ethics committees have a tendency to keep sensitive matters quiet. It is certainly appropriate for such deliberative bodies to maintain the confidentiality of an accused professional prior to an adverse finding, and discretion may be used in the manner and extent of publication of case results. However, publication at some level (e.g., through professional newsletters or local newspapers) does serve to provide a clear message that the profession is responsive to the public's valid expectation of trust and responsibility, while also informing other members of the profession that certain behaviors are clearly unacceptable.

Selection of Professionals for Key Roles

Health professionals are often called to assist in the processing of ethical complaints. They may serve as members of ethics committees and licensing boards, as expert witnesses, and as board-appointed supervisors. The fair treatment of both complainants and professionals accused of violations depends heavily on the competence, diligence, integrity, and sensitivity of such individuals, and they should be chosen with extreme care.

Case Disposition Procedures

Stone [37] and Sinnett and Linford [35] have discussed problems in how licensing boards handle disciplinary cases. States and professional organizations share an equal responsibility to ensure that licensing statutes and related rules and regulations are set up to deal with disciplinary cases in an appropriate manner, that competent, conscientious legal counsel is available, and that all participants are afforded their due process rights.

Review of Ethical and Legal Standards

Professional and community standards of behavior in the clinical setting can be more effectively communicated and enforced if they are specifically defined in criminal and licensing statutes and in professional codes of ethics. Professional societies and licensing boards can contribute to this need by actively and openly discussing the issue, reevaluating existing standards, and working to enact necessary changes.

Resources for Impaired Professionals

Cases of sex-related offenses reported in the literature reflect extremes of both misbehavior and punishment. Yet depending on the circumstances and extent of the misconduct, it may be possible to rehabilitate a health professional. This may be especially true when the professional has acted with sincere but misguided conviction that a sexual intervention was helpful to the patient.

Many professional societies have successful programs for the treatment of impaired professionals. Although these programs tend to concentrate on problems of alcohol and drug abuse, one might ask whether they also deal with problems of sexual impairment. Such programs could provide confidential, preventive intervention. Professional ethics committees and licensing boards might also consider referral to such programs as a condition for reinstatement of membership in a professional society or of a license that has been suspended or revoked.

Additional Research

Because of the sensitive nature of the problem of sexual exploitation of patients, little reliable data are available on the incidence of sexual misconduct in various professional settings, its impact on the patients involved, the disposition of complaints, and the effectiveness of either punitive or rehabilitative measures. Furthermore, an examination of the references appended to this chapter reveals that available data and discussions come from a relatively narrow range of sources. Additional research is necessary if the problem is to be dealt with appropriately and fairly. To succeed, these efforts need the active support of the professional community.

NOTES

The authors are indebted to Timmerman Tepel Daugherty, Paul H. Ephross, Lois T. Flaherty, Judith M. Plaut, Jennifer L. Robbins, and Sherman Ross for their critical comments on the manuscript and to Dorothy Anderson for her assistance in its preparation. The authors assume full responsibility for the views expressed.

1. American Psychological Association. 1981. *Ethical Principles of Psychologists.* Washington, D.C.:American Psychological Association.

2. *Board of Medical Examiners v. Cutshaw,* 6 Ariz.App. 330, 432 P.2d 474 (1967).

3. Bouhoutsos, J., J. Holroyd, H. Lerman, B. R. Forer, and M. Greenberg. 1983. "Sexual Intimacy between Psychotherapists and Patients." *Professional Psychology: Research and Practice* 14:185-96.

4. Burgess, A. W. 1981. "Physician Sexual Misconduct and Patients' Responses." *American Journal of Psychiatry* 138:1335-42.

5. Butler, S., and S. L. Zelen. 1977. "Sexual Intimacies between Therapists and Patients." *Psychotherapy: Theory, Research and Practice* 14:139-45.

6. *Cardamon v. State Board of Optometric Examiners,* 165 Col. 495, 441 P.2d 25 (1968).

7. *Cooper v. Board of Medical Examiners,* 49 Cal.App.3d 931, 123 Cal.Rptr. 563 (1975).

8. Dahlberg, C. C. 1969. "Sexual Contact between Patient and Therapist." *Contemporary Psychoanalysis* 6:107-24.

9. *Decker v. Fink,* 47 Md.App. 202, 422 A.2d 389 (1980).

10. *Doyle v. Veterans Administration,* 667 F.2d 70 (Ct.Cl. 1981).

11. *Dresser v. Board of Medical Quality Assurance,* 130 Cal.App.3d 506, 181 Cal.Rptr. 797 (1982).

12. Edelwich, J., and A. Brodsky. 1982. *Sexual Dilemmas for the Helping Professional.* New York: Brunner/Mazel.

13. Finney, J. C. 1975. "Therapist and Patient after Hours." *American Journal of Psychotherapy* 29:593–602.

14. Hall, J. E., and R. T. Hare-Mustin. 1983. "Sanctions and the Diversity of Ethical Complaints against Psychologists." *American Psychologist* 38:714–29.

15. Hare-Mustin, R. T. 1974. "Ethical Considerations in the Use of Sexual Contact in Psychotherapy." *Psychotherapy: Theory, Research and Practice* 11:308–10.

16. Herrington, B. S. 1985. "APA Moves to Discourage Sexual Misconduct in Therapy." *Psychiatric News,* January 1985, p. 17.

17. Holroyd, J. C. and A. M. Brodsky. 1977. "Psychologists' Attitudes and Practices Regarding Erotic and Non-erotic Physical Contact with Patients." *American Psychologist* 32:843–49.

18. Kardener, S. H. 1974. "Sex and the Physician-Patient Relationship." *American Journal of Psychiatry* 131:1134–36.

19. Kardener, S. H., M. Fuller, and I. N. Mensh. 1976. "Characteristics of 'Erotic' Practitioners." *American Journal of Psychiatry* 133:1324–25.

20. _____ . 1973. "A Survey of Physicians' Attitudes and Practices Regarding Erotic and Non-erotic Contact with Patients." *American Journal of Psychiatry* 130:1077–81.

21. Kermani, E. J. 1982. "Court Rulings on Psychotherapists." *American Journal of Psychotherapy* 36:248–55.

22. *In re Kincheloe,* 272 N.C. 116, 157 S.E.2d 833 (1967).

23. Kirstein, L. 1978. "Sexual Involvement with Patients." *Journal of Clinical Psychiatry* 39:366–68.

24. Marmor, J. 1972. "Sexual Acting-out in Psychotherapy." *American Journal of Psychoanalysis* 22:3–8.

25. *Martinez v. Texas State Board of Medical Examiners,* 476 S.W.2d 400 (Tex.Cir.App. 1972).

26. "Nursing Ethics: The Admirable Professional Standards Survey of Nurses—A Survey Report." 1974. *Nursing* 4:34–44.

27. *Peer v. Municipal Court of the South Bay Judicial District,* 128 Cal.App.3d 733, 180 Cal.Rptr. 137 (1982).

28. *People of the State of Ill. v. Rudi,* 94 Ill.App. 3d 856, 419 N.E.2d 646 (1981).

29. Perry, J. A. 1976. "Physicians' Erotic and Non-erotic Physical Involvement with Patients." *American Journal of Psychiatry* 133:838–40.

30. Pope, K. S., L. R. Schover, and H. Levenson. 1980. "Sexual Behavior between Clinical Supervisors and Trainees: Implications for Professional Standards." *Professional Psychology* 11:157–62.

31. Reaves, R. P. 1984. *The Law of Professional Licensing and Certification.* Charlotte, N.C.: Publications for Professionals.

32. Riskin, L. L. 1979. "Sexual Relations between Psychotherapists and Their Patients: Toward Research or Restraint." *California Law Review* 67:1000–27.

33. *Ross v. State of Florida, Division of Professions et al.,* 342 So.2d 1023 (Fla.Dist.Ct.App. 1977).

34. *Shea v. Board of Medical Examiners,* 81 Cal.App.3d. 564, 146 Cal.Rptr. 653 (1978).

35. Sinnett, E. R., and O. Linford. 1982. "Processing of Formal Complaints Against Psychologists." *Psychological Reports* 50:535–44.

36. Stone, A. A. 1983. "Sexual Misconduct by Psychiatrists: The Ethical and Clinical Dilemma of Confidentiality." *American Journal of Psychiatry* 140:195–97.

37. _____ . 1976. "The Legal Implications of Sexual Activity between Psychiatrist and Patient." *American Journal of Psychiatry* 133:1138–41.

38. Taylor, B. J., and N. N. Wagner. 1976. "Sex between Therapists and Clients: A Review and Analysis." *Professional Psychology* 7:593-601.

39. *Texas State Board of Medical Examiners v. Koepsel,* 159 Tex. 479, 322 S.W.2d 609 (1959).

40. Turkington, C. 1984. "Women Therapists Not Immune to Sexual Involvement Suits." *APA Monitor,* December 1984, pp. 3-4.

41. *Vigilant Insurance Co. v. Kambly,* 114 Mich.App. 683, 319 N.W.2d 382 (1982).

42. Voth, H. M. 1972. "Love Affair between Doctor and Patient." *American Journal of Psychotherapy* 26:394-400.

43. Wabrek, A. J., and P. M. Feldman. 1972. "Human Aspects of Medical Sexuality." *Obstetrics and Gynecology* 39:805-06.

PART 2

The Patient's Perspective

The patient's act of seeking help from the health profession requires a suspension of self-protective strategies. Trust in and reliance on the helping person is essential. In cases of professional misconduct, the offender forces the patient to adjust his or her thinking regarding the inappropriate behaviors in the professional. Doubt in the mind of the patient is resolved when both patient and offender normalize and justify the exploitative behavior.

For offending health professionals, insight into the patterns of patient accommodation results in skillful maneuvers to obtain and maintain control over the patient. Furthermore, this maneuvering is carried over to dealings with other colleagues and with the legal system. When threatened, offending professionals often show themselves to be adept at using the press and other potential means of intimidation. Although confrontation disrupts their sense of control and power, their ability to parry accusations further enhances their sense of superiority and influence. Consequently, accusing a health professional of sexual exploitation is often difficult.

The boldness manifested by offending health practitioners reflects both moral collusion with society and moral confusion within society. To better understand this interaction, we present two patient accounts of sexual exploitation by, in these cases, male physicians. In both cases, neither the authors nor the identities of the individuals involved are identified in order to preserve confidentiality.

The first case, "The Good Deed Undone," is a mother's account of the sexual exploitation of her 13-year-old daughter by a pediatrician neighbor. This case demonstrates how legitimate access to a patient's body is used for sexual purposes. The doctor not only takes advantage of the privileged contact, but also plays on the basic fears and anxieties of the patient who has come for help. The dilemma of the parents, the violation of the child's rights by the doctor, and the response of the legal system all underscore the compounding trauma of disclosing the sexual abuse. The professional associations confuse and minimize the issue, which illustrates the attitudes that ultimately condone and protect the exploiter. Not only is the family torn apart, but so is the community.

The second case, "Trying to Forget," recounts the abuse of a woman by her cardiologist. The dialogue in this case reveals how the offender can gain control, in part, by assuming values similar to those of the patient. As the patient recounts how a vacation trip was marred somewhat by the behavior of a group of people, the doctor readily claims his dislike for that particular ethnic group. He then recounts his own vacation, introducing sex into the conversation and attributing his penile erection to the patient's discussion. He challenges her by asking her what she is going to do about his erection.

These two cases show that the physicians involved are not transgressing for the first time. They are accomplished at what they are doing and their deep sense of entitlement is revealed in their boldness and in their defensive strategies. From these cases, we learn not only about the plight of the victims, but also how the exploitative practitioners undermine every effort of the patient to end the pathological relationship.

The Good Deed Undone

Anne K——, a bright 13-year-old, was referred to a pediatric surgeon for possible appendicitis. At the hospital, Anne and her parents were pleasantly surprised to find that the pediatric surgeon on call was Dr. E——, a neighbor they liked and trusted. He had recently moved to the area to teach at the local university, and his duties included serving as staff surgeon at the university-affiliated children's hospital.

Upon examining Anne, the surgeon discovered she had an imperforate hymen, a congenital condition that made the escape of menstrual fluid impossible. The large amount of fluid that had collected was causing her immediate symptoms. Dr. E—— performed a brief, simple, surgical procedure to open and drain the hymen, allowing the discharge of menstrual fluid. Anne felt well enough to go home later that evening and by the next day seemed completely recovered.

The second day after surgery, Anne spent the day shopping with her mother; three days later she attended her weekly all-day ski lesson. She reported no pain and no bleeding and stated that she felt "just great."

The surgeon had told Anne's parents that he would stop by in a few days to check on Anne. In fact, he visited the very next day. Two additional visits followed. Although Anne's parents appreciated the doctor's home visits, three visits in eight days made them suspect a complication in her recovery. After the third visit, Mrs. K—— asked the doctor if something was wrong. His explanation upset Anne's mother, and she suggested consulting a gynecologist. Dr. E—— responded that he should care for Anne and that she needed monitoring. Anne continued to feel fine and actively participated in all her normal activities.

Anne and her family left on a skiing vacation, and Anne skied every day. During the vacation, Anne told her mother that she did not wish to see Dr. E—— again and that if he called or visited he should not be allowed to see her. Anne's mother asked if she wanted to see a different doctor, and Anne replied that she was only willing to see a female physician.

When the family returned from their vacation, Dr. E—— made several attempts to see Anne again. He stopped at the K——'s house the same night they returned, only to find them on their way out to eat. Two days later he called, asking to see Anne for a few minutes to make certain everything was all right. Anne refused, saying her parents were not home. A few days later Dr. E—— called again; Anne's mother told the doctor she would be taking Anne to a gynecologist.

For the first time, Mrs. K—— began to wonder if something was seriously bothering her daughter. Her questioning triggered Anne to sob uncontrollably before finally describing the doctor's checkups. Dr. E——, their trusted friend and neighbor, had been sexually abusing Anne. Anne's mother told the family pediatrician about the abuse, and the pediatrician made arrangements for Anne and her parents to see a counselor at the county center for sexually abused children.

THE MOLESTATION DISCLOSED

Anne was able to relate, both to her mother and later to her counselor, what had happened during the visits by Dr. E——. On each of the three home visits, the doctor had examined Anne in her bedroom with the door closed. The first visit was brief and normal. However, on each of the next two visits Dr. E—— told Anne to take off all her clothing; he remained in the room and watched her disrobe. He then "examined" Anne, on her bed, without placing any sheet or covering over her. The doctor began the examination by rubbing Anne's genital area for what she described as "forever," telling her, "I'm doing this so you'll be nice and relaxed when I examine you." She said he continued to do this until she began to feel "twitchy, yucky all over."

Anne was also disturbed by the way the doctor looked at her, by his smiling, and by his labored breathing. She said she felt embarrassed and humiliated by the examinations. Dr. E—— said she didn't have to talk about the examination to her parents or anyone else, telling her "they're kind of embarrassing at your age." In addition, the doctor described Anne's vagina as "the place where the man's penis goes." Mr. and Mrs. K—— recalled his saying the same thing at the hospital before Anne's surgery and thought it was a strange, nonmedical term to use.

Anne did not recognize the abnormality of the examinations because she had never had a pelvic exam before. She later testified that the experience left her terrified of what she believed would be a lifetime of similar examinations.

Anne found it difficult to tell about what had happened to her. She was a shy child and at 13 was sensitive about her changing body. However, her counselor explained that the molestation was not Anne's fault and that the surgeon had a serious problem and probably had molested other children. The counselor also supported the family as it dealt with difficult decisions, the most important being whether or not to report the doctor to the authorities.

Anne's parents were concerned with protecting their child from any further damage that might result from a courtroom trial. Their counselor told them that the trial would be a difficult experience and that it might generate substantial publicity.

RESPONSE TO DISCLOSURE

As soon as Dr. E—— discovered the molestation had been disclosed, he began to pressure Mr. and Mrs. K—— to drop the case. He telephoned them repeatedly. He also called their pediatrician to try to discredit Anne's report, and he even telephoned the sexual assault center where the family was receiving counseling. In addition, Dr. E—— persuaded his minister to call Anne's parents and tell them what a "wonderful, Christian man, brilliant doctor, and loving father and husband" he was. The minister urged Mr. and Mrs. K—— to forgive and forget.

During this period, the K—— family grappled with their overwhelming feelings of anger, grief, shock, betrayal, and disbelief. They began to be suspicious about Dr. E——'s move to the area, at what must have been a considerable reduction in income. Anne's parents felt anger and guilt directed at themselves for not having protected their child. They felt they should have recognized the inappropriateness of lengthy home visits following a five-minute, minor surgical procedure. Despite their awareness about child sexual abuse, they had failed to recognize the intentions of a good friend and neighbor and had trusted him completely. To them, a doctor was the one person who had the license to touch all parts of the body.

THE MOLESTATION REPORTED

After careful review, Anne's parents decided to report the incident to police and to allow prosecutors to file charges. Anne met with the prosecutors and told her story with a policewoman and a counselor present.

The prosecutors had given the K——'s an approximate schedule for filing charges, for the defendant's preliminary court appearances, and for the trial. However, it soon became clear that the prosecutor's office was ambivalent about filing charges. Anne was once again asked to tell her story, this time to the chief prosecutor. By this time, family unity was crumbling under the pressure; family members wanted to forget the whole thing.

HOSPITAL REACTION

As they attempted to deal with the possibility that a staff surgeon was a child molester, hospital administrators requested an interview with Mr. and Mrs. K——. Because Mr. K—— was unable to keep his composure at the meeting, Mrs. K told about the abuse.

The investigating committee, made up of ten physicians, voted unanimously to place Dr. E—— on probation and to impose sanctions on him. The hospital's medical director explained the conditions of the sanctions: Dr. E—— had to undergo psychiatric examination by a hospital-selected therapist, he had to enter ongoing therapy with someone experienced in treating sex offenders, and he had to remain in therapy until the hospital and the therapist agreed that he no longer needed treatment. On resumption of his duties at the hospital, the offender would be allowed to see patients only with a chaperone in attendance and would be barred from treating adolescents. He also would not be allowed to see patients outside the hospital, thus prevented from setting up a private practice.

The medical director, also a physician, expressed his personal belief in Anne's story and pledged that the hospital would cooperate fully with the prosecutor's office. However, he implied that he felt the molestation might be an isolated, one-time slip. He told them of Dr. E——'s remorse and of how he had willingly placed his signature on the hospital's sanctions.

EARLIER INCIDENTS

Anne's parents felt that Dr. E—— had shown practiced smoothness in gaining access to Anne. They recalled that a year earlier the physician had visited their younger daughter, then 11 years old, after she had been hospitalized for a severe case of flu. The child had said nothing at the time, but now, when questioned, told how Dr. E—— had removed her pants and underwear and asked her if she had started to develop yet.

A young boy from the city where Dr. E—— had previously practiced reported to his mother that two years earlier the doctor had molested him on five separate occasions. The 13-year-old boy had been too embarrassed to tell anyone, although he had complained about having to see the doctor. After hearing about the charges against Dr. E——, the boy's mother questioned her son further.

The boy described being directed to kneel on his knees and elbows on the examination table. Dr. E—— then fondled the boy's penis for 10 to 15 minutes with a fixed stare and a smile on his face. Even after the doctor had moved away and was back visiting the area, he arranged to check on the boy during the visit and molested the youth again. At the time, the boy's mother believed the doctor to be an unusually dedicated and caring physician.

After her son's disclosure, the mother contacted the hospital medical director where Dr. E—— was on probation. Her testimony convinced the medical director and the hospital board of trustees to fire Dr. E——. They also pledged to support prosecution efforts if charges based on the new evidence were filed.

THE CHARGES FILED

Charges of indecent liberties were filed against Dr. E—— five months after Anne first reported the molestation. Originally, the charge was to have been statutory rape, but prosecutors believed it would be too difficult to prove against a physician. The prosecutor's optimism for a guilty plea from Dr. E—— was premature. The doctor was not going to plead guilty to charges that would result in automatic loss of his license.

The K—— family began to feel the stress of their experience and were no longer unified in their decisions. Anne's mother favored prosecution as a way to protect other children, while Mr. K—— believed a trial would devastate not only Anne, but the rest of the family as well.

Up to this point the K——s had been able to protect Anne's privacy. This privacy was shattered when Dr. E—— and his wife hired a private detective to find out as much as possible about Anne and her parents. The detective called neighbors, friends, teachers, and even casual acquaintances of Anne's family and stated that Anne had falsely accused a fine surgeon of molesting her. Anne's privacy was destroyed. However, the detective never testified for the defense, as she was unable to gather any evidence against the family.

As the trial date neared, the K—— family became more fragmented. Mr. K—— had business that took him out of the country for the entire month prior to the trial. In addition, Anne's counselor took a three-month maternity leave and was thus unavailable to Anne until the time of the trial.

PRETRIAL MANEUVERS

During the discovery phase of the proceedings, the defense counsel was entitled to access to all witnesses for the prosecution. Defense attorneys requested interviews with Anne and her mother. By the time the separate interviews were finished, the unease mother and daughter felt over the upcoming trial had increased. Mrs. K—— was especially outraged at certain questions the defense attorney had asked her regarding whether or not she practiced sexual "self-gratification."

It became clear during these interviews that the defense planned to concentrate on discrepancies in dates and times and not on the behavior of Dr. E——. It also appeared that defense attorneys would focus on Mrs. K—— rather than on Anne. Shortly before the trial, Mrs. K—— learned that in a pretrial hearing a judge had granted the defense's request to subpoena records of her past visits to a psychologist. Dr. E——'s wife had reported that Anne's mother had a pathological hatred of doctors and had suffered a breakdown requiring antipsychotic drugs and psychiatric care. The K——'s saw this action as an attempt to make them withdraw charges before the case went to trial.

Even though the defense was unsuccessful in getting the K——'s to drop the charges, Mr. and Mrs. K—— drifted further apart as a result of this additional struggle. Anne's father felt frustrated and wanted to drop the matter before his daughter and wife were hurt any more, and he began to mistrust everyone connected with the case—the prosecution as well as the defense. Mrs. K—— began to feel increasingly abandoned and alone as the trial date neared and as she realized her husband's inability to support her emotionally. She did, however, remain determined to see the case through and to provide support for Anne throughout the ordeal.

Realizing that the prosecution would dwell on dates and times, Anne prepared herself the week before the trial by writing down everything she could remember, using the family calendar for reference. Although this was painful for her, she feared her nervousness at being on the witness stand might cause her to forget details. However, the prosecutor had failed to inform Anne that the defense attorney would have a right to review her notes.

THE TRIAL

The trial commenced nine and one-half months after Anne reported the molestation to her mother. The morning she was to testify, Anne was requested to meet in the prosecutor's office to discuss her notes with defense attorneys. Mrs. K—— protested yet another questioning by defense attorneys over notes intended for private references. The prosecutor convinced Mrs. K—— that failure to turn over the notes could result in a mistrial.

The "brief" meeting lasted one and one-half hours. When it was over, Anne emerged crying and refusing to testify. It took the combined efforts of the prosecuting staff, the counselor advocate, and Mrs. K—— to persuade Anne to proceed with her testimony.

Anne reported that defense attorneys questioned her about her detailed notes and about such unrelated matters as the correct order of the Catholic Mass. Apparently the defense was attempting to confuse Anne to prove her inaccuracy of recall. Anne did not deviate from her original story of the molestation.

In its opening statement, the defense team called the whole episode a "witch hunt." The attorneys declared that a tragic mistake had been made by the victim, a mistake followed by hysteria from the victim's mother and the sexual assault workers. Dr. E—— was described as a wonderful doctor who had saved the child's life, a man now caught in a nightmare caused by the runaway fantasies of a 13-year-old girl and the overreaction of her mother.

The prosecution focused entirely on Dr. E——'s behavior in his examinations of Anne. The prosecuting attorney acknowledged that Anne could have mixed up some times and dates, yet stressed Anne's consistency in her story of the molestation.

When Anne took the stand she was asked how many times she had told her story. Even the prosecutor was surprised that Anne could remember seven different instances. The defense attempted to demonstrate inconsistencies in times and dates and questioned her intensely for nearly two hours. Defense attorneys claimed that Anne had changed her story and that Anne's mother had provided Anne with the details for her notes.

Mrs. K—— took the stand after Anne. The prosecution asked her about the conversation she had with Anne about the molestations and about her recollections of the details of the doctor's visits. Defense attorneys objected to nearly every answer Mrs. K—— gave. At one point, the judge cleared the jury from the courtroom and instructed the defense team to discontinue their intimidation.

The defense suggested that Mrs. K—— had been negligent in caring for Anne by allowing her to become ill. They also suggested that the mother had not given Anne any sex education; this was why Dr. K—— had felt it necessary to explain certain sexual facts to Anne during his examinations.

The defense also questioned Mrs. K—— about a book she had been reading during the family ski vacation and read aloud a sexually explicit passage from the book. It was not revealed that the book was part of an assignment for a class Mrs. K—— was taking toward an advanced degree. Mrs. K—— left the witness stand feeling degraded and humiliated.

Mr. K—— was called as a prosecution witness testifying to the one instance when he and Anne were home alone and Dr. E—— came to examine Anne. Dr. E—— denied having made this visit.

The boy victim and his mother also testified about molestation by Dr. E——. Although this influential testimony lasted nearly an entire day, it was not reported in any of the three local newspapers. When Mrs. K——

telephoned one newspaper about this, she learned that although an article had been submitted, it was not printed because of lack of space. However, although Anne was not identified by name, newspaper stories described her specifically enough so that her anonymity was destroyed.

One of the turning points of the case was the appearance of a nationally known pediatric surgeon as character witness for the defense. This man, who ten years earlier had been one of Dr. E——'s teachers, testified that he encouraged his students to make home visits. He also indicated that girls can easily misinterpret a physical examination. The physician did say, however, that he would never ask a young girl to disrobe completely for an exam without his using a cover and without being chaperoned.

The jury voted for acquittal. After delivering their verdict, several jurors embraced Dr. E—— and his wife as the doctor thanked them for their "fairness." The newspaper accounts mentioned the ten-month ordeal of Dr. E—— and his family; the ordeal of the two child victims and their families was not noted. Dr. E—— was reinstated with probation at the children's hospital.

THE AFTERMATH

Both families still live in the same community, and the K——s have done their best to put the trial behind them. Their greatest difficulty has been in coping with the community that took sides over the case. Anne's parents are unable to discuss the trial with each other, and they both feel angry over its outcome and the ordeal they endured. However, Mrs. K—— still believes the family did the right thing.

Until recently Anne had been unwilling to visit a doctor, but now Mrs. K—— has found a female practitioner that Anne is willing to see. Anne reports that she feels frightened about the prospect of having a pelvic exam and that sometimes she feels she is "different" from other girls. To her, the trial was a painful, meaningless, and degrading experience. Mrs. K—— says she hopes that Anne will listen to her assurances that the bravery she displayed throughout the ordeal may perhaps have helped other children to avoid a similar experience.

Trying to Forget

I have avoided writing this story. I've lived with this memory for five years, and I will live with it for the rest of my life. Every time I visit someone in a hospital, every time I have a checkup, and sometimes when I least expect it, I start thinking about it.

I've kept all my notes and correspondence regarding this matter, although I don't know why I saved everything. I hate this whole thing. Although I promised to write this account, thinking it would help others, it is taking its toll.

THE VICTIM'S ACCOUNT

It was August; I'm not exactly sure of the date. I had had an appointment with Dr. Y—— for several months for my annual cardiac exam; it's essential because I have a minor congenital heart defect. The general procedure at the hospital was to have an electrocardiogram (ECG) before proceeding to the doctor's office for the cardiac exam. I had been a patient of Dr. Y—— for six or seven years; he was a prominent cardiologist at a large hospital.

I was finished with the ECG quickly, so I had to sit in the corridor outside Dr. Y——'s office for almost one hour to wait for someone to arrive. I had brought a book with me and I read it while I waited to see the doctor. When he did arrive, he acknowledged my presence but did not remember my name. I only see him once each year. The following is an account of the conversations and occurrences that took place at that time (D = doctor, P = patient).

D: How are you? You look great!
P: I'm fine. How are you?
D: You look terrific.
P: Thanks. I just got back from a trip to Bermuda with my husband. We had a fantastic time!
D: Where did you stay?
P: Castle Harbour. I would really recommend it. The service was terrific, and it has a lot of charm. It was expensive but worth it.
D: How expensive?
P: One thousand dollars.
D: And how much for the air fare?
P: That included air fare. (He wrote down the name of the hotel. I spelled it for him, and he made a joke about my accent.)
P: The hotel was really nice, but one group of people was offensive.
D: I bet they were------. (He identified an ethnic group.)
P: Yes.
D: I can't stand them.
P: We had a great time. Our room was terrific because we had such a beautiful view. We also rented bikes and went from one beach to another. We even found one very private beach. Everything is so beautiful in Bermuda.
D: We took a six-week trip to California with the five kids and had a good time, but there was no time for sex while traveling with the kids. We also visited a friend who had a communal hot tub. Six of us got in with clothes on, but by the time we got out we had all our clothes off.
P: That wouldn't interest me.
D: Nothing really happened.
(Conversation was interrupted by a telephone call from another physician concerning a patient with a heart condition and a gallbladder problem.)
D: Sorry for the interruption. How are you feeling?
P: I do get some chest pain when mowing the lawn.
D: What about during intercourse?
P: I occasionally have shortness of breath after an orgasm.
D: Let's see how you're doing.

I proceeded to take off all my clothes except my underpants, and I put the smock on. The curtain wasn't drawn—I'm not sure that there was one. I was sitting on the end of the examining table when he approached me. He said, "Look what all this conversation has done."

I turned and looked at him and he had his hand on his erect penis inside his pants. He grabbed my right hand and put it on his pants over his erection. I didn't say a word. I just pulled my hand away in panic. I did not know what to do. I was not dressed, and he was between me and the door. I just wanted to get out of there without any more problems. I was frozen on the table when he started to take my blood pressure. It was very high, because I was really scared.

Then he listened to my heart—both in front and in back. He checked my pulse in my neck and ankles and then took the stethoscope and placed it on my groin and listened for a long time, saying he heard a noise. I started to get off the table when he put his arm around me and kissed me on the lips. I pulled away and started to dress as fast as possible.

After I was dressed, I asked him what the noise had been. He called me over to the desk where he sat to listen again, telling me to lift up my skirt. Stupidly, I did it. He said the noise was gone, and told me to get back up on the table. He listened again. He said he could hear it, and held the stethoscope so I could listen. Although I couldn't hear a thing, I said I could. I just wanted to get out of there. As I started to get off the table he tried to kiss me again, but I bent down quickly and put my sandals on. He went to his desk and wrote something down, and he said I needed an x-ray. I said I didn't have time. He told me not to worry about the murmur that he heard. He got up and came toward me. He asked me what he was supposed to do with his erection, which he had his hand on. I had my hand on the door and said I did not know. I left quickly.

When I left his office, I was very upset. I kept thinking about the whole thing and started to cry driving home. Then I got angry. My husband came home from work, and although I had planned to wait to tell him until after the children were in bed, I couldn't. I blurted it out to him the moment he came in the door. I didn't sleep all night and in my mind kept going over the whole thing. My husband was very upset, but I knew then there was nothing we could really do. It would be my word against the doctor's, and he's a very well-known and respected cardiologist.

The next day my son had an appointment with his pediatrician. My husband called the pediatrician before I arrived and told him in generalities what had happened. The pediatrician had been my pediatric cardiologist, and I had been seeing him for almost 30 years. He now treats both my children. This doctor discussed with me what had happened, and he was very angry. He gave me the name of a new cardiologist and told me there was not much I could do about Dr. Y——. He also questioned the medical reason for Dr. Y——'s listening to my groin so intently. The doctor indicated he would no longer refer patients to Dr. Y——.

My husband contacted his cousin, who is with the state police and is also a licensed attorney. The cousin had had previous professional dealings with the medical board of registration, and he offered to get the information necessary for filing a complaint.

Later that month another physician, Dr. S——, saw me in an emergency due to uterine hemorrhaging. My husband and I were together. Dr. S—— had originally referred me to Dr. Y——, but I did not discuss with

Dr. S—— what had happened for several reasons: (1) I was concerned about my immediate medical problem, (2) Dr. S—— treats Dr. Y——'s wife, and (3) Dr. Y—— is Dr. S——'s personal physician. In our presence, Dr. S—— called Dr. Y—— to discuss various medications he was going to prescribe for me. It was a very tense and difficult time for my husband and me.

The next day, I contacted the lawyer to discuss the matter. I then proceded to write a complaint and file it with the medical board and the hospital where the incident occurred.

Several weeks later, Dr. Y—— called me on the telephone. He asked me about the notification to the board, and I told him I had leveled a complaint because of his sexual advances toward me. He said he didn't think hugging and kissing a patient could be considered a sexual advance. I immediately refreshed his memory, saying that having an erection and forcing me to touch it was definitely a sexual advance.

There was silence, then he started to apologize. He was very upset, and he kept saying how devastated he was and that he really didn't mean to do it. He claimed that it had never happened before and that he was sorry. Dr. Y—— asked what the board was going to do with the issue. I told him probably nothing would result, considering his professional position and reputation.

I also told Dr. Y—— that I took this action to protect other people and that I wasn't out for vengeance. He said he had a wife and five children, and this could hurt him deeply. I said I had a husband and two children and that I had already been hurt deeply. He wanted to know if he could appeal to me again to prevent the complaint from becoming public. I said I didn't know, but that I thought it probably would not get that far. Dr. Y—— then began crying and again apologized to me and my husband. He made a second appeal concerning publicity, and with a final apology he hung up.

THE LAWYER'S FOLLOW-UP STATEMENTS

Sent account of physician encounter to the board of medicine. Board's immediate remark: "This lady is a flake." Board then saw the seven-page report and speculated on whether this was a pattern with the cardiologist or a one-on-one stress situation.

Patient goes to a new cardiologist: "He asked me why I left Dr. Y——, and I said, 'He tried to seduce me.' I told him I had been [Dr. Y——'s] patient for years and that it had shocked me. He said I didn't have to worry with him because his wife was the secretary. I asked if he had a nurse in the room for the examination. He replied that cardiologists don't use nurses for exams. He put his arm around me and hugged me as I left."

Client and husband told another physician of the experience. That doctor said, "In that small office?" Client thought to herself, "You don't need a gymnasium."

Client's cousin, who is a nurse at the hospital, said Dr. Y—— had a reputation for sleeping with the nurses.

Client realized the head of the board of medicine was on the staff at the hospital. Dr. Y—— filed a response with the board of medicine saying the client made this incident up and he wants to file a slander suit against her. Dr. Y——'s lawyer called a "street fighter."

Board invited client in to determine whether or not to go forward with the complaint. Dr. Y—— later told the board he routinely hugs his patients and that he did nothing unusual that day. He denied everything the client stated happened, and his lawyer threatened her legally if she continued to pursue the complaint.

Client called the board and was told Dr. Y—— had appeared and had been given a lecture on ethics. As far as the board was concerned, it was all over. Board voted only to warn him.

Client was very angry. Board asked what action she wanted. She said Dr. Y—— should have psychiatric help for his problem. The board said the doctor was shaken by the incident. Client felt let down and knew it couldn't go any further, as it was her word against his.

EPILOGUE

I will always have this dark secret. When I went to visit someone at the hospital where it happened, I was almost paranoid about running into Dr. Y——. I kept looking around the whole time I was there. I don't ever want to step foot inside the hospital again.

Now there are suspicions that I am developing more cardiac problems. I just recently was referred to another cardiologist for a consultation. He asked who my original cardiologist was, and naturally Dr. Y——'s name came up again. I made no comments; I just cringed. I can't seem to get away from reminders of that incident.

I feel the most angry and bitter about the fact that I don't know if Dr. Y—— ever lost a night's sleep over this. He had the gall to call crying on the phone to me, then he hired a lawyer and insinuated that I might get sued for defamation of character. The man definitely needs psychiatric help, but no one would enforce the judgement. Since this incident, I have confided in only a few people about what happened.

I sometimes wonder if I should have carried some of the blame for the incident. I then say *NO*. I believe in always striving to do the right thing, yet I can't describe how difficult it has been to write about what happened.

PART 3

The Consultant's Perspective

After the trauma of sexual exploitation by a trusted health professional, the victim turns to other individuals for help in dealing with the ordeal. This assistance often comes from professionals in psychiatry, social services, and law. In Part 3, we examine patient sexual abuse from the perspective of the therapist, the counselor, the lawyer, and the medical board prosecutor.

The accounts of these different consultants have several themes in common. First, the authors found deep institutional and professional resistance to acknowledging the extent of the problem. Second, the inaction of individuals with knowledge of the exploitation allowed the offending health professionals to continue their abusive behaviors at the expense of additional victims.

We begin Part 3 with observations by the therapist of a man who was sexually exploited for over eight years by his former therapist. Frederic E. Oder discusses not only his professional response to this unusual case, but also what the victim revealed about the effects of long-term sexual abuse by a trusted mentor. The chapter also points out the reactions of other health professionals, both to the account of the abuse and to the offending therapist, and recounts the consequences of those reactions.

The private lawyer's perspective is presented by Daniel Burnstein in Chapter 5. A cross-section of cases and several suggestions for lawyers prosecuting similar cases are included, and excerpts from a detailed recollection by the same male victim discussed in Chapter 4 provides insight into the insidious, practiced manner in which the offender gained the trust and confidence of his victim.

Chapter 6, by Audrey W. Mertz, documents the interprofessional struggle in reporting sexual abuse in a startling account of molestations by a hospital-affiliated anesthesiologist. The chapter offers an insider's view of how the institutional and medical hierarchies protected the offender and allowed him to continue sexually molesting anesthetized patients. When the abuse finally became public, women who may have been victimized as well as the community at large reacted with shock and anger.

Two different aspects of one case of sexual abuse of numerous patients by a gynecologist are discussed in Chapters 7 and 8. Marylin Beck and Lori Long, in their presentation of a medical board's investigation and decision in a case of sexual misconduct, reveal the strategies, issues, and problems arising during the board's consideration of the case. The chapter provides yet another example of how the inaction of medical colleagues allowed the exploitative practices to continue after they became known. In the follow-up chapter, Ann Burgess offers a therapist's insight into these same female victim's thoughts and feelings during the abusive examinations, immediately after the sexual abuse, when determining a course of action, and after the medical board's decision.

Perceptions that a health professional's sexual misconduct generally involves one isolated incident are challenged by B. Joyce Dale in "The Rape Crisis Center View." From the time when the first victim reported the incident to the arrest of the accused gynecologist three years later, 24 victims came forward. The account also illustrates how the knowledge that other victims have been abused by the same health professional aids victims in overcoming their feelings of futility when deciding whether to disclose abuse.

The final chapter in this part suggests that the training of health professionals needs to acknowledge the possibility of sexual feelings surfacing in both patient and therapist. In "Workshops on Patient-Therapist Sexual Relationships," Marjorie Braude discusses issues that have been raised in her workshops. The results of a questionnaire for participants give additional perspectives on how psychiatrists view the problem of therapist-patient sexual relationships.

4

Observations on a Case of Patient Sexual Abuse

Frederic E. Oder

Several years ago, the young man in the following case came to me for treatment. He had spent many years with a psychiatrist who regularly had sexual contact with him during therapy sessions. What follows are my observations about this case.

BACKGROUND

When my patient, Mr. R——, first consulted his former therapist, Dr. L——, he was 25 years old, working in a boring factory job, friendless, and recovering from a psychiatric discharge from the navy. He was one of four children (one sibling was his identical twin) who grew up in marginal poverty in a small, New England town. His father was alcoholic, passive, and ineffectual; his mother paraded her promiscuity and was spiteful and sadistic in dealing with her children. Deceit, envy, and hatred characterized most of the family interactions, and when Mr. R—— first sought treatment, he was estranged from his twin. Although he was bright, he had dropped out of high school because of panic attacks that had begun in his sophomore year. He was fearful of women and had no significant sexual experience.

Dr. L—— proved to be charming, warm, and supportive. By the end of the second month, Dr. L—— initiated sexual contact with Mr. R——, telling him that it would be part of the treatment and delivering the first of many convoluted lectures about his world view and philosophy. Mr. R—— was sexually exploited by his therapist for nearly ten years. Apparently, the therapy took place once or twice each month in the therapist's office. Use of alcohol and marijuana and participation in sexual activities were frequent.

Mr. R—— quickly came to feel special to Dr. L——. Their meetings were held during the doctor's last session of the day, a time that the doctor said he kept for his favorite patients. A member of a minority group and of humble origins, the doctor was quick to point out the hypocrisy and corruption, the intolerance and narrow-mindedness of the middle class, a group that Mr. R—— had struggled fruitlessly to join. Dr. L—— proclaimed himself to be Mr. R——'s teacher and delivered innumerable homilies and parables designed to show that he was sharing a special wisdom that would enable Mr. R—— to move through the world with the same finesse as his mentor.

Dr. L—— also offered advice that touched every aspect of his patient's life. Much of it ran counter to ideas tentatively put forward by Mr. R——. At one point, Mr. R—— considered ending a relationship with a woman he felt was too smothering; Dr. L—— enjoined him to marry her because her family was wealthy and would support the couple. When Mr. R—— said he might try to learn something about computers, the doctor urged him instead to become a psychiatric nurse so they could run a clinic together.

Advice often led to action, at times trivial and at other times serious. To improve Mr. R——'s appearance, Dr. L—— took him shopping for clothes or to the hairdresser. To change the appearance of his penis, Mr. R—— was sent to a urologist for a circumcision. This behavior made Mr. R—— feel like he was being made over. Unsophisticated but not stupid, Mr. R—— questioned his doctor from time to time about his seemingly unorthodox techniques. Dr. L—— responded with lengthy diatribes about the stupidity and lack of originality of his colleagues.

The relationship was not without its problems as the years passed. Mr. R——, despondent over his lack of progress and his continuing panic attacks, took a drug overdose. Dr. L—— admitted him to the small, private hospital where he worked and pointedly told his patient that if he told anyone about his treatment, he would be sent to a state hospital.

This marked a turning point. Sessions became less frequent, and the doctor seemed less interested and available. Still, the attachment was so strong that Mr. R—— has wondered whether he might still be with Dr. L—— if the doctor had not suddenly moved to another city. There was no termination or referral by the doctor when he left.

Predictably, Mr. R—— felt abandoned, and he agonized for months over whether or not to contact his doctor. However, one day he saw a talk show on sexual abuse by therapists. He began to recognize what he had wasted in time, money, and opportunity for change. Over the next few years he seriously contemplated suicide; instead, he contacted a lawyer.

TREATMENT ISSUES

Credibility

I was not the first psychiatrist whom Mr. R—— contacted. A colleague who saw him before me was skeptical of the abuse, and Mr. R—— nearly gave up seeking assistance. However, as I had treated another of Dr. L——'s patients some years earlier, I was familiar with his methods. Yet the skeptical response from the first new therapist fulfilled Mr. R——'s worst fears as well as filled him with shame.

Psychological Diagnosis

Mr. R—— suffered from classic panic attacks with severe anticipatory anxiety and avoidance behavior. When I first met him, his wife and her family were virtually the only people in his life. Fairly good control of the panic attacks has now been achieved with medication, and he is comfortable in many social situations.

The initial work with this problem provided a safe activity during the first year, when Mr. R——'s capacity to trust me was tenuous. Spending time with symptoms, side effects, and medications in a traditional doctor-patient situation helped ease Mr. R——'s persistent fear that I might initiate bizarre activities.

Mourning

Much of the work that Mr. R—— has done in therapy has been grieving. He has repeatedly reviewed the minute details of his relationship with Dr. L—— and has come to terms with the fact that this relationship may prove to be the most important he will ever experience. He has relived the pain of his abandonment, realizing that he did not occupy the special place he sought in the heart of his doctor. He also has struggled with the idea that his therapist used him without interest in or capacity to understand his patient's needs.

Throughout this process, Mr. R—— experienced considerable anger and sadness. He now has a more dispassionate, if not forgiving, view of Dr. L——. Dr. L—— no longer assumes such importance in Mr. R——'s therapy, and it appears that at last they have terminated.

The Legal Process

When Mr. R—— came to see me, he had already initiated a malpractice suit against Dr. L——. I had to decide whether to remain relatively neutral or to be supportive and eventually participate in this process. I chose the latter, guided by Mr. R——'s conscious conviction that this was preferable to destroying physically and professionally either Dr. L—— or himself. The sublimation thus far has worked.

A second benefit from the lawsuit did not become apparent for some time. For years, the lawsuit has kept Mr. R—— in another legitimate professional relationship. Mr. R—— participated actively in the process of the lawsuit; he had many good ideas that his attorney used. At one point, Mr. R—— advertised in a local newspaper for other former patients of Dr. L—— who would be willing to discuss their experiences with him. He received over 50 replies and personally interviewed many of them. Not only did he discover one individual who was instrumental in resolving the case, but also he was able to dispell feelings that it had been something in him that had encouraged Dr. L——'s behavior. Mr. R—— was asked thousands of questions about his relationship with Dr. L—— as the process of discovery proceeded, which proved important to his work with me. Mr. R—— has borne considerable disappointment and frustration and has seen his attorney behave in a decent, professional manner.

QUESTIONS FOR THE PROFESSION

The first of Dr. L——'s patients that I saw told me that Dr. L—— had lost his license, had left the area, and was no longer practicing psychiatry. Among colleagues who had also learned of the doctor's flagrantly unethical and unprofessional conduct, the general consensus seemed to be "good riddance."

However, not only was Dr. L—— still practicing psychiatry, but he had an important position in a large, well-known hospital in another city. Not a single complaint had been filed against him at the state licensing board in nearly fifteen years of practice. Yet his behavior was fairly common knowledge within the profession and was so widespread that I had seen two of his former patients in less than three years. Neither I nor my colleagues had thought to verify the report that Dr. L—— was indeed out of business. I had reasoned that Dr. L——'s behavior was so frequent and outrageous that the information must have been correct.

This illustrates the much-publicized difficulty the medical profession has in policing itself and also shows the uncanny ability to survive that marks many practiced individuals like Dr. L——. Finally, it shows the inherent procedural problems in bringing a complaint against Dr. L——. (If Dr. L—— had indeed left the area and was not a member of any national medical organization, in what jurisdiction should a report be filed? What legal problems might one face in filing charges?) Only with increased attention to these issues, whether through laws mandating the reporting of sexual abuse or through regulation of licensing on a national level, can progress be made against the continuing practices of health practitioners who exploit their patients.

5

Sexual Malpractice Litigation

Daniel Burnstein

As recently as 25 years ago, private lawyers did not handle cases involving sexual abuse by health professionals. At best, lawyers would sympathize with victims and tell them that sexual abuse had not been determined by the courts to be malpractice. Now, the average lawyer is more apt to be approached by a victim, and a body of case law has developed.[1]

In my ten years as a civil litigator, I have had ten clients who were sexually abused by their therapists. This chapter describes some of the wrongs perpetrated on patients and the outcome of legal action in some of these cases. It also discusses the various parts of a case and some of the special issues involved in bringing legal action against health professionals; suggestions for attorneys are incorporated into the discussions.

OVERVIEW OF CASES

My first sexual malpractice case involved allegations so bizarre that I spent six months investigating them before accepting the case and sending a notice of claim. Usually, this notice is sent within a few weeks. The client told a confusing story about having been asked by her psychologist, Dr. A——, to seduce a male patient while Dr. A—— was present. The client successfully undertook this and another assignment and became intrigued with the idea of working with her therapist as a sexual surrogate.

With encouragement from Dr. A——, the woman rented an apartment and placed an advertisement in a weekly newspaper to test the market for sexual surrogates. She gave up the idea after the psychologist pulled out of the arrangement shortly thereafter. Several years later, these surrogate activities were discovered by her husband, from whom she was separated at the time she first went to Dr. A—— for marital counseling. When the woman returned to Dr. A—— for a letter to use in the divorce proceedings, the doctor instead seduced her. In a sworn deposition, the doctor admitted that he had been in his office while sexual activity occurred but claimed he had turned his head away and that at the time the woman was no longer his patient. He admitted in depositions not counseling her on the implications of surrogate work on her marriage and not having her obtain a physical examination.

The aspect of the case to which the doctor admitted was settled the day after the trial started. The sum was made up of amounts contributed by the doctor ($72,500), his supervisor ($25,000), the clinic ($25,000), and the successor clinic ($23,000). Because the doctor denied any seduction on his part, a jury heard the case against Dr. A—— and awarded the woman an additional $60,000 for the seduction.

Six years later, the licensing complaint is still ongoing; the psychology board of registration has not held a hearing on the complaint. The lawyer for the psychologist has been able to encourage the board's inertia by opposing the complaint on procedural grounds. Only after two newspaper articles appeared did the board even meet with the victim.

In another case, a woman client alleged that her psychiatrist tried to seduce her, but that he had been impotent and did not achieve penetration. The client further charged that her psychiatrist insulted her sexuality on numerous occasions for about one year thereafter, when she finally had enough courage to change therapists. The woman did not want to publicize her allegations, to file a lawsuit, or to file a licensing complaint. A negotiated settlement won the client all her therapy costs ($5,000) and attorney fees ($2,500), even though the doctor's insurance company initially claimed it would not cover him for such nonprofessional charges.

Another case involved a psychiatrist, who was also a law school graduate, accused of seducing his female patient. A jury verdict was rendered for the defendant. It has been speculated that a major factor in the verdict was the trial judge's instruction that if the patient knew or should have known that having sex with the doctor was wrong, then she could not recover damages. The case has been appealed on the grounds the judge's instruction was in error because the woman's mental status prevented her from comprehending the appropriateness of her actions and because a mental patient, judged legally incompetent, cannot give informed consent.

Several cases involved Dr. L——, a male psychiatrist accused of seducing male patients in his office. One client was subjected to eight and one-half years of sexual abuse and marijuana and alcohol use during his therapy sessions. The client also charged the doctor with failing to treat him for his suicide attempts and anxieties. The doctor admitted his failure to treat the patient for these problems but defended his practice by saying the patient had never raised the problems as issues.

The doctor denied the allegations of sexual exploitation and drug and alcohol use. Three years of investigation and advertisements placed in local newspapers resulted in five psychiatrists giving depositions about the defendant being fired or not rehired because of similar activities. Also, five additional male patients came forward and stated that they had been similarly abused with the aid of marijuana or alcohol during therapy sessions.

About a year and a half after the case was filed, the defendant's lawyer offered $25,000. In making this offer, he indicated that although he felt the charges against the doctor were "fantastic," there was some risk posed to the defendant by the various possible trial outcomes.

Three years after the lawsuit was filed, the defendant's lawyer offered $150,000. At that point, a key issue was whether the federal judge who would preside over the jury trial would allow the other victims to testify at a trial. The law generally does not allow evidence of prior negligence or "prior bad acts" to be introduced into evidence unless a jugde is convinced that the prior bad acts are proof of a similar scheme or plan.[2] The federal judge assigned to the case indicated in a pretrial conference that he was leaning toward admitting the evidence of prior bad acts.

A month later, immediately before the trial was scheduled to start, the offer was raised to $225,000. (This offer represented the full insurance amount available from the three insurance companies covering the doctor.) This final offer came after an individual responding to one of the newspaper ads indicated that Dr. L—— had boasted to him about having sex with a number of his patients, including the client, and that these patients were "like puppets on a string." Several other men have filed notices of claims, and another case has been filed in federal court.

The plaintiff accepted the offer of $225,000. He also notified the relevant authorities about the details of his case. The psychiatrist was dismissed from his job and lost his license to practice medicine after the authorities completed an independent investigation.

The original client in this case wrote a chronology of events to aid his psychiatrist and his lawyer in preparing his case. Excerpts of this account follow. The document is unique in the client's exceptional ability to recall and convey mesmerizing words of his psychiatrist.

November

Initial appointment with Dr. L——.

If there is only one thing I have learned from my experience with Dr. L——, it is that the only ones who are fully aware of and understand the influence, the control, and the power another can have over us are those who have been abused by it.

Dr. L—— asked me my reasons for seeking treatment. I told him I was afraid [and] depressed and felt panicky most of the time. I felt isolated—my life existed between my job and the apartment I shared with my father (I said that I lived with my father because I was afraid to live on my own). I told Dr. L—— I wanted to live a normal life. I said that it was important to me to work, but I wanted very much to have something that was worthwhile. I wanted to be able to make friends, begin dating, and someday marry and raise a family.

Dr. L—— asked me if I had had any past therapy treatment, besides that of Dr. ——.

I told him about my navy experience, Stanford University (he remarked that he had done his residency there), and the one or two visits with Dr. ——.

Dr. L—— asked if it was correct that, besides Dr. ——, I hadn't had any therapy experience. I said yes.

I told Dr. L—— that I had attempted suicide that past May. I had felt, as I did then, that I would always be a prisoner of my fears and depressions.

Dr. L—— asked me questions concerning my family. I told him of my alcoholic father (who seemed to be always frightened of something) and my cold, aloof mother who carried on a number of affairs.

When I told Dr. L—— that my older brother was homosexual, Dr. L—— wanted to know more about him. He asked if my brother had told me himself that he was gay or was this an assumption I had made on my own. I said that my brother had told me.

Dr. L—— asked if my attitude toward my brother had changed any because of his homosexuality. I said no, I didn't believe that it had.

Dr. L—— told me that after this first session, he would not dwell any further on my family background. He told me that any further information would be irrelevant. He said that other therapists would dig further—only to lengthen the time of treatment, adding unnecessarily to its cost.

November/December

I don't recall how many sessions I had with Dr. L—— during November–December. I saw him on the average of once a month throughout my treatment, beginning [the following] January.

At my next session, Dr. L—— showed me the front left panel of his desk. The panel, when lowered, revealed a hidden bar.

He explained that it was his custom to have coffee available during the day for his "regular" patients, beer and alcohol at night for his "special" patients. I declined the drink he offered at first, but he was persistent. Dr. L—— said that resisting a drink was part of my problem. He explained to me that by refusing to drink, I was retreating into a shell. I did not know how to enjoy life, he told me.

Dr. L—— explained that we all have a natural right to enjoy life—even if it was illegal. He said that the trick was to realize it was only the unenlightened, "square" middleclass that passed laws against having fun. But there were ways around these laws. Using himself as an example, he said he would love to walk along a beach, on a warm summer morning, with no clothes on. It would be natural to enjoy strolling naked, feeling the sand beneath his feet and a warm breeze and ocean spray on his body. But he realized that if he were to do so, he would be arrested. The small-minded middle class had the power to enforce its beliefs.

The way around the situation was to [walk on the beach] fully dressed—but naked in his mind.

Dr. L—— told me that both the upper and lower classes were very much alike. They shared the same opposite views from the middle class. The upper and lower classes were free in their lifestyles in that one had the power of money and the other had nothing to lose. Dr. L—— said that because the two shared like outlooks and both felt only disdain for those in the middle, the two classes could and do live side by side. He said that when the middle class lived in the city, the other two would coexist out in the suburbs. When the middle class moved to the suburbs, the other two shifted to the city.

Dr. L—— told me that as far as he could see, my homosexual brother was the only one in my family who was enjoying life. "He was out there doing things." Unlike me, he was at least involved in some form of sexuality. Dr. L—— told me that I was asexual.

I asked Dr. L—— if he meant that I would be better off being homosexual. He replied no. He explained that there were three stages of sexuality: homosexuality, heterosexuality, and bisexuality. He said that to develop sexually we must all pass through each stage in that order.

[The] homosexuality stage need not be physical. Its completion led into heterosexuality, which must be physical. Bisexuality was the apex, the ultimate level that could be achieved. A rare few, he being one, reached this top level.

Dr. L—— told me that anyone not reaching bisexuality was "stuck" in one of the lesser stages. He told me that my older brother, for whatever reason, was stuck in the lesser stage of homosexuality.

I told Dr. L——, as I had earlier, that I had had a sexual relationship. He replied that since it had been a chance encounter, not initiated by me, the experience had no real meaning. He asked if I were, at that time, involved in any sexual relationships. When I answered no, he told me that this was proof of his point.

Dr. L—— explained to me that I was asexual because I had not developed an ego—the ego being essential for entrance into sexuality.

Dr. L—— told met that we have three elements to our psyche: the id, the superego, and the ego.

The id is our natural, or animal, desires (food, sex, etc.). The superego is our civilized, or moral, conscience. And between the two is our self-evolved ego.

Dr. L—— used an example to illustrate how the three interact. He told me to imagine myself standing on a street corner, when suddenly a woman walks into view. Watching her approach, I become sexually aroused. My id, wanting simple satisfaction, urges me to attack her. But the equally strong superego intervenes and prevents this. There is, therefore, Dr. L—— explained, a stalemate.

If the situation were left as is, anxiety and depression result. What is needed is a referee—a mediating ego. The ego provides compromise between the two conflicting forces. In [the] example, the most likely solution would be allowing the id to accomplish its desire, but only after following some preset, civilized rules—courtship and marriage.

Dr. L—— told me that my treatment would consist of his stepping in and becoming my surrogate ego—while directing me to develop an ego of my own. As my ego, he would see to the satisfying of my id while placating my superego. The development of an ego of my own would necessitate my trying different experiences. He told me it was not going to be easy. And it was not necessary that I like any of the experience—but it was important that I try them if I was to succeed in therapy.

And I was desperate to succeed—particularly now that such hope was being held out to me.

I understood Dr. L—— to mean he intended me to enter the first stage of sexuality by becoming my "best friend," by becoming a nonphysical, intensely medically trained guide.

I thought I would reach the second stage of the hierarchy, heterosexuality, by his guiding me in developing relationships with women. I believed Dr. L—— to mean that he might even go so far as to use a woman, a sexual surrogate.

Dr. L—— told me he would keep in mind that I was a twin. As a twin I would have had unique experiences. He said he had twin sons and would treat me in light of his own experience as a father to them. Because he had twins, he said, he looked upon me in a special, even fatherly, way.

Dr. L—— asked me about my treatment with Dr. ——. I told him that after three or four sessions with hypnosis, we generally talked during a session. I said that Dr. —— had related to me some of his case histories and [I] told these to Dr. L——. The histories, I said, although giving me added confidence, made me somewhat uneasy. Uneasy because I couldn't help wondering if Dr. —— ever talked to other patients about me.

Dr. L—— told me that since Dr. —— was not really qualified, the stories were meant only to give himself credibility. I asked what he meant by Dr. —— not being qualified and was told that Dr. —— was not a psychiatrist. Not being a physician, [he] did not have the knowledge, authority, or control over his patients. His use of hypnosis was only a gimmick.

Dr. L—— went on to say that, as a patient of a psychiatrist, I had placed myself in his hands. He told me that the state gave him power over my freedom—that he had the right to place me in an institution at any time.

January

During my next appointment, Dr. L—— suddenly took out a marijuana joint, lit it, and took a puff. Without saying a word, he offered it to me. I was completely taken by surprise. I had never tried marijuana, let alone with a doctor during an office visit.

Believing this was what Dr. L—— had meant by trying new experiences and that I was being tested, I accepted it.

I believed that this was an important test of trust. Dr. L—— told me he was surprised but pleased that I was willing to risk trying a new experience, the marijuana.

We smoked marijuana with a few exceptions, at every session during the eight and one-half years of my treatment.

February

The first time Dr. L—— sexually abused me.

Smiling as he walked around from behind his desk, Dr. L—— motioned for me to stand. He embraced [me] and began kissing me on the lips. He fondled my genitals. Stepping back, he began undressing and told me to do the same. When I didn't move, he told me that I was again retreating into a shell.

Dr. L—— told me I had to trust him. He said he was acting as my ego and that as such he was taking me into the first stage of sexuality.

Dr. L—— told me that if I didn't trust him, I would never be rid of my anxieties and depression.

He unbuttoned my shirt and I finished undressing. Following his lead, I left my underpants on. He led me over to his black leather couch and told me to lie down.

Dr. L—— lay next to me. He fondled my genitals and again began kissing me on the lips. He moaned and made other erotic sounds. He took off his underpants and told me to do the same. He put my hand on his penis and motioned for me to masturbate him. He put his hand on my penis and began to masturbate me.

Dr. L—— had an erection, but I remained flaccid. After ten minutes or so his moaning grew louder and more intense.

He put my hand on his testicles and told me to squeeze and fondle them as he masturbated. He masturbated to orgasm—ejaculating semen over us and the couch. He embraced and kissed me while murmuring endearments.

Dr. L—— got up, telling me not to move, and went into the bathroom. I heard water running, and soon he brought out a damp washcloth and told me to wipe myself off.

While I was doing so, he dressed. After I had dressed, he again embraced and kissed me. Dr. L—— joked and laughed as we left his office—as if nothing had happen.

Dr. L—— repeated this scenario with a few variations throughout my eight and one-half years of therapy.

When I got home I took a shower. I did so after every session.

INTERVIEW, INVESTIGATION, NEGOTIATION, AND TRIAL

The initial interview of a victim of sexual abuse is almost always painful for the prospective client. The individual has been violated by a trusted health professional. No professional will ever be fully trusted again, and a new lawyer is no exception. Thus, it is critical to conduct a low-key, open-ended interview and not to expect to hear or understand all the facts immediately. Trying to establish exact dates and events only frustrates victims because they have often tried to forget much of what has occurred.

The attorney must fill in the gaps. The best way to do this is through successive interviews. As trust is built, more information is provided. In addition, attorneys need to obtain all the client's medical and therapy records; these records provide critical dates, facts, and perhaps information about problems for the case. Because defense attorneys will also have access to these records, it is important to know what they contain.

A second vital aspect of the cases's early phases is the establishment of a good working relationship with the client's current counselor. This relationship assists the lawyer in articulating a coherent, consistent, and accurate picture of what occurred and how the actions of the defendant damaged the patient. Unless a significant and permanent change in the victim's condition can be shown, it is difficult to win an acceptable recovery.

Clients should be appraised that their most intimate experiences will be brought up if the case goes into discovery and trial. Once damages are claimed, the defense has the right to delve into the client's emotional state before and after the malpractice. Thus, it is generally useful to consult with the client's counselor or therapist about the ability and advisability of the client's participation in this stressful experience.

Clients need to know their options for redress: taking action at the regulatory board level, filing criminal charges, filing civil actions, and notifying other responsible authorities. Unless the local district attorney is going to move the case enthusiastically, I do not recommend criminal complaints because of the high standard of proof required—proof beyond a reasonable doubt. There is a strong possibility that the client will be additionally victimized by the criminal justice system; the various participants in the legal process often cannot visualize how a patient was forced into sexual activity. Masters and Johnson have characterized sexual malpractice as rape,[3] but this view has not been widely adopted by prosecutors.

Typically, the first step in a civil case is notifying the therapist of the charges. Then the defendant's employer, the state licensing board, and the professional association of the defendant are notified of the client's claims. It is also advisable to notify current employers so they cannot claim to have had no notice of the plaintiff's charges. The employer most likely will wait to see how the case develops.

Early in the process, clients need to know that they can take the civil action one step at a time and decide exactly how far to go. It is important for clients to realize that the first step is simply sending out the notice of claim. After further investigation and negotiation, the client may decide to drop the case. A properly drawn contingent or hourly fee agreement will protect both parties and thus should not influence any decision of whether to continue with the case.

A critical aspect of developing and investigating cases is finding other victims. This is necessary, even if only to make the defendant's insurance company take the case seriously. The most effective way to locate other victims is through advertisements in local papers; the ads state that a lawyer or a patient of Dr. —— seeks to locate other former patients to compare treatment experiences. Attorneys must avoid prejudicing potential witnesses as well as take steps to minimize contact between a potential witness and the client. Witnesses should not be given the details of your case or advised of their legal rights. Instead, lawyers should listen carefully and, if possible, get a sworn statement. The statement can be useful for settlement purposes, for preparation of a deposition, or for convincing a judge that evidence is relevant to the case. In addition, victims with similar experiences make the client's story seem more believable. Their accounts may, depending on the judge, be admissible into evidence as an indication of a common scheme or plan.[4]

Other corroborating evidence is also helpful. In the case above involving Dr. A——, the jury appeared to take great interest in a bottle of perfume sent to the patient and charged by the therapist at a local department store. Although a civil case can be won simply through the testimony of the patient, some corroborative evidence is generally useful: people who saw both parties together in social settings, letters, knowledge of physical attributes of therapist's body and home, patterns of late hour therapy sessions with no nurse or secretary present, excessive intrusion into patient's private life, and gifts.

The negotiation phase of a case seems to occur at specific times in the progression of the case. One such period is before a case is filed. The next serious time of negotiation is immediately before a scheduled trial. With a case in litigation, insurance companies are reluctant to examine closely a case until the pretrial conference with the judge.

The role of the attorney during negotiations is similar to the attorney's role during the trial. The lawyer must convince the defense and the judge that the story of the plaintiff is more credible than the story of the defendant. Most information pertinent to the case will end up on the negotiating table before the trial.

SPECIAL ISSUES

Certain issues influence the legal proceedings against a health professional who has abused patients. Insurance coverage is one factor that increasingly impacts legal outcomes. A significant factor in several cases discussed earlier is that the doctor or therapist changes insurance companies more than once during recent years. The current law in most states is that the maximum coverage of the policy that one person abused by a psychiatrist could collect against would most likely be the maximum for a single claim in single year (i.e., $100,000 in a $100,000/$300,000 policy). However, these single claim limits may be "stacked," or added together, to get the maximum coverage if the health professional changes during the period the patient is abused.

In addition, insurance coverage for sexual misconduct may soon cease altogether if the current trend of policy denial continues.[5] This will mean that the average health practitioner will be denied an insurance lawyer for defense purposes and the funds to pay a settlement or judgment. In turn, this will make it harder for plaintiffs to recover damages and for physicians to defend themselves. However, courts may eventually force insurers to provide coverage as a matter of fairness.

Another special issue concerns the statute of limitations. This is particularly important in cases of sexual misconduct because victims of sexual abuse are often so traumatized that they wait several years before seeing a lawyer. Victims often spend much time in therapy before confronting a former therapist. However, the law usually allows approximately two or three years for the victim to file a malpractice lawsuit. In most states, this time period begins when the victim knew or should have known that he or she (1) had suffered damages (2) as a result of the malpractice of a former health professional. There is further protection for the victim in states where health practitioners are presumed to know that they wronged the patient. Because the health professionals have a fiduciary duty to inform the patient of the wrong, the patient's right to bring a claim is not lost.

Civil suits for damages alone are an inadequate tool. If insurance companies are involved, they merely pay the settlement or judgment and then raise the malpractice premiums. In turn, health practitioners pass on the added costs to their patients. The end result is that in certain cases, the insurance companies make more money from malpractice suits because they take their profits as a percentage of the total, increased premiums. Thus, civil suits quietly pursued have no lasting results in themselves other than recovering sums of money for the victim, sums that are never enough to compensate for the loss of trust and self-worth. A concerted effort combining civil suits, licensing actions, and community education may have a more long-term effect on reducing the sexual exploitation of patients.

A surprisingly broad spectrum of individuals display a lack of sympathy for victims of sexual malpractice. In selecting jurors, attorneys need to consider that members of certain demographic groups expected to empathize with these victims may instead see them as "deserving of what they get." In addition, this widespread lack of sympathy indicates the need to educate the jury, through the plaintiff's account and the testimony of expert witnesses, about the nature of the transference reaction. Freud described the dangerousness of transference love, or the patient's projection of earlier love experiences onto the therapist.[6] Such a reaction is to be expected; it is the health professional's engaging in sex with the patient that is condemned by the mental health and medical communities. If this can be conveyed to juries, they will render a verdict for the victim of sexual exploitation by a health professional.

NOTES

1. *Landau v. Werner,* 105 Sol.J. 1008(1961); *Zipkin v. Freeman,* 436 S.W.2d 753 (Mo.banc 1968); *Roy v. Hartogs,* 81 Misc.2d 350, 366 N.Y.S.2d 297 (1975), *aff'd on condition of remittitur,* 85 Misc.2d 891, 381 N.Y.S.2d 587 (1976).

2. Evidence of other crimes, wrongs, or acts is not admissible to prove the character of a person in order to show that he acted in conformity therewith. It may, however, be admissible for other purposes, such as proof of motive, opportunity, intent, preparation, plan, knowledge, identity, or absence of mistake or accident. Fed.R.Evid. 404(b).

3. W. H. Masters and V. E. Johnson, "Principles of the New Sex Therapy," *American Journal of Psychiatry* 133 (1976): 553.

4. *United States v. Free,* 574 F.2d 1221, 1223 (5th Cir. 1978); *Hamman v. Hartford Accident and Indemnity Co.,* 620 F.2d 588 (6th Cir. 1980); *Croce v. Bromley Corp.,* 623 F.2d 1084 (8th Cir. 1980); *United States v. Billups,* 522 F.Supp. 935 (E.D.Va. 1980); *Crawford v. Yellow Cab Co.,* 572 F.Supp. 1205 (N.D.Ill. 1983); *People v. Sylvia,* 54 Cal.2d 115, 4 Cal. Rptr. 509, 351 P.2d 781 (1960); *People v. Ing,* 65 Cal.2d 603, 55 Cal.Rptr. 902, 422 P.2d 590 (1967); *Gunthorpe v. Daniels,* 257 S.E. 199 (1979); Stone, *The Rule of Exclusion of Similar Fact Evidence: America,* 51 Harv.L.Rev. 988 (1938); Morgan, *Admissibility in Criminal Prosecutions of Proof of Other Offenses as Substantive Evidence,* 3 Vand.L.Rev. 779 (1950); Weinstein and Berger, 2 Weinstein's Evidence §404 [08] (1975); 143 A.L.R. 1194, 1199 (1943); 2 Wigmore, Evidence, §§202, 275, 300–373 (3d ed. 1940); Trautman, *Logical or Legal Relevancy—A Conflict in Theory,* 5 Vand.L.Rev. 385, 406, n. 84 (1952); McCormick on Evidence, §§41–44, 190–191, 193–195 (2d ed. 1972).

5. New policies issued by the American Psychiatric Association, American Psychological Association, and National Association of Social Workers attempt to exclude sexual activity from insurance coverage. Whether the courts will uphold these exclusions remains to be seen. Cases that have considered insurance coverage include: *Zipkin v. Freeman*, 436 S.W.2d 753 (Mo.banc 1968); *Security Insurance Group v. Wilkinson*, 297 So.2d 113, (Fla.Dist.Ct.App. 1974); *Hartogs v. Employers Mutual*, 89 Misc.2d 468, 391 N.Y.S.2d 962 (1977); *Greenberg v. McCabe*, 453 F.Supp. 765 (E.D.Pa. 1978); *St. Paul v. Hawaiian Insurance and Guaranty Co.*, 2 Hawaii 595, 637 P.2d 1146 (1981); *Vigilant Insurance Co. v. Kambly*, 114 Mich.App. 683, 319 N.W.2d 382 (1982); *Hirst v. St. Paul Fire and Marine Insurance Co.*, 106 Idaho 792, 683 P.2d 440 (1984); *Smith v. St. Paul Fire and Marine Insurance Co.*, 353 N.W.2d 130 (Minn. 1984).

6. Sigmund Freud, "Observations on Transference-Love," in *Collected Papers*. Vol. 2, *Further Recommendations in the Technique of Psycho-Analysis*, ed. Ernest Jones, trans. Joan Riviere, (New York: Basic Books, 1957).

6

Sexual Abuse of Anesthetized Patients

Audrey W. Mertz

COMMUNITY RESPONSE

Community residents were shocked when a prominent anesthesiologist was arrested for sex acts with anesthetized female patients. The physician had orally copulated with women in the operating room, while surgery was in process, many times during a two-year period. Citizens found it incredible that this activity could continue undetected. Immediate community response was disbelief and outrage. It became apparent that although the behavior had been reported by nurses, the hospital had taken no action.

As nurses began their grand jury testimony, the community learned that two years earlier, a circulating nurse had observed the anesthesiologist, standing behind opaque drapes at the head of the operating table, with his penis in the patient's mouth. Stunned, the nurse asked another circulating nurse to verify what she saw. Both nurses reported the incident to the operating room nursing supervisor; after the operation all three talked with the surgeon and examined the stains on the drapes. The surgeon did not believe their account, did not order lab tests on the stained material, and told the nurses not to discuss the matter.

The supervising nurse then reported the incident to the head of anesthesiology. When the nursing supervisor, the anesthesiology chief, and the surgeon confronted the anesthesiologist, he denied the charges. No further reports were made.

The nurse who had made the first observation continued to witness suspicious behavior by the anesthesiologist in the operating room and discussed her concerns with supervising nurses. Although the allegations were relayed to the hospital administrator and the president of the hospital board of trustees, no action was taken.

After the charges filed through hospital channels failed to bring results, the operating room nurses decided to gather evidence and take it directly to the hospital administrator. Approximately two years after the initial incident and after observing suspicious movements by the doctor with a 12-year-old patient, the nurses collected a specimen of secretions from the patient's suction tubing to test for the presence of semen. They prepared a report, submitted it to the administrator, and received no response. The nurses then presented their report to the state medical licensing board.

The county medical society's executive director and president met with the reporting nurses and with the society's attorney. This attorney informed the hospital that the doctor should be suspended from the hospital medical staff and the case reported to the state medical licensing board. County medical society officials told the doctor of their actions and urged him to seek counseling. He had already resigned from the hospital and made an appointment with a psychiatrist.

Without citing specific reasons, the hospital one month later notified the licensing board of the doctor's suspension from the medical staff. The board immediately investigated and brought the information to the district attorney, who filed felony charges. The doctor attempted suicide and was hospitalized.

After the abuse by the anesthesiologist became public, hospital officials, the hospital licensing agency, the hospital accreditation commission, local and state medical societies, and the district attorney were bombarded with questions about what actions they were taking and why they had not acted earlier. The state nurses' association immediately held a press conference to urge nurses at the hospital to speak out regardless of a hospital gag order and to point out the advantages of association membership. (Some months earlier, the hospital nurses had voted against a contract with the state nurses' association after the hospital administration promised to set up grievance procedures.) In addition, five women's organizations formed a coalition—Women Against Medical Oppression—and staged a rally outside the hospital to protest the offenses by the anesthesiologist, the cover-up at the hospital, and other aspects of victimization of women by the medical establishment.

An editorial in the community newspaper gave this view of events: "Thus a complaint whose seriousness would have been instantly recognized if it had come from a doctor was dismissed because it came from a nurse. And that—and the rigid sex barriers with which this nurse/doctor situation is still laced—is also how the possibility that a doctor had criminally abused women patients would lead a nurse to outraged sympathy with the patients, while a doctor-administrator would be more solicitous of the mental health of his colleague."[1]

OFFICIAL RESPONSE

Soon after public disclosure of the abuse, the hospital executive director was suspended, with pay, pending internal investigation. After the investigation was completed, he was fired. Medical staff bylaws were changed to tighten procedures, and the composition of the board of trustees was altered so that physicians no longer constituted a majority. Although the joint commission on accreditation of hospitals revoked the hospital's accreditation after an unannounced survey, it was later reinstated.

The state medical quality assurance board and the board of registered nursing moved to suspend the licenses of two doctors and three nurses for "gross negligence and unprofessional conduct" in failing to investigate and report the offenses. On appeal, the superior court judge ruled that two of the nurses should retain their licenses. The court of appeals ruled that the physician chief of staff was not subject to discipline by the medical licensing board because he was acting in an administrative capacity, rather than as a physician. The state supreme court let stand the previous rulings concerning these three professionals.

A state administrative law judge ruled that the second doctor, the surgeon in the original incident, was not guilty of gross negligence or unprofessional conduct. The remaining nurse, the operating room supervisor, had her license revoked. However, a superior court judge later ruled that she should have a new hearing because she was denied due process in the previous revocation proceedings.

CONSEQUENCES TO THE ANESTHESIOLOGIST

The anesthesiologist pleaded no contest to three felony counts involving three patients. As a result of the plea bargain, four other counts involving three additional patients were dropped. After a court-ordered psychiatric evaluation, the doctor was committed to a state hospital as a mentally disordered sex offender. The physician's medical license was revoked. On the basis of being mentally disabled, he filed for Social Security benefits to meet his child support obligations. Benefits were first denied, then awarded. As of early 1986, the offender had been released from the state hospital and was enrolled in an outpatient program in another city.

CIVIL SUITS

When the district attorney prepared the criminal case, he gathered 1,500 patient records to identify people who were anesthetized by the physician and thus might have been victims. The anesthesiologist had stated to psychiatrists that he victimized approximately two patients monthly for several years, carrying out a compulsive, secret ritual expressing hostility to women.

Eventually, 158 civil suits were brought together by a plaintiff steering committee. The superior court judge was able to bring the opposing parties, represented by a total of 35 attorneys, to agreement in nine days of negotiating. Insurance carriers for the defendant doctors and nurses and for the hospital contributed to a fund for paying damages. After review of each case, awards were made in accordance with liability and damages. The judge's accomplishment saved approximately five years of litigation and millions of dollars in court costs.

PATIENT RESPONSE

"Why do they always rape me?" was the first response of a middle-aged woman when she learned she had been victimized by the anesthesiologist. She remembered receiving injections and hearing attendants talking but had no other recollection of the operation until she awoke. At that time, the woman noticed a wet area on the anesthesiologist's pants and thought he had urinated or spilled something. She had no apparent ill effects from the operating room experience until contacted by the district attorney two years later. The woman had been positively identified as a victim because nurses had seen the doctor's penis in her mouth during the operation.

Disclosure of the abuse reawakened a series of memories of being sexually exploited in early childhood. The woman felt dirty and ashamed as well as anxious, angry, and depressed; she blamed herself for bringing out evil urges in men. The victim suffered increased marital conflict and began to drink more heavily.

Victims' grand jury testimony about their recollections of the operating room experience varied. Some victims recalled nothing, while one woman, who was not unconscious during the abuse, was fully aware of oral copulation. When she told her husband in the recovery room what had happened, he did not believe her.

After accounts of the offenses appeared in the news media, hundreds of women who had been anesthetized by the doctor searched their recollections for clues about whether they had been victimized. Some women recalled postsurgery bad taste in the mouth, nausea, vomiting, anxiety, sleep disturbance, or vague feelings of something being wrong. Many patients experienced a change in sexual response after the operation.

The possibility of having been victimized elicited a strong, emotional response in many women. One former patient, a college professor in women's studies, reported her panic when she confirmed that the doctor had been her anesthesiologist. She had difficulty concentrating and working, forgot appointments, slept and ate poorly, and experienced backaches and stiffness. Realizing that her reactions were typical of rape victims, she called a rape crisis counseling center. Many women felt antagonism toward doctors and hospitals and either turned to alternative health care or decided to avoid any future health care.

AFTERMATH

Denial of the unwelcome truth is still heard from doctors and hospital staff who do not believe that their respected colleague could act in such an aberrant manner. Others criticize the victims' claims of injury and say that because anesthetized patients do not feel anything, they could not have been injured—and are wrong in suing for money. These critics say that the media coverage created the victims; the patients had no adverse effects before their knowledge of the sexual abuse.

Although it may be true that for the deeply anesthetized patient oral copulation could occur without perception, several victims did present some physical and emotional response in the operating room or soon afterward. Other patients felt damaged, long afterward, at the discovery that they were or might have been victimized. And the community remained outraged that a hospital could allow such behavior to continue.

NOTE

1. Editorial, the Sacramento *Bee*, April 25, 1979.

7

Gynecologist-Patient Sexual Abuse: I. A Medical Board's View

Marylin Beck and Lori Long

One particularly disturbing aspect of many cases of sexual abuse by health professionals is that the offender's conduct was known by professional colleagues even before patient complaints were lodged. No steps were taken to protect patients from the sexual exploitation; no attempts were made to obtain appropriate psychiatric help for the offenders. By the time these cases were reported to medical registration boards, many patients had been injured.

There are several reasons why official action is often delayed; victims are reluctant to lodge complaints, avenues of complaint are lacking or unknown, physicians tend to disbelieve such complaints, medical colleagues will not confront the offender, and identifiable forums or guidelines for dealing with the issue have not been established.

Each of these factors was present in three cases we prosecuted for a state board of registration in medicine. The history of one of these cases illustrates how these factors contributed to an escalation of the problem.

CASE HISTORY

The case involved a gynecologist who had been conducting sexually abusive internal examinations for fifteen years. The physician's public profile was impeccable. A middle-aged man with a family and with a busy, successful practice in a closely knit suburban town, he was known as a kind, gentle doctor. He was active in the medical community and had held various leadership positions at the local hospital.

The complainant to the medical registration board was a 26-year-old mother of two who had seen the physician during both her pregnancies and who had just delivered her second son. Although she previously had been pleased with his care, she felt she had to complain about the "unprofessional" examination she had been given. At the end of her six-week, postpartum examination, the nurse who had been present during the routine exam left. As the patient prepared to dress, the physician told her he had forgotten to check something and asked her to lie down again so he could reexamine her. Using a large amount of lubricating cream, the doctor rubbed and manipulated her genitals, particularly her clitoris, for approximately 20 minutes. At no time did he have one hand on her abdomen, as in a normal internal exam.

While this was happening, the patient's thoughts alternated between questioning the doctor's actions and fearing that he had found something seriously wrong. When she asked him what was wrong, he told her not to worry, that it would only take a few more minutes. After masturbating the patient to orgasm, the physician abruptly stopped and washed his hands as though nothing unusual had happened. The patient, very shaken and confused, left the doctor's office without confronting him.

Upon arriving home, the woman told her husband about the incident. Together they wrote a letter of complaint to the physician. The physician responded by telephone. Without addressing the allegations, he instead stated that he was sorry the patient had been troubled by the examination.

Unsatisfied with the physician's response, the patient discussed her experience with a few close friends and with her childbirth nurse-instructor. The nurse encouraged her to pursue the matter and offered to speak to the hospital's chief of obstetrics on the patient's behalf. The chief of obstetrics referred the nurse to the medical society, which suggested that the patient file a written complaint with the board of medical registration.

By this time, the patient had learned of two other women who had experienced similar treatment from the physician. She referred to these women in her letter of complaint.

The board comprises five physicians and two lay members. Upon receipt of a complaint, the board determines whether the alleged conduct is a licensure infraction and whether there is reasonable cause to believe the allegations are true. A preliminary investigation is conducted. If findings are positive on both counts, the board institutes formal disciplinary action by issuing a complaint, known as an order to show cause.

When the board members first received the complaint in this case, their immediate reaction was that the story was unlikely to be true. The members felt the incident could not have occurred without the patient's cooperation, especially as she admitted to having an orgasm. Nevertheless, board investigators were instructed to contact the other two women mentioned in the complaint and to request that the physician respond to the allegations.

The physician answered promptly and briefly. He did not deny the charges but explained that the woman had not complained during the exam and that his busy schedule would have precluded him from spending with her the amount of time she claimed.

Although the other two women were initially reluctant to become involved, they eventually agreed to file official complaints. The incidents they described had occurred five and nine years earlier.

One of the stories was almost identical to the incident described in the original complaint. The abusive exam had occurred after a routine exam. The woman reported the same excessive use of lubricating cream, and the exam ended when she finally told the doctor to stop because he was hurting her.

The incident reported by the third woman was somewhat different. It occurred in the physician's private office after the examination was finished and the patient had dressed. While talking with the physician at his desk, the patient mentioned that she had been experiencing a pain in her side. Rather than asking the woman to return to the examination room, the physician asked her to stand up and roll down her pants. She was flustered, but nevertheless complied. The doctor crouched in front of her and began to manipulate her genitals. She protested and asked him to stop, to which he responded that he was almost finished. When he did stop, he told her that everything appeared to be fine. The patient was too shaken to confront the physician, and she tried to convince herself that the incident was not irregular and that the doctor's motivations were purely medical.

On the basis of these three allegations of improper conduct, the board initiated formal disciplinary proceedings and voted to issue an order to show cause. The order charged the physician with three counts of manipulating patients' genitals without legitimate medical purpose.

Once an order to show cause is issued, the licensing board removes itself from active involvement in a case and turns it over to its prosecutor for further investigation and presentation at a fact-finding hearing. Because the board will judge the case, due process considerations require that it not communicate with its prosecuting staff about the case while it is pending. All communications are made in the context of legal proceedings.

The prosecutor in a disciplinary case is not unlike a criminal prosecutor, being responsible for presenting a full and accurate picture of the defendant's misconduct and establishing that the allegations are true. In this case, we prosecutors decided it was important to assemble as much evidence as possible against the physician. The physician's reputation was immaculate, and as in most cases of sexual victimization, the victim's credibility and reputation's undoubtedly would be an issue. Thus, we believed it would be easier to convince the board of the allegations if more women could testify about similar experiences. Therefore, additional witnesses were sought.

CASE INVESTIGATION

Obtaining evidence proved to be the most difficult phase of the case. We followed leads offered by the three witnesses to identify other women with similar experiences. None of these new potential witnesses would agree to meet with us or to allow their identities revealed because they feared retaliation and a negative impact on their families. To communicate with them, we drafted a general letter explaining the case and what their involvement as a witness would entail. This letter was given to the three complainants to give to potential witnesses. The charges were mentioned only in general terms, and the doctor was not identified.

After several weeks, a few women came forward. Each one described a similar incident that had occurred as much a ten years earlier, and each witness knew of someone else with a similar experience. A few also said they had reported the incident to other doctors in the community. Every woman we talked with also agreed to join the growing pool of witnesses. However, we were never confident that these witnesses would remain with us throughout the proceedings.

Because several witnesses indicated that the medical community had prior knowledge of the problem, physicians who had allegedly been told of incidents involving the defendant were contacted. The chief of obstetrics and gynecology at the hospital where the defendant saw most of his patients, had seen two of the witnesses as private patients after their experience with the defendant. This physician had been informed by both women of the defendant's "unprofessional exams" and more recently had referred the original complainant to the state medical society. When we spoke to him, he denied having had any earlier knowledge of the problem. Although his own notation on one woman's records referred to her complaints about the defendant, he dismissed it, explaining that the patient was probably just a "poor reporter." He blamed the defendant for not having a nurse in the room to protect himself from malicious accusations. The other physicians contacted likewise denied having heard any complaints against the defendant, calling the accuracy of the witnesses' recollections into doubt.

Shortly thereafter, two significant pieces of evidence were brought to our attention by medical insiders. The childbirth educator who had supported the original complainant contacted the new chief of obstetrics, whom she knew well, and at our request asked him if he had heard of any complaints against the defendant. This physician acknowledged that a patient had complained to him about an examination by the defendant six months *after* the board's order to show cause had been issued. The physician presented the patient's complaint to the chief of the medical staff at the hospital, not knowing that board action had been initiated.

These two physicians, acting as hospital officers, met with the defendant and informed him of the woman's complaint. The defendant offered to telephone the patient to apologize for anything she thought may have been improper. The officers advised the defendant to seek professional help and warned him that further incidents would be met with sanctions. They never officially recorded the meeting or checked whether the defendant followed their advice.

When we met with these two hospital officers, they cooperated and appeared concerned. However, they refused to believe the defendant was a danger to his patients unless the board could prove yet another incident had taken place after their confrontation with the defendant. They seemed to attach little significance to the fact that the incident they had investigated occurred after the defendant already knew of the board's involvement in an earlier case.

The second piece of evidence against the defendant came from a young woman who had been victimized by the defendant and who had confided in her employer, a local general practitioner. Although the woman declined any involvement in the case, she did authorize us to talk to her former employer.

This practitioner said the woman told him about the incident immediately after it occurred, and that he took the complaint to an obstetrician who practiced at the defendant's hospital. The general practitioner informed us that he then met with two obstetricians from the hospital and that both men told him they knew about the defendant's behavior and had been trying to make him stop "for years." However, both these obstetricians refused to talk to us, telling us their lawyers had advised them not to cooperate.

Despite this lack of cooperation from the physician community, we had enlisted 14 witnesses. At this point, the defendant petitioned the board to limit witnesses to this number. Apparently convinced by the defendant's argument that the investigation alone, if unchecked, would destroy his reputation, the board granted the motion.

Although we felt that the women who had agreed to testify would benefit from group therapy, concerns about defense claims of conspiracy against the defendant necessitated our requesting that the women refrain from speaking with each other. We instead encouraged witnesses to contact us to voice concerns and ask questions. In short order, this became so time-consuming and emotionally draining that an outside consultant with experience in dealing with victims of sexual abuse was sought. The consultant became our contact with the witnesses, and from that point we talked or met with witnesses only when legal preparations required such contact.

With the investigation phase over, formal discovery and trial preparation began in earnest. Each of the 14 witnesses was interviewed by a team of lawyers. The defendant was permitted by the board to interrogate the witnesses through deposition testimony. This would provide him with an opportunity in advance of the hearing to intimidate the witnesses, women who were already reluctant to speak against the well-respected doctor. It was clear that the defense attorney intended to attack their credibility and to develop the theory that they were conspiring against an innocent man. However, settlement was reached before any of the witnesses were deposed.

SETTLEMENT NEGOTIATIONS

It is usually in the interest of a state agency to negotiate a settlement and avoid a trial when the proceedings are likely to be protracted. Resources generally are limited, and when all resources are allocated to one case they are unavailable to others.

Settlement of a disciplinary proceeding presents some special problems. In civil litigation, a case is usually settled by two opposing attorneys acting with authority to represent their client's interests. In criminal cases, the prosecutor agrees on sentencing with the defense counsel and recommends the agreement to the judge, who is free to accept or to reject the agreement. If the judge rejects the agreement, the case goes to trial before a new judge and jury with no knowledge of the defendant's prior admission of guilt. In a disciplinary proceeding the board both finds the facts and imposes sanctions. An administrative agency cannot challenge itself and transfer the case if the proposed settlement is not acceptable.

As the board's prosecutors, we could neither bind the board to a negotiated settlement nor try the case before an alternative factfinder if the proposed settlement was rejected by the board. In a disciplinary proceeding, the defendant has to take the risk that the board will accept a proposed settlement. In most cases when a disciplinary action is tried, the facts are presented to one board member who is designated by the entire board to hear the case. The hearing officer makes findings of facts and recommends a decision that the board considers in making a final determination. The hearing officer is excluded from voting on the final decision.

In preliminary settlement discussions, board prosecutors and defense counsel agreed that if the allegations were true, the defendant's conduct reflected deep-seated mental and emotional problems. To assist both sides in reaching a fair result, we agreed to give considerable weight to an independent psychiatric evaluation of the defendant, conducted by a mutually acceptable psychiatrist experienced in working with impaired professionals. Both sides readily agreed on a psychiatrist but had great difficulty determining the approach the psychiatrist should take in examining the defendant and the evidence.

The parties finally agreed to submit a summary of the prosecution's evidence to the psychiatrist, with instructions that he was to assume the evidence was true. He was asked to examine the defendant to determine whether he could be rehabilitated and, if so, to recommend areas of medical practice unlikely to trigger similar problems. Both parties agreed on a series of questions to be answered by the expert psychiatrist. The expert was not to make any determinations about the truth of the allegations. However, the defendant would have access during the evaluation to the psychiatrist without the presence of the board's counsel and would thus have an opportunity to impress his view on the psychiatrist. The defendant persistently maintained his innocence.

Unfortunately, the psychiatrist's report was quite ambiguous; although the psychiatrist stated that the defendant definitely needed help, the report emphasized the stress the defendant was under during the protracted disciplinary proceedings and encouraged the defense's conclusion that the problem would disappear once proceedings were terminated. It appeared that the psychiatrist had chosen not to believe all of the evidence and felt great compassion for the physician.

The psychiatrist who had examined the defendant appeared before the board in executive session to answer questions about the defendant's condition. Board members were unanimously unimpressed with his suggestion that the charges had caused any of the defendant's problems.

The negotiated agreement included specific and general admissions to the misconduct and the ongoing nature of the problem. The settlement called for the revocation of the defendant's license and the immediate issuance of a limited license to enable the defendant to enter a two-year retraining program in anesthesiology. The defendant had been accepted to a training program at one of the leading local medical centers. By agreement, the defendant would continue in therapy with his own psychiatrist, who would report the physician's progress to the board at regular intervals. The defendant's retraining would be monitored by the board through regular reports from the defendant's supervisor. In order to supplement his income during retraining, the defendant was permitted to assist in general surgery under the close supervision of the chief of surgery, with the provision that the chief of surgery would be fully informed of the defendant's problems and his need for supervision. On successful completion of his retraining program, the defendant would be issued a license restricted to anesthesiology. The board met with the defendant in closed session and informed him of their intent to approve the settlement. Seven months later, the board issued a final order consistent with the agreement.

Following the board's private notification of the defendant that it had accepted the terms negotiated and recommended by both parties, the defendant closed his private practice and began his residency program. He sent letters to his former patients, informing them of his change of specialties and offering to transfer their medical records to another physician.

This generated a variety of responses from his patients. Some called the board to complain about the physician's abandonment of his patients; others called about rumors concerning the defendant's misconduct. The local newspaper became interested in the commotion surrounding the close of the defendant's practice and called the board for more information. A reporter examined the board's file, which did not yet include a final order. When the defendant learned that the press had examined his disciplinary file, he moved to amend the settlement agreement because of changed circumstances and requested that the board limit his license without first revoking it.

The board refused to modify the terms of the settlement. When the final order was issued, the local newspaper did a full-page feature article on the case. The article was picked up by the largest newspaper in the state, and five months later the largest regional newspaper printed a feature story on the case in the editorial section of their Sunday paper. Nevertheless, because identities were changed, only people already familiar with the case recognized the principals involved.

8

Gynecologist-Patient Sexual Abuse: II. An Evaluation of Victims

Ann Wolbert Burgess

Sixteen women were sexually exploited by their male gynecologist during physical examinations. This chapter presents what they related about their victimizations and their reactions to medical board actions and news media accounts concerning the incidents of sexual abuse.

PATIENTS' BACKGROUNDS

At the time of the victimizations, all 16 women were married. Their ages ranged from 23 to 37 years and the majority were at home raising their children in traditional homemaker roles. Their families saw private physicians for health care services and lived in suburban, middle-class communities.

The sexual abuse incidents occurred over an eight-year period. Five of the women saw the physician only once or twice for a specific gynecological complaint (e.g., abdominal pain, vaginal discomfort). However, ten of the 11 women who had several appointments with the physician before the incident had been seeing him for obstetrical care for a minimum of eight months; one woman had seen him over many years for general gynecological care and diet medication.

The physician had an established practice at the time of the early complaints. The women characterized him as fatherly, friendly, casual, professional, kind, and cordial. Most of the patients liked his professional style, saying that he did not rush them, that he answered their questions, and that he made them feel relaxed. As one patient said, "He was the ideal doctor. He took an interest in his patients. He knew your name, and he would take time to sit and talk to you. Patients love him." The majority of the women stated he had been highly recommended by either a family member, another physician, or a trusted friend.

THE ABUSIVE INCIDENT

The sexual exploitation described by the women took place during gynecological examinations. When asked to describe features of the examinations that seemed unusual, the patients identified the following:

1. Lengthy examination. The main complaint by all patients was the length of the examination ("It took an eternity"). This complaint escalated when the women learned that the time taken by other physicians was one to two minutes.

2. Misuse of the physician's hands. Most of the women reported that the physician touched them all over the perineum and genital areas; they also reported that the physician's thumb rubbed the clitoris. Patients said that he used an in and out motion with his examining hand and that he did not keep his left hand on the abdomen.

3. Absence of a nurse during the examination. The women reported two settings in which the abuse took place: (1) on the examining table when the nurse was never present or when the physician said he needed to check something after the nurse had left the room, and (2) a "stand-up" examination in the physician's outer office after the regular examination had been completed and the patient had dressed.

4. Excessive use of lubricant. Most patients commented on the use of lubricant during the internal examination in terms of amount ("There were gobs and gobs"), noise ("There was so much it made a squashing noise"), and location ("It was all over my thighs by the end of the examination").

Coping with the examination. Although all the patients became aware of the unusual length of the examination, 12 women did not stop the physician for three reasons: (1) four thought the exam was lengthy because something was seriously wrong internally, (2) four trusted that the doctor was conducting an ethical examination, and (3) four felt powerless to interrupt him. Most women, rather than terminating the examination, coped in various ways, such as asking questions ("What is taking so long?" "Is all this necessary?" "What are you doing?"), making polite requests ("Please hurry up," "Please stop"), physically moving on the examing table (squirming, moving away, pulling back), dissociating themselves from the experience ("I counted the squares on the ceiling"), and trying distraction techniques. In response, the physician made placating remarks ("In another minute," "I'm just checking something"), gave instructions ("You must relax"), made interpretations ("You are upset and nervous"), and asked questions ("Am I making you nervous?" "What are you thinking of?"). The women experienced a variety of feelings during the examination, primarily disbelief ("I wouldn't believe he was doing anything wrong"); anxiety and fear ("I suspected what was going on, but I was too scared to do anything"); and annoyance, anger, terror, and panic. They most often were immobilized ("I didn't want to cause a scene so I didn't stop him").

Physiological response. Two specific physiological responses were reported by the women: sexual arousal and physical discomfort. Ten of the women reported feelings of sexual arousal, and eight described having an orgasm. None of the women reported any subjective pleasure with the physiological response, but rather used phrases such as "felt something warm" or a "funny weird feeling". Five women reported shaking and perspiring ("My back was soaked when I got off the table").

The eight women who described feelings of physical discomfort and two of those who had orgasms complained of the pain during the internal examination ("I think he pushes on the uterus to distract you; it hurts, but his thumb is also on your clitoris"). They described feeling scared, nervous, and physically upset ("I thought I was going to vomit"). These women tended to be visiting the physician for specific gynecological complaints and were concurrently experiencing vaginal discomfort ("I was still sore from delivery").

Ending the examination. The examination ended in a variety of ways: by the women confronting the physician ("You'll have to stop; it hurts; I'm blacking out"), by the women physically changing position ("I sat up"), by the women recalling rumors about the physician ("The minute his thumb started rubbing me, I thought of my friend and what she had said and told him to stop his examination"), immediately after an orgasm ("He stopped right after I climaxed"), or after the physician terminated the examination himself.

All the women reported negative reactions to the incident. All were upset and confused and reported feeling dirty, humiliated, degraded, embarrassed, and nauseated. Four women expressed anger; one woman walked out of the office, past other women sitting in the waiting room, and thought of warning them; four women cried on the way home; and three took baths as soon as they were home.

DECISIONS AFTER THE INCIDENT

After being sexually abused, all of the women had to make decisions about continuing medical care with the gynecologist and about disclosing the incident. All 16 women terminated their medical care with the physician either immediately (ten women), after one more visit (four women), or after several more visits (two women). The women who made one more visit usually had immediate medical concerns. Pregnant women were under greatest stress to make a decision. As one woman who returned to the doctor stated, "I didn't want to go back, but what could I do? No doctor will take you in your eighth month. I changed [doctors] as soon as I had my baby." This woman told the office nurse that she wanted an additional person with her in the examining room, thus adding a safety factor for her return visit. Other pregnant women consulted their mothers, who tended to be defensive of the physician and told their daughters that he was "probably doing a thorough examination" or that "this kind of thing can happen."

Sometimes the decision to return to the physician was based on the woman's denial of the incident. For example, one woman had talked herself into thinking the incident was all in her imagination; however, she felt very upset sitting in the physician's waiting room at her next visit and thought, "What am I doing here?" The exam was very difficult for her. The physician noted her anxiety and did not do anything unusual, but she never went back.

The women disclosed the incident to a range of people, including family, friends, health professionals, and clergy. Initially, the majority of women told someone in the immediate family, such as a husband, parent, or sister. A few women had difficulty in admitting to themselves what had happened, describing the incident as an "overly extensive examination."

Disclosure to family and friends added to the women's stress. Often they had to deal with people's reactions to hearing about the incident, and often they felt they had to explain their behavior. For example, one woman said her girlfriend asked her how she could have let a physician examine her standing up. The woman said, "I told her he made it sound logical. I had a uterus suspension and had told him I was having pain. He said he wanted to check my uterus from a different position and for me to stand up. I'm not a doctor. I did what he said."

The most notable reaction described by the women—their powerlessness in dealing with the incident individually—had several facets. Immobilized by the physician's actions, the 16 women did not know what to do. Only one woman indirectly confronted him with his behavior: when responding to his inquiry about why she was upset, she said, "Come on now, don't be so stupid," and walked out of the room. The women were confused ("I thought, my God, why me? Why would a doctor do this?"), questioned themselves ("Did I say something to lead him on? I'm a friendly person—was I overly friendly?"), felt inadequate ("I was young; it was my first baby; I didn't know what to expect"), and minimized the physician's behavior ("It wasn't like a violent rape where he grabbed me and tied me; he didn't threaten my life").

The women talked of being upset with themselves over their inability to respond; one woman said, "When it happened I had a poor self image. [I] thought I handled it ineffectively. [I] didn't tell him of my rage, and that confirmed my feeling I was a jerk. [I] asked myself if I said or did anything to indicate I encouraged it [and] was relieved to find out others had the same thing happen."

The physician's behavior came as such a shock and surprise to the women that they did not know what to do or whom to tell. The women readily admitted that they wanted to take action ("I wanted to report it but did not know to whom"), but felt their credibility was at risk ("I felt I wouldn't be believed"). Some of the women were initially unsuccessful in having their complaints taken seriously ("Even my own brother didn't believe me at first"). They emphasized the unequal power status ("What good would it do—my word against his"), identified the physician's defense ("Doctors are so well-protected), and tested reactions.

The women also felt powerless when they realized that physicians are loyal to other physicians. Except in one instance, physicians who were told of the exploitation did not side with the patient. One woman talked with her father-in-law, who was a physician. He advised, "It is not worth it to pursue [the incident] because such a charge is impossible to prove." Physicians would admit having heard similar information from other patients, and some even said they would do something ("I'll talk to him about it"); however, one physician made it clear he did not believe the abuse had occurred ("Yes, I hear lots of patients complain, but I have no facts"). Some women felt betrayed a second time by physicians who, while appearing to believe them, would permit the offending physician to substitute for them while they were on vacation. One woman described her reactions as follows:

> The next doctor I went to asked why I was changing. I turned red and became flustered and thought he wouldn't believe me and would think I was a weirdo, but said, "I didn't think his exams were professional." He said I was not the only one. A few years later, I called the physician while he was on vacation and his answering service said to call [the offending physician]. I said, "I'd rather drop dead first."

Two strategies were useful to the women to help neutralize the powerlessness they experienced: (1) support from their husbands, and (2) collective action. All the women were significantly influenced by their husbands' reactions to the experience, regarding both possible action and emotional support. Although the husbands' reactions ranged from anger at the physician ("He wanted to go after him"), to minimization ("Don't let it bother you"), to rationalization ("He just tried to get away with something"), several husbands actively supported their wives' taking action against the physician. Some husbands expressed concern over negative publicity, the legal process, and possible retaliation by the physician. Some women who were not encouraged by their husbands to do anything were disappointed ("I wish I had a different type of husband—he said to let sleeping dogs lie").

The women thought and were led to believe that they would be unable to influence an investigation into the physician's actions. Not until the women developed a network to act collectively did they discover that they were not alone in their complaints and that there was an official board that would respond to these complaints.

MEDICAL BOARD DECISION AND COMMUNITY RESPONSE

The case was settled without a hearing. The physician's license to practice obstetrics and gynecology was revoked, but he was issued a restricted license that allowed him to retrain as an anesthesiologist—a speciality that the licensing board believed would prevent unsupervised contact with the patients—and to assist in surgery during his two-year residency.

When the board of medicine's final order was issued, the local newspaper published a full-page article reporting that the doctor had turned in his license to practice medicine after admitting to sexually abusing various women. Also quoted was the doctor's admission to the board of his ongoing psychological problem, which had affected his medical practice to the extent that he had engaged in inappropriate conduct with female patients. The article also stated that the doctor was retraining as an anesthesiologist. In a second article on the same page, the chairman of the department of anesthesiology at the medical center where the doctor was being retrained described how his desire to give the doctor a second chance influenced his decision to admit the gynecologist into his residency training program.

The newspaper then published a series of letters—both for and against the doctor—and replies to these letters. Letters supporting the gynecologist argued that for the few women who were abused by him, there were "hundreds of patients who were absolutely devastated when he gave up his practice." In a similar pro-doctor letter, a delivery-room nurse who worked with the doctor for over six years stated that a relatively few anonymous women should not be able to destroy the reputation of a fine doctor and suggested that maybe words and actions were misconstrued, misinterpreted, and misunderstood.

Letters countering this view described the trauma of the experience and urged that the publicity of the case demonstrate to women that they no longer need to remain silent in cases of sexual abuse. Another person commented that it was incredible that some people felt that a self-admitted sex offender should be allowed to continue to practice medicine.

PATIENTS' REACTIONS

All 16 women were contacted after receiving board notification of the case's conclusion and were asked for their reactions. The women made several spontaneous comments in response to the therapist's questions.

How do you feel? All women except one were distressed to see that the doctor was allowed to retrain and practice in another speciality. The women were specific in what they thought should have happened. They said the gynecologist should have been sent to jail, should have had his license revoked, or should not be practicing medicine. Only one woman felt it was acceptable for him to be retrained, commenting that she was glad he was not allowed to practice as a pediatrician. Other responses were that "the medical profession protects its own" and "no one else would be given such a lenient punishment." Some of the women expressed concern that they might encounter the doctor in his new role ("What if I had an accident and came into the emergency room when he was on duty?").

Why did he do it? The majority of the 16 women stated they believed the gynecologist was mentally ill. However, one woman said, "Sick is too simplistic a term. Maybe his masculinity was threatened." Others speculated that he knew he could get away with it, that he was curious about what women would do, and that he was compulsive. Several women believed the doctor hated women. One cautioned that because he was unable to control his behavior, he would try the sexual abuse again in a new setting. Several women commented on his cleverness and how well he was able to conceal his behavior.

Why did this happen to you? In some cases, the women could give no reason for why they had been victimized. As one woman said, "I don't know why he did it to me. He knew me and he knew my husband. There were women of all different ages [who were victimized]."

It is striking that some women blamed themselves for the doctor's behavior. They did not directly state this, but their answers indicate this was so:

- He knew I had never been to another gynecologist.
- I was naive. He did an emergency Caesarean section on me and he was my hero. I felt he saved my baby. [During the] checkup, the nurse left the room. He inserted his finger into me and said I had such a deep abdominal incision that my nerves might be damaged and I'd have no sensation for sex. Maybe he thought he could get away with it.
- At the time I was 24 and [had] three young babies. [I was] married at 18. I felt my whole life passed me by, [and] had doubts about myself. I liked to go [to his office]. He made me feel he cared about me—maybe I sent him signals.
- I think he saw me as vulnerable at that time. I didn't express any feelings. I was horrified.
- Maybe he picked on me because I was naive. I was 27 and it was my first child.
- Maybe he chose a certain personality type—like I was a victim of opportunity.

There were a few women who placed the problem on the doctor for the behavior, as follows:

- I used to question him and maybe he didn't like that. Maybe he wanted to have power over me because I was questioning his intelligence. One time he had moved my baby, and it hurt. I said to tell me when it was going to hurt next time.

Some women were aware of the escalation and dangerousness of the doctor's behavior. They were able to talk about that, as follows:

- Mine was so well planned. I had a 1:00 P.M. appointment. No one was in the whole building. When I came out, there was still no one there. When I think of what could have happened. . . I was so upset. I didn't want anyone to see me. I thought of rape—he could have done that.
- My girlfriend and I wonder why he picked us. Maybe it was something I did or said. He wasn't friendly, and I wasn't either. [I] haven't figured it out.
- This was rape. Another person would have been prosecuted. It isn't fair that someone was protected by his influence and position.
- It is fortunate we didn't go off the deep end or he didn't do anything else. If nothing happened maybe he would have done something worse. He was stopped, and that is the most important thing.

One woman was very clear in her anger and her blame of the doctor. She said:

- I blame him for a lot of things. He was so busy playing his little games that he missed a lot. I trusted him so much. He was treating me for infertility. It was so haphazard, the drugs and treatments he was prescribing for me.

Do you think of it? Some women denied thinking about the abuse when the case was completed. Other women reported being reminded whenever a medical situation occurred. For example, one woman talked of her son requiring minor surgery. She worried that he would need anesthesia and that the anesthesiologist would be her former gynecologist. Several women reported nightmares and flashbacks ("I still have nightmares where I wake up and find him standing there").

Two women described aggressive, angry feelings. One woman wanted her husband to find the doctor and physically assault him. Another woman reported her fantasies:

I have fantasized so much. I wanted to harm him. It just pops into my mind. I'd like to put him in a cage and starve him and do mean things to him. I'd like him to know I wasn't a fool. I've thought of going to his house and confronting his wife or to his office and announcing he is a sex maniac.

There is a sequel to this case. The woman who made the original complaint did so after her six week checkup and the insertion of an intrauterine device (IUD). Four years later she became pregnant. This news instigated a series of flashbacks for her. When she went to her first prenatal visit, she burst into tears when the nurse asked about the pregnancy. Her new doctor said he would have to remove the IUD for her to continue the pregnancy, and the woman insisted her husband be present. Her greatest fear—which did not materialize—was that on delivery she would have to face her former doctor.

OBSERVATIONS

The theme of false accusation has held a dominant place in the literature on sexual assault as well as had a major impact on those institutions and personnel who deal with sexual assault. Hale's (1734) cautionary rule on rape, "It must be remembered. . . . that it is an accusation easily to be made and hard to be proved, and harder to be defended by the party accused, tho' never so innocent," enjoyed wide acceptance in the courts for over two centuries. It significantly influenced American medical and law texts until the mid-1970s, when rape research challenged and reversed the view (Burgess and Holmstrom 1979, Geiss 1978).

From a clinical standpoint, there were several clear indicators regarding the credibility of the victims in this case. Most notable was the traumatic response to the incident in terms of psychological and behavioral changes. The emotional impact of the incident on the women ranged from none to considerable. One husband made it clear the he felt his wife would "never get over the trauma." The fact that the majority of women took assertive action to remove themselves from the abusive situation may account for some of the less severe symptoms reported; this behavior is consistent with faster recovery of rape victims (Burgess and Holmstrom 1979).

The clarity of the details of the incident as reported by the women suggests that the incident remained a psychologically unresolved issue ("It has been clear in my mind for eight years now," "I can see the examination as if it was yesterday, and I go back ten years on this"). Changes in sexual interest and/or activity varied from acute, aversion reactions ("I didn't want to have anything to do with sex that night") to more long-term effects ("It has had a major effect on my sex life").

Many women avoided future gynecological care. Some women waited a long time before deciding on a new doctor or seeking care. Most women took careful measures to validate a physician's medical credentials and reputation. Some women chose general practitioners rather than gynecologists; others chose doctors with contrasting characteristics ("My doctor is an old-timer—no bedside manner," "I'll only go to a female physician now"). The women with teenaged daughters expressed concern over how to warn their daughters about "such doctors," and some said they would insist in the future on being present during examinations.

Flashback symptoms were described by some women ("If my husband touches my genitals I still see [the physician's] face"). Another woman described her panic during a subsequent gynecological examination when her feet went into the stirrups and the covering sheet interfered with her ability to see the doctor; her anxiety decreased only when she lifted the sheet to watch the physician's actions. In their negotiations with their new physicians, the women tended to do three things: ask the length of an internal examination, tell the physician and nurse of the prior experience, and insist that a nurse be present.

REFERENCES

Burgess, A. W., and L. Holmstrom. 1979. "Adaptice Strategies and Recovery from Rape." *American Journal of Psychiatry* 136 :1278-82.

Geis, G. 1978. "Lord Hale, Witches, and Rape." *British Journal of Law and Society* Summer.

Hale, M. 1734. *Historia Placitorum Coronae*. London: Nutt & Gosling.

9

The Rape Crisis Center View

B. Joyce Dale

Late one spring afternoon in 1977, a 16-year-old girl disclosed to her mother that she had just been sexually assaulted by her doctor during a routine gynecological examination. The girl's mother immediately took her daughter, Sandra, to the emergency room of the hospital adjacent to the doctor's office. Sandra was given a routine rape evidence examination, and the hospital reported the incident to the police. The hospital also contacted the local rape crisis center, Women Against Rape, to provide counseling and medical assistance to the victim.

Detectives investigating the incident interviewed both the victim and the offending physician several times. Laboratory analysis of the medical evidence revealed the presence of seminal fluid and nonmotile sperm. Results of polygraph exam administered to the victim were "uncertain"; the physician "passed the polygraph, but not with flying colors," according to detectives. Police decided not to initiate criminal prosecution of the physician, Dr. D——, because of inconclusive evidence.

Nearly three years later, another woman called Woman Against Rape to report that she had been assaulted by Dr. D—— during an otherwise routine pelvic examination earlier that week. The victim's description of the incident was almost identical to the assault described by Sandra three years earlier. Although the victim, felt it was important to report the crime to police, she decided to take some time to consider a course of action and to seek guidance from her parents. She continued to receive supportive counseling from the rape crisis center. She also disclosed the sexual assault to friends and acquaintances, hoping that other victims might find the courage to come forward.

Almost a month after she reported the incident to the rape crisis center, Joan received a telephone call from a woman who identified herself as a victim of Dr. D——. The woman, Anne, told Joan that she had heard "through the grapevine" about Joan having been assaulted by Dr. D——, and that she needed to talk to someone about her experience. Within a few days, Anne told a counselor at Woman Against Rape that she had been raped by Dr. D—— three years earlier during a routine gynecological exam. Ironically, the assault occurred at approximately the same time that Sandra was being examined for evidence of sexual assault in the hospital emergency room.

Both Joan and Anne sought the advice of an attorney and eventually reported the incidents to police. Within a few weeks, the doctor was arrested and charged with two counts of rape. The arrest of Dr. D—— was highly publicized in the news media, and other patients began to call Women Against Rape and/or police to disclose sexual assaults by Dr. D——. As a result, he was charged with raping two more women patients.

Prior to trial, charges in one case against the doctor were dismissed because the two-year statute of limitations had expired. After a week-long trial, the jury acquitted the doctor of the remaining three rape charges.

However, by the time the criminal trial was concluded ten months after Joan and Anne reported the assaults to police, a total of 31 former patients of Dr. D—— had reported rapes and other sexual assaults to Women Against Rape, and several of the victims had made formal complaints to the state medical board. Some of the victims also reported the sexual assaults to police. A year later, four victims initiated a civil suit against the hospital where Dr. D—— practiced medicine and against the doctor himself. As of early 1986, the civil suit was pending.

The medical board eventually cited Dr. D—— for 38 violations of state medical standards, including for having sexual intercourse with nine patients. After almost two and one-half years of investigation, witness interviews, and hearing date continuances, the medical board settled their case against Dr. D——. The settlement, reached without victim consultation or consent, restricted the doctor's license by prohibiting him from having direct patient contact.

THE VICTIMS

Dr. D—— practiced gynecology at a medical facility in an affluent suburb of a major metropolitan area. The victims' ages ranged from 16 to 49, and almost all victims came from middle to upper-class backgrounds. Most were college educated, and were intelligent and articulate.

The reported sexual assaults occurred over a period of 17 years. Of the women who eventually reported incidents to the rape crisis center, 24 were assaulted sometime during the three-year period between when Sandra first reported the rape to the emergency room and when Joan and Anne reported their rapes to police.

Of the 31 victims, 19 disclosed to the rape crisis center during the eight-month period following Joan's initial telephone call to the center. As a rule, these victims had heard rumors of the police investigation or had found out about the existence of other victims as a result of the publicity surrounding the doctor's arrest.

Seven additional women came forward during the criminal trial and admitted to having been victimized by the doctor. Three more victims disclosed to the rape crisis center in the months immediately following the trial.

In all, 15 victims reported rape and sexual assault incidents to the police: 11 before the criminal trial began, and four either during or after the trial. In several cases, the statute of limitations for criminal prosecution had expired. In others, the victims chose not to go through the ordeal of prosecution. Of the 31 victims, 12 also reported the incidents to the state medical board responsible for the licensure of physicians.

THE VICTIMIZATIONS

Of the 31 victims who disclosed to the rape crisis center, 26 reported having been assaulted by Dr. D—— during the course of an otherwise routine gynecological examination. Joan's description of the incident is typical.

On the day of the rape, Joan had gone to Dr. D—— for her regular checkup. A nurse was present in the room while the doctor checked Joan's breasts and began the pelvic exam. The doctor took a pap smear and instructed the nurse to take it for testing. The nurse then left the examination room.

According to Joan, the doctor then told her to turn her head so that she was facing the wall and instructed her to cough. She felt his body move very close to hers and felt his lab coat brushing against her thighs. Joan said she then felt the doctor insert his penis into her vagina and move it in and out in a steady, rhythmic motion. During the assault, the doctor continuously told Joan to breathe deeply and asked her personal questions about her family and her sex life. When Joan turned her head to look at the doctor, he told her again to turn her head to the wall.

Joan related that after the rape, Dr. D—— told her to remove the sheet covering her naked legs and pelvis and to stand up. He instructed her to stand with one foot on the step of the examining table and one foot on the floor, he then gave her another internal examination using his fingers.

When the doctor finished, he left the examination room. Joan quickly dressed and left the office. She said she was afraid and just "wanted to get out of there." When she arrived home, she telephoned a friend and disclosed the assault to her. Her friend advised her to call Women Against Rape.

All of the victims reported that the doctor asked them personal questions, often sexual in nature, during the assault. The victims all interpreted the questions as designed to distract them. The doctor also instructed many of them to face the wall and to cough or breathe deeply while the assault was taking place.

Five of the 31 victims reported sexual assaults other than intercourse. Some described "stand up" examinations during which the doctor inserted his fingers into their vaginas. Others said that the doctor stroked their hips, thighs, and genitals while they were standing in front of him. Dr. D—— told one victim that this exam was to determine if her hips were wide enough for childbirth.

Another victim reported being sodomized by Dr. D——. After the assault, the doctor told her to get up on her hands and knees on the examining table so that he could show her exercises for her tilted uterus. In another instance, Dr. D—— told a victim that she had abnormal genitals and took a photograph of her genitals, for "teaching purposes," without her written consent.

One victim was a patient of another doctor who was an associate of Dr. D——. When the patient went into labor, her own doctor was unavailable and Dr. D—— substituted for his absent colleague. The victim reported that Dr. D—— sexually assaulted her while she was in labor by manipulating her external genitals as he was checking the dilation of her cervix.

All 31 of the victims reported that the nurse always left the examining room before the end of the examination. No nurse was ever in the room at the time of the sexual assault, the victims said.

VICTIM REACTIONS DURING THE ASSAULT

Almost all victims reacted to the realization that they were being assaulted with shock, disbelief, and denial. Anne said that during the assault she thought, "My God, what is he doing; why is he doing it; what am I going to do?" Susan said, "I couldn't believe what he was doing to me because I trusted him. He was my doctor. I just wanted to believe that it wasn't happening to me." Another victim said she thought, "He can't really be doing this; he's supposed to be a reputable doctor."

Most of the victims also reported being afraid of the doctor and of his reaction if he were confronted during the assault. Anne said, "I was scared. I didn't know what he would do. If he was capable of doing this, he could do something else. . . . I was the only one there. If I screamed no one would hear me and no one would believe me." One woman said that she was afraid of Dr. D—— and didn't know what to do because he "had a funny look on his face, sick and smug."

Many of the victims described themselves as relatively passive individuals and felt they had reacted passively during the assault. One said, "I wouldn't know how to stand my ground. I'm not a fighter. I don't want to hurt feelings." Several victims said that they believed the doctor perceived them as "passive" or "vulnerable" and that he had deliberately chosen them as victims because of that perception. Most of the victims said that after the assault they left the doctor's office as quickly as possible and that they were too shocked and frightened to disclose the assault to anyone in the doctor's office.

One victim said she confronted the doctor during the assault by refusing to comply with his instructions to turn her head toward the wall and to pant. She said, "Why are you doing this?" Highly agitated, he abruptly left the examining room.

Another victim recounted how she heard the doctor unzip his pants before he assaulted her. Although she was certain that he had his penis in her vagina, she confronted him by asking, "What are you doing? Is that your finger?" The doctor stopped the assault, laughed, and told her she was being "ridiculous."

VICTIM REACTIONS IMMEDIATELY FOLLOWING THE ASSAULT

All the victims described themselves as being extremely upset immediately after the assault. One victim reported that she was so distraught that she could not locate her car in the parking lot. Another woman said that she had difficulty driving home, and a third woman described crying all the way home.

Victims also experienced considerable stress over disclosure and reporting issues. Most of the victims left the doctor's office and, after the initial shock and disbelief subsided, disclosed the assault to a trusted family member or friend.

Almost all victims expressed concern over whether they would be believed. In fact, all of the people to whom the victims initially disclosed did believe them, although most of them discouraged the victims from taking action because they were afraid of the doctor's power and influence in the community. Many felt anger over the betrayal of trust by their doctor and the belief that they were powerless to take any effective action.

Although most victims initially disclosed the assaults only to family members or friends, a few of them confronted the doctor during, immediately after, or a few days after the assault. One victim, who was deaf, immediately reported the incident to the doctor's nurse. She also asked the nurse if anyone else had reported that the doctor had sexually assaulted them. Despite the fact that the incident occurred after the doctor already had been investigated by police, the nurse replied that no one had accused the doctor of this before. The nurse then quickly left the room and returned with the doctor. When the woman confronted the doctor, he told her that she was mistaken and that many women had problems being examined and were "hung up" about sex.

Linda and her husband, Frank, confronted Dr. D—— together after Linda disclosed she was sexually assaulted during an examination. The doctor denied the incident, saying he wouldn't dare risk his career for something so "stupid." He then showed them both the examining table, pointing out that the table was too high for the incident to have occurred in the manner Linda described. However, the table was adjustable, and Linda and Frank were convinced that it had been raised prior to their meeting with the doctor.

When another victim confronted Dr. D——, she made an appointment to see him in his office. There she angrily accused him of assaulting her and told him of the serious psychological impact of the incident. Dr. D—— denied it.

LONG-TERM IMPACT OF THE ASSAULT

Without exception, the women reported the victimization as being one of the most stressful events in their lives. All the victims reported having recurring intrusive thoughts of the sexual assault incidents, and many reported these symptoms continuing even years after the assaults. Some of the women had dreams and nightmares of the incidents. A few of the victims reported having major sexual problems that they attributed to the assault. All victims found other doctors, and many refused to see anyone other than a woman gynecologist. A few avoided health care altogether, even when aware of medical problems requiring the attention of a physician.

Patricia's reaction to the betrayal by her doctor was perhaps the most severe. The psychological trauma was so overwhelming that she had suppressed even the fact that the sexual assault had occurred. For over a year, she had no recall of the incident until she read the account of the doctor's arrest in the newspaper. During that year of blocking out what had happened, she continued to see Dr. D—— for regular gynecological care. However, each time she visited the doctor she became extremely anxious and broke out in a rash. After Patricia remembered that she had been sexually assaulted by Dr. D——, she sought the assistance of a psychiatrist to help her cope with the trauma. The psychiatrist eventually referred her to the rape crisis center for further support.

RESPONSE OF THE CRIMINAL JUSTICE SYSTEM

The arrest of Dr. D—— was highly publicized in area newspapers and television news reports; the publicity triggered additional reports of rape by the doctor. Fifteen of the 31 victims known to the rape crisis center reported to the police; however, some of the assaults no longer fell within the statute of limitations for prosecuting Dr. D——. Nevertheless, police were prompt and thorough in their investigation and treated all victims with dignity and respect.

The trial, however, was less praiseworthy. The behavior of the judge was so questionable that one newspaper described him as the "ringmaster" in the "circus" trial and called for an investigation of his actions. Despite a state law forbidding such questioning, the judge forced one victim to answer defense questions about the number of sexual encounters and partners prior to the assault. In addition, an expert prosecution witness, a prominent psychiatrist, was not allowed to testify concerning the power dynamics in sexual assaults by authority figures.

During the trial, the defense requested additional seating in the courtroom for the doctor's family and friends; the judge granted the request and had several folding chairs brought in for them. The victims, on the other hand, had to wait with the general public in line each day for seats. One day when the courtroom was full and one of the victims could not find a seat, the judge denied her request for special seating.

All the victims testified that the nurses had left the examination room when the sexual assaults occurred. The doctor's nurses, testifying for the defense, said that they had never left the doctor alone in the examination room with a patient. When the nurses' testimony was reported on the evening news, the prosecutor was inundated with telephone calls from women who claimed to have been examined by Dr. D—— when nurses were not present. Eight of those women agreed to testify the next day as rebuttal witnesses. Although the women agreed to testify only that they had been examined without the nurses present, the judge refused to allow the testimony of all but one woman because the women also admitted to having been sexually victimized by Dr. D——.

When the defense presented its case, Dr. D—— denied sexually assaulting any of his patients. He claimed that he used a "European technique" during the pelvic exams and that the women had mistaken this technique for sexual intercourse. His defense attorney told the jury that what the women felt during the examinations was actually "vigorous probing." After deliberating for more than seven hours, the jury returned a verdict of not guilty.

RESPONSE OF HELPING PROFESSIONALS

The unofficial response by the doctor's colleagues in the medical profession to disclosure of the victimizations was protective of him. Not only did the doctor's nurses testify that no abuse ever occurred, but in the case of the deaf woman the nurse told the victim she was "absolutely wrong" about just previously having been assaulted. When Sarah, the victim who said she was assaulted by Dr. D—— while she was in labor, told her own doctor about the abuse, he replied, "Well, there's nothing I can do about it." A new doctor who saw Anne said, "I don't know why you left Dr. D——, and I don't want to know."

OFFICIAL RESPONSE OF THE MEDICAL COMMUNITY

After the not guilty verdict at the criminal trial, the victims felt that their last resort was the state medical review board. They knew that the standard of proof would not be the same as in a criminal trial and that there was no statute of limitations, thus the number of victims who could testify would increase substantially.

Twelve victims who reported the sexual assaults to Women Against Rape also reported to the state medical review board. Over two years later, after interviewing the victims and conducting an investigation, the medical board issued a citation charging Dr. D—— with 38 counts of violating state medical standards. The charges included engaging in grossly unethical, immoral, and unprofessional conduct with nine women patients over a period of ten years.

After months of delays of the scheduled hearing date, the victims were notified that they were to testify before the medical board examiner. Three days before the scheduled hearing date, the victims were notified that the medical review board had reached a settlement with Dr. D——. This settlement initially had been recommended for disapproval by the hearing board examiner; his recommendation was overruled. The doctor was cited only for administering a fertility drug without full disclosure, and his license was restricted to research. One member of the medical board commented that the doctor had a problem with sex and that the settlement would prevent him from having contact with patients. The issue of sexual misconduct was never addressed, nor were the victims consulted about the proposed agreement.

The victims, the general public, and the news media were highly critical of the medical board's disposition of the case. The chairman of the medical board responded to the criticism by saying that other matters before the board were more important than "this doctor chasing girls." As a result, a prominent state senator called for the chairman's immediate resignation, saying his comment was "inexcusable and intolerable" and that the board's action had been a "travesty." In addition, the lawyer who had been scheduled to preside as the hearing examiner and who had disapproved of the recommendation for a settlement resigned in protest over the action of the medical review board.

The medical review board eventually responsed to public pressure and reviewed its decision. This review was nothing more than an attempt to justify the original disposition in the case. The settlement remained in effect. The issue of sexual misconduct by Dr. D—— was never fully addressed or resolved by the state board mandated under law to police its own profession. As a local newspaper commented in an editorial, the standards of good medical practice should be better than the standards of proof for the not guilty verdict—or at least we, as patients, would hope so.

10

Workshops on Patient-Therapist Sexual Relationships

Marjorie Braude

DEFINING THE PROBLEM

Psychotherapy is a professional interaction that places two people alone in a closed setting to discuss intimate thoughts and emotions. The possibility of sexual feelings surfacing inevitably arises. It is critical for therapy that these feelings be appropriately acknowledged and not used as a basis for action. I was introduced to this problem after I received a consultation request from a patient hospitalized for depression. She reported that her daily sessions with her male psychiatrist were focusing almost exclusively on discussions of sexual feelings, his as well as hers. She was intensely disturbed over the sessions and felt a threat to her equilibrium. However, she was attracted to her therapist and was unwilling to change psychiatrists.

Shortly after our consultation, the woman was accosted while asleep in her hospital bed by a male hospital patient. Her psychiatrist appeared unconcerned over her alarm, and the hospital staff labeled her as a seductive. As a result, she asked me to be her therapist.

One week later her former psychiatrist approached her, and they had sexual relations. The psychiatrist told me and several other psychiatrists about the relationship. Two weeks later he stopped seeing her, and the patient's defenses crumbled. She became self-destructive and had suicidal and psychotic periods. The woman was hospitalized for a year, and her recovery to survival functioning was long and difficult. During her second year of therapy, it emerged that she had been an incest victim.

Although the hospital and the psychiatric society temporarily suspended the psychiatrist, the suspension was not reported to the public. The state board of medical quality assurance investigated the matter, but relinquished jurisdiction because the sexual activity took place when the woman no longer was the psychiatrist's patient. No sanctions were imposed by the psychiatrist's psychoanalytic society. Nevertheless, the patient won a six-figure malpractice settlement in civil litigation.

DEALING WITH THE PROBLEM

This case demonstrated the profession's gap in understanding sexual feelings in the therapeutic situation. To enable psychiatrists to learn more about the problem and to explore their own responses, the women's committee of a state psychiatric society developed a workshop on sexuality between psychiatrist and patient. A workshop format was chosen in order to maximize informality and to encourage each participant to speak freely.

We found one of two ingredients necessary for the workshop's success. Either psychiatrists must be willing to present a detailed case history that includes both specifics of interactions and psychiatrist's thoughts and responses, or an anonymous questionnaire should be administered to participants to aid in triggering recall of important details of any sexual incidents.

Several patient-therapist situations repeatedly came up for workshop discussion. One of these centers on the patient who develops an intense, long-standing relationship with the therapist. That patient may entreat or demand that the therapist extend the relationship in sexual or other ways. Responding to these overtures may have serious results; the patient may become suicidal or threaten some form of acting out when the special relationship is withdrawn or no longer sufficient.

Another situation involves incest victims, who may present themselves in erotic and destructive ways. They consciously or unconsciously wish to repeat the sexual drama with a new parent figure—the psychiatrist—and are likely to exhibit elements of past anger, masochism, or symptoms of abuse.

In a third type of situation, the patient may threaten or hint at violence along with the sexual demand. In psychiatric practice, such patients are usually borderline or psychotic in functioning. Psychiatrists need to find a combination of firmness and respect for the patient so therapy can continue without rejection of the patient or harm to the psychiatrist.

The psychiatrist who refuses to recognize or discuss the patient's sexual feelings is another problem that lends itself to workshop discussion. In one case, a patient committed suicide when the therapist acted in this manner.

QUESTIONNAIRE RESPONSES

Our experience with the questionnaires and the case materials brought to the workshops greatly reinforces the ethical, psychotherapeutic, and practical wisdom of maintaining the boundaries of the basic therapeutic contract. The patient comes for help and healing to a psychiatrist who is licensed by the state and receives money to provide these services. No patient, not even one who asks for or demands an extension of the therapeutic relationship into sexual contact, can be considered to be making an equal or informed decision.

Responses from 35 anonymous questionnaires used at two workshops—one held at an annual meeting of the American Psychiatric Association and a second at a Southern California Psychiatric Society Meeting—have shown interesting results. Although not a statistically valid survey of participants, the questionnaire results do indicate how certain aspects of the problem of psychiatrist-patient sexual relationships are viewed by a small subpopulation.

In response to a question regarding the patient's expression of sexual feelings for the psychiatrist, several respondents stated that the expression of sexual feelings was a healthy and expected part of each patient's development in therapy and that this should be acknowledged by the therapist and utilized as contributing to the patient's growth. Therapists responded that sometimes, but not always, they were able to use the patient's expression of sexual feelings to benefit the therapy, such as when a patient's expression of sexual feelings for the psychiatrist led to associations about similar responses in other situations. Another group of respondents said they did not acknowledge sexual feelings expressed by the patient because they felt such feelings impeded therapy.

Most respondents who described situations in which patients attempted to act on sexual feelings were concerned with declining the overture in such a way as to preserve the therapy. In a few instances, the patient left therapy after the therapist refused to respond to the sexual advance.

The questionnaire also asked participants to describe a situation in which they had sexual feelings toward a patient and to state whether they acted on this feeling. All but three of the 20 males responding described situations in which they were attracted to patients; most said they did not reveal their feelings to the patient. They also stated that their feelings did not hamper the therapy, and some even said it improved the therapy by heightening their awareness of the patient. Only one male said his feelings were a detriment to therapy. In two instances, male psychiatrists acted on their sexual feelings. In one of these cases, the therapist married and subsequently divorced the patient.

Of the eight female psychiatrists responding, five said they enjoyed their sexual feelings toward patients to some degree, and three said they did not. In some instances, the female therapist was intimidated or fearful of a male patient who made advances. In no instance did a female act on her feelings.

The main points elicited by the questionnaires can be summarized as follows:

1. Sexual feelings, both heterosexual and homosexual, do arise in therapy on the part of both the psychiatrist and the patient.
2. Sexual feelings need to be acknowledged as one dimension of the interaction that occurs in the therapeutic setting.
3. Sexual feelings can be considered part of the normal development of therapy and can be used constructively in therapy.
4. Sexual feelings can create problems for the therapy.
5. Situations in which patients wish or demand to act on sexual feelings are especially sensitive because:
   a. When the psychiatrist declines the invitation, the patient's feelings of rejection could interfere with or terminate the therapy.
   b. A few patients make sexual overtures as part of an ongoing behavioral pattern, which produces a difficult management problem.
6. There are some differences between male and female psychiatrists in the area of psychiatrist-patient sexual feelings:
   a. Female psychiatrists reported no instances of acting on sexual feelings.
   b. Male psychiatrists were more likely to experience sexual approaches as flattering while female psychiatrists described them as intimidating or frightening.

Finally, there were differing opinions among psychiatrists about the boundaries of appropriate behavior between patient and therapist. Some felt that hugging or hand-holding could be therapeutic, while other psychiatrists felt such actions were inappropriate. Perhaps the essential question is one of intent: did the psychiatrist's behavior have a specific role in illustrating or working on a specific patient problem, or did it occur for some other reason and thus give substance to any fantasies the patient might have? These workshops have proven a useful tool to raise consciousness in a critical area. Other groups are encouraged to use similar programs.

NOTE

For copies of the workshop questionnaire, interested groups of psychiatrists should contact the author at 11973 San Vicente Boulevard, Los Angeles, CA 90049.

PART 4

The Social Context

In the fourth part of our exploration of sexual abuse of patients by health professionals, we broaden our view of this problem by examining it in a social context. The three chapters in this part reveal how different facets of our social structure—law enforcement, professional associations and regulatory boards, and print media (in this case, a sexually explicit magazine)—react to patient sexual abuse. Because of these institutions' influential positions in our society, their reactions play an important part in determining how we all look at patient-health professional sexual interaction.

In Chapter 11, titled "When the Pediatrician Is a Pedophile," Carolyn Moore Newberger and Eli H. Newberger examine the moral conflicts of the responding institutions in a case of child sexual abuse by a pediatrician. The authors' step-by-step "moral analysis" of the case illustrates how police and medical registration board responses served their own interests while failing to address those of the community at large. The chapter also defines intervention goals for the constituencies involved and suggests options for meeting those goals.

The normalization through cartoons of sexual abuse by health professionals is examined in Chapter 12 by Judith A. Reisman, Deborah F. Reisman, and Barry S. Elman. The authors studied nearly 200 cartoons of health professionals that appeared in a popular, sexually explicit magazine and found that sexual activity was illustrated in two-thirds of them. Their research highlights a dominant male attitude toward females (adults or children), an attitude that condones abuse and exploitation.

An effort to explore intraprofessionally the possible tacit condoning of professional sexual exploitation is discussed by Nanette K. Gartrell, Silvia Olarte, and Judith L. Herman in "Institutional Resistance to Self-Study: A Case Report." The authors outline the resistance that met their efforts to carry out a survey among fellow members of a professional psychiatric association. Because professional organizations influence training, licensing, and regulating of professionals, it is imperative that their resistances to investigating sexual abuse be detailed and addressed. It is then possible to develop procedures that can support fairly the investigation of sexual exploitation.

11

When the Pediatrician Is a Pedophile

Carolyn Moore Newberger and Eli H. Newberger

As recently as ten years ago, child sexual abuse was considered extremely rare. Recent retrospective surveys, however, suggest that from 3 to 6 percent of males and from 12 to 38 percent of females are sexually victimized during their childhoods (Finkelhor 1979; Russell 1983). Although there is variation from study to study in estimates of incidence, the magnitude of the problem is clear. During the past few years, cases of child sexual abuse have involved day care centers, prominent families, and respected institutions (Trainor 1984).

Little is known about adults who commit sexual acts with children. Available data suggest that 95 percent of the sexual abuse of girls and about 85 percent of the abuse of boys is committed by men, most of whom are known to the child. The offenders come from all ethnic and income groups and may be community leaders who exploit their positions of prestige to gain access to children. They are more likely than the general population to be outwardly religious and rigid about sexual mores (Finkelhor 1984).

Most child sexual abusers appear normal to the rest of the world, and their deviancy is frequently not recognized by their wives, friends or colleagues. They may be homosexual, heterosexual, or bisexual; they may have sexual relations with adults as well as children or only with children. Some individuals prefer sustained relations with one child, while others favor brief sexual encounters with many. They may rape infants or "initiate" adolescents. Some sexual abusers operate "sex rings" in which groups of children become involved with one or more adults, usually through some neighborhood or recreational activity (Finkelhor 1984; Burgess et al. 1984).

Pedophiles, individuals whose sexual preference is for children, may select professional contexts in which access to children is assured. Within the medical profession, pediatrics offers such access. The pediatrician, usually a beloved and trusted member of the community, has intimate and often private contact with children's bodies. When the pediatrician is a pedophile, the interests and needs of many parties are compromised: the children's needs to be free of abuse and exploitation and to trust adult caregivers, the medical profession's needs to maintain its standards for care and its status within the community, and the community's needs to maintain social order and to trust those on whom it relies for the care of children.

Such multiple needs and interests are reflected in our society's confusion over what to do about the sexual abuse of children. This confusion reflects a fundamental set of moral conflicts: (1) the conflict between personal and institutional needs and the assumption of responsibility for others, and (2) the conflict between responding with standard rules of justice and responding with individualized prescriptions for care. In this chapter, we present a case that illustrates these central moral conflicts and discuss how we might resolve them in ways that achieve an enlightened, moral response.

WHOSE INTERESTS ARE SERVED?
THE CASE OF THE PEDIATRICIAN PEDOPHILE

When we are confronted with sexual abuse, especially abuse by a powerful professional, all too often every interest but the child's seems to take priority. This appears to be true in the case of a pediatrician we call Dr. Smith.

Dr. Smith was the subject of a disciplinary proceeding before a state board of registration in medicine. The pediatrician is a respected, prestigious, and powerful member of his community. He is married and an active member of a local church.

During the routine physical examination of a 14-year-old boy, Dr. Smith removed the child's undershorts while the boy lay on the examining table and began stroking his genitals and asking questions about injury to the penis, sperm color, and problems with ejaculation. After masturbating the child to ejaculation, the doctor hugged the boy, saying "I'm a pretty cute guy," and then kissed him on the neck. By this time, the child became very nervous and confused. He was subjected to several more hugs before leaving the examination room. After the boy and his mother left the doctor's office, he told her what had happened.

Shortly after, the boy's family called police. Although an initial contact was made, the police inquiry apparently then stopped. No criminal charges were filed, and there was never any public disclosure of the incident. Rather, the matter was addressed six months later in a closed hearing of the state board of registration in medicine. The board retained a private attorney to conduct its own investigation and to serve as the prosecutor in a closed meeting in which the complainant, other witnesses, and the doctor would appear.

During the closed inquiry, the doctor claimed that boys often had ejaculations during physical examinations and revealed the names of two other boys. His records showed a private shorthand for the events and lavish descriptions of the boys' bodies. He also said that he served often and without compensation as a lecturer on teen-age sexuality, that he worked as both a school and a camp physician, and that his examinations of boys' genitals often lasted more than five minutes. He steadfastly maintained that there was no harm in what he did.

The doctor's license was suspended for 30 days and he was placed on probation for ten years, during which time he was to seek psychiatric help until discharged by the psychiatrist. Dr. Smith was instructed to have a third person present during the examinations of his patients throughout the probationary period. Responsibility for arranging for that third person was left with the doctor.

The parents of Dr. Smith's patients were not notified of the hearing or its findings, and public communication was limited to a small notice in the local newspaper. The self-monitoring and limited public communication, especially in light of the doctor's failure to acknowledge any wrong doing, made the effectiveness of controls over Dr. Smith's practice questionable. Dr. Smith discontinued psychiatric treatment following an evaluation period.

In the meantime, two other cases of past abuse were revealed. The victims were boys who had approached Dr. Smith with problems after a sex education class during which he invited children concerned about sexuality to consult with him. One boy had worries about homosexuality; the other was worried about venereal disease and about whether he had impregnated his girlfriend. These disclosures prompted a reopening of Dr. Smith's case by the state board of registration.

The deliberations of the second hearing, 18 months after the initial disclosure, resulted in Dr. Smith's permanently losing his license to practice medicine. Dr. Smith again refused to admit wrongdoing. During at least part of this time, he had continuing opportunity to molest his young patients.

Dr. Smith demonstrates some of the classic characteristics of pedophilia (Lanning 1984):

- The perpetrators are male.
- They select a particular age and gender of victim.
- They choose professions (medicine) and specialties (adolescent pediatrics) that provide legitimate reasons for sustained (and in the doctor's case, intimate) contact with the children they prefer.
- The perpetrators keep a personal record that permits prompt retrieval of material about their victims.
- They protect themselves.

Several aspects of this case are particularly interesting. First, after being contacted by the parents of the child who first reported the abuse, police contacted the boy's school before even contacting the doctor. The school secretary was asked to check the boy's records, and she found four minor disciplinary infractions. No mention is made in the police records of whether this was done with the permission of the child or family. The implicit statement in the police action is that the child's behavior in school will have something to do with how the police will respond to the accusation. This means that the victim, rather than the act, is the first line of investigation, at least when the accused is a powerful member of the professional community.

Second, according to Dr. Smith's testimony, he was informed by the state and national offices of the American Academy of Pediatrics and by the American Medical Association that there are no guidelines for dealing with this offense. In light of new estimates of the prevalence of the sexual abuse of children, of the likelihood that the abuser is known and trusted, and of the probability that pedophiles choose positions where they have access to the victims, these organizations have an obligation to establish clearly articulated values and procedures.

Third, following a brief period, the discreet police inquiry stopped. There were no criminal charges or public disclosures. The doctor continued in his practice, while the board of registration in medicine conducted an investigation that resulted in a closed hearing six months later. These procedures served to protect the physician and his profession, but failed to protect the public.

A final highlight of these cases is that Dr. Smith's conduct was found by the board to be improper, inappropriate, and unprofessional. This is tantamount to saying he was a "bad boy" and does no justice to the seriousness of the charges and to the effects of the abuse on the victims. Because there was no public disclosure, Dr. Smith could take a month-long vacation and thus camouflage the suspension. He arranged for his own chaperoning. When the case was reopened after the two previous patients came forward, he stated on deposition that he did not believe that he needed treatment, that what he had done was not wrong, and that his actions had no effects on the children.

A MORAL ANALYSIS OF THE CASE OF DR. SMITH

The issue of morality is not an issue simply for the sexual victimizer, but also for the systems and individuals that respond to the victimization. How do we articulate a framework for moral choice to guide public and private behavior, especially when the interests of powerful adults threaten to obscure the rights and needs of children?

When we examine professional practice and policy in relation to child sexual abuse, moral tensions and conflicts between self-interest and responsibility and between justice and care are present. Some of the confusion and conflict around the sexual victimization of children centers on the extent to which we feel we should take public responsibility, and when we do, whether a morality of justice or a morality of care is the appropriate response.

The Conflict between Self-Interest and Responsibility

The conflict between self-interest and responsibility is generated in this case in at least three ways.

1. Dr. Smith's sexual desires for his patients versus his responsibility to these children as a pediatrician.
2. The inferred need on the part of the police to stay in favor with the powerful medical community versus their responsibility to investigate openly a case considered a crime by community standards.
3. The desire on the part of the medical community to protect its reputation by secrecy versus its responsibility to the public to protect children from sexual exploitation and to allow parents informed choice about whether they want their children to be treated by a man who molested other children in his care.

Clearly each of these were resolved on the side of self-interest.

The first step in applying moral choice is interpersonal awareness, or being aware of the effects of actions on others. Dr. Smith appears not able to make that first step, insisting that what he is doing is not wrong and does not effect his patients. That he acted out his own needs, rather than his patients', is clear. Less clear is how self-interest and responsibility are defined by his professional peers, who suspended his license to practice for a brief period but did not take steps to ensure that additional children would not be victimized. Is it self-interested not to inform people that their pediatrician is a pedophile? Does it protect the image of the profession that has the task of judging him? Or does it protect people from the knowledge that caregivers might be capable of hurting them, knowledge that might cause harm if people then fail to seek medical care?

The Conflict between a Morality of Justice and a Morality of Care

The justice versus care dilemma in child sexual victimization might be articulated as follows: *How can we maintain social order and justice, while at the same time respond to individual needs for healing and care?*

As a society, we are confused whether to treat adult sex with children as a crime to be punished or as a symptom of pathology to be cured. This confusion has led to a continuing conflict, with some people arguing for universal criminalization of child sexual abuse and other people advocating a more family and treatment-oriented approach.

The conflict between a morality of justice and a morality of care is evident in several aspects of this case:

1. On the part of the police, the conflict was between whether to treat this case as any case of sexual molestation would be treated (i.e., to apply a standard of equal justice with the consequent exposure of a member of the medical community), or whether to respond to the needs of the medical community by turning the case over to its own governing body.
2. On the part of the board of registration, the conflict was whether to treat this case as a violation of medical conduct, which requires loss of the privileges of the profession, or to approach it as a case of a sick physician who needs to be cured.

The issues of justice *or* care in relation to the victims appear not to have been considered.

Resolving the Moral Conflicts of Sex with Children

For everyone who must respond to the sexual victimization of children (families of victims, clinical providers, protective workers, members of the criminal justice and judicial systems, and architects of social policy), there is a need to recognize the moral conflicts the victimization presents. Can we face the problem when it conflicts with our own needs and interests? Can we provide justice while not neglecting individual needs for healing and care?

Three orientations toward persons and problems can be viewed as characterizing how individuals and institutions have responded to sex with children. We suggest that these orientations define a developmental progression of response to child sexual victimization.

An egocentric orientation. The problems of child sexual victimization are avoided, denied, or responded to out of individual need. In the case of Dr. Smith, the response was in terms of protecting a powerful profession and a colleague rather than the children.

A conventional orientation. Criminal or clinical rules and procedures bind and constrain action on child sexual victimization. Individual differences are not understood or acknowledged. For example, a conventional interpretation of sexual victimization as a criminal act leads to the universal prescription of prosecution and punishment. A conventional interpretation of sexual victimization as psychopathology leads to a universal prescription of psychotherapy. Although responsibility for responding to sex with children is assumed, response tends to be rigid and ideological. In this case, psychotherapy was ordered without considering the doctor's motivation to change. His steadfast belief in the normalcy of his behavior and his consequent failure to follow through with treatment means that unless other options can be considered and applied, children with whom he has contact will continue to be at risk.

An individualized orientation. Evaluation of each situation in terms of its own particular needs and realities guides response, which considers the needs of the child for emotional support and protection, the offender's need for corrective intervention, and our institutions' needs to do their jobs. A variety of options are available to be applied in the service of both justice and care.

TOWARD RESPONSIBILITY IN THE CASE OF DR. SMITH

Can we define a response to Dr. Smith's victimization of his patients that will protect children from further abuse and will permit intervention to be *both* fair *and* individualized? As a first step, we identify goals of intervention for the four primary constituencies in this case: the community, the medical profession, the victims, and Dr. Smith.

The task of the responding institutions is to identify flexible and realistic options that would satisfy as fully as possible all these goals. Our

Constituency	Goals
Community	To maintain laws that deter others and provide equitable redress for crimes To apply the law without favoritism To protect its population from harm
Medical profession	To uphold the ethical imperative to do no harm To maintain public trust and confidence
Victims (past and future)	To have an opportunity to recover from the abuse and to know the abuse was not their fault To be protected from sexual exploitation
Dr. Smith	To be removed from situations where he can sexually abuse others To be rehabilitated to assure that he assumes responsibility for his acts and will not sexually abuse others

preference is for a system of interdisciplinary practice, with members from the mental health, law enforcement, legal, and medical communities, to evaluate such cases. The protection of children must be the primary concern, with the protection of the needs of offenders and institutions secondary.

In our opinion, justice was not served by the doctor's treatment as a special case, and the care of children was violated by the failure to inform parents of the risk of child sexual abuse by Dr. Smith. In addition, the goal of rehabilitation was not served by the prescription of mental health treatment in the face of Dr. Smith's denial of a need for change. In this case, criminal action may have been warranted in order to impress upon Dr. Smith the seriousness of his behavior. Strong external controls may be necessary, at least initially, in the face of minimal internal acknowledgement.

Although the ultimate removal of Dr. Smith's license to practice medicine may be a removal from opportunities to abuse children sexually, this action may protect the medical profession more than it protects children from Dr. Smith. He will no longer have access to children as a pediatrician, but it does not prevent access to children in other ways. The power of sexual desires and preferences in pedophiles is extremely strong, and pedophiles often form rings and networks that enable them to have contact with children. In this context, Dr. Smith is a pedophile first and a pediatrician second. He should be treated not as an errant pediatrician, but as a pedophile who remains a threat to children.

REFERENCES

Burgess, A., C. Hartman, M. McCausland, and P. Powers. 1984. "Impact of Child Pornography and Sex Rings on Child Victims and Their Families." In *Child Pornography and Sex Rings*, edited by A. Burgess, pp. 111–26. Lexington, Mass.: Lexington Books.

Finkelhor, D. 1984. *Child Sexual Abuse*. New York: The Free Press.

————. 1979. *Sexually Victimized Children*. New York: The Free Press.

Lanning, K. 1984. "Child Pornography and Sex Rings." Paper presented at the annual meeting of the American Orthopsychiatric Association, Toronto.

Russell, D. 1983. "The Incidence and Prevalence of Intrafamilial and Extrafamilial Sexual Abuse of Female Children." *Child Abuse and Neglect* 7:133–46.

Trainor, C. 1984. "Sexual Maltreatment in the United States: A Seven-Year Perspective." Paper presented at the Fifth International Congress on Child Abuse and Neglect, Montreal.

12

Sexual Exploitation by Health Professionals in Cartoons of a Popular Magazine

Judith A. Reisman, Deborah F. Reisman, and Barry S. Elman

Popular sexually explicit magazines reach millions of readers each month and transcend virtually all socioeconomic boundaries. Although some such magazines are known for their sexual content, others are diverse publications carrying articles, commentaries, advise columns, letters, illustrations, cartoons, and special features on many contemporary subjects.

Our research focused on the exploitation of patients by health professionals as a popular cartoon theme in a prominent, sexually explicit publication. The purpose of our research was to analyze such depictions of exploitation using a formal content analysis instrument.

BACKGROUND

Why study sexually explicit magazines? The more prominent among them rank high in magazine sales revenues and reach millions of readers. Much of this readership can be classified as relatively well educated. Cartoons are an important component of many of these magazines, and adult readers commonly rate cartoons as favored features (Stauffer and Frost 1976). According to Harrison (1981), these cartoons are chosen with great care. In some cases, 200,000 cartoon ideas may be examined each year with only a few hundred chosen for publication.

Why study cartoons? The cartoon has its own artistic and historical tradition. Similar to other art forms, the cartoon demonstrates a view of life, of an issue, of an event, or of a people. By its very nature, the cartoon has a way of overstating, stereotyping, and exaggerating its case. Moreover, due to its single-frame concept, the use of deceptively simple lines, and its generally few characters, the cartoon seems honest, truthful, and "of the people." With it seeming lack of class pretension, the cartoon often appears as light and guileless humor. But it most certainly is a sociopolitical art form, communicating concepts that describe people and events in short and visually dynamic language.

The cartoon has served and continues to serve as a powerful editorialist, educator, and seller of ideas. It has been used by great European artists such as Goya, Daumier, and Philipon to articulate and advocate the rights of the downtrodden and oppressed. It has also been used effectively, however, to disparage, debase, demean, humiliate, belittle, or otherwise victimize the subject of the "joke" (e.g., Bogardus 1945; Zillmann, 1983; Zillmann, Bryant, and Cantor 1974; Zillmann and Cantor 1972). During World War II, for example, the Allies circulated thousands of propaganda cartoons mocking and ridiculing our Axis enemies, while at the same time, Germany, Japan, and Italy circulated thousands of propaganda cartoons mocking and ridiculing the Allies. The general and scholarly literatures are replete with cross-cultural examples of nationalistic, racist, and sexist cartoon humor.

Scholarly investigations of the cartoon as a powerful and influencial form of expression and mass persuasion can be traced at least to the 1930s with the works of Schaffer (1930) and Johnson (1937). Scores of scholars have since entered this field of study, each contributing to the literature from a range of disciplinary perspectives (e.g., Bogardus 1945; Bryant, Gula, and Zillmann 1980; Gombrich 1980; Harrison 1981; Ryan and Schwartz 1956; Saenger 1955).

A great deal of recent scholarly attention and public concern has centered on the possible effect that cartoons and other forms of mass media communication may have on human attitudes and behavior. While there is considerable debate regarding the precise nature and degree of different mass media effects on receiving publics (e.g., Austin and Myers 1984; Cantor and Sparks 1984; Singer, Singer, and Rapaczynski, 1984), few would contend that mass media does not have *some* effect on the human mind (e.g., Comstock et al. 1978; Eysenck and Nias 1978; Gerbner et al. 1978; Runco and Pezdek 1984).

In light of the cartoon's historical role as a tool of propaganda and mass persuasion and of the growing real-life problem of patient sexual exploitation by health professionals, it seems meaningful and appropriate to examine any continued, widescale circulation of cartoon messages about the health professional-patient relationship. For this reason, our research characterizes the quantity and quality of cartoons depicting exploitation by health professionals in a leading sexually explicit magazine.

METHODS

To carry out the investigation, content analysis was used. As a research methodology, content analysis has a long and distinguished history.

Standard practice in scholarly content analysis has been to investigate media materials that command the largest circulation and respect within a given genre as well as those materials that have similarities in audience, purpose, and content.

In this investigation 141 issues of a sexually explicit magazine, dating from January 1973 through December 1984, were analyzed for their health professional cartoon content. Three magazine issues from this time period were unavailable and, therefore, not included in the analysis. Any cartoon depicting or referring directly to one of the following health professionals was selected for examinations: general physicians, nurses, psychiatrists/psychologists, marriage counselors, sexologists, gynecologists/obstetricians, dentists, sex therapists, social workers, and others (e.g., surgeons, pharmacists, dermatologists). A total of 187 cartoons were analyzed.

Following the Reisman Model for Child Cartoon Analysis (1984), a preliminary cartoon content analysis coding instrument (CCACI) and standard coding sheet were designed to classify and record information contained in the health professional cartoons. The final version of the CCACI consisted of a set of 28 questions regarding the activities, setting, and individual characters depicted in the health professional cartoons. Although we minimized the need for subjective judgment on the part of the trained coders, no analysis technique currently available can guarantee complete objectivity in any examination of effective material.

RESULTS

Cartoons portraying health professions were a prevalent feature in the magazine during the 12-year study period, with the regular reader encountering 187 such cartoons. Although a few of the cartoons contained complex imagery, most cartoon imagery was simple and direct. Hence, most cartoons readily lent themselves to the classification and codification of the textual and visual activities, setting, and characters.

Activities

The majority (87 percent) of health professional cartoons during the period of study involved activity that was illegal, unethical, sexual, morbid, or violent in nature (see Figure 12.1). Such activity was explicit in approximately 93 percent of the cartoon cases in which it occurred.

Illegal or Unethical Activity

More than 55 percent of the 187 cartoons protrayed some form of illegal or unethical activity (see Figure 12.2). In nearly 100 cases, this involved

FIGURE 12.1.

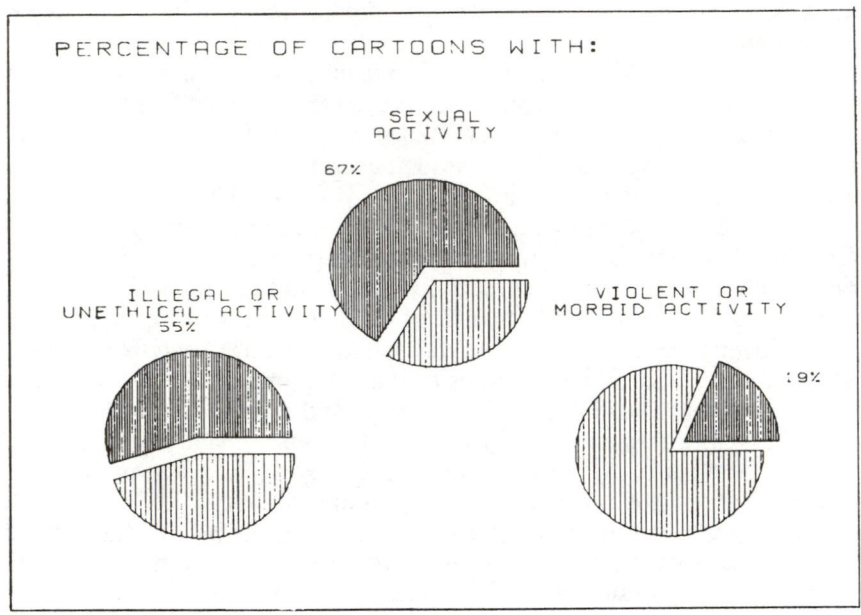

Source: Compiled by the authors.

misconduct on the part of the health professional. The health professional in 25 of these misconduct cases employed some type of trickery or deception. The illicit use of drugs was the subject of two cartoons, extortion was the subject of one cartoon, and exhibitionism was the subject of one cartoon. There were two cases of blatant sexual assault: a male gynecologist publicly raped a female, and a female patient sexually assaulted a male physician. There were also two cases of child sexual abuse.

Sexual Activity

Approximately two-thirds of the health professional cartoons involved an activity or interaction that was sexual in nature (see Figure 12.3). More than 55 cartoons related to sexual intercourse. Nearly 50 additional cartoons contained nudity, a sexual overture, or some sexual activity or interaction short of intercourse. Another 16 cases involved masturbation, venereal disease, or some other sexual motif.

FIGURE 12.2.

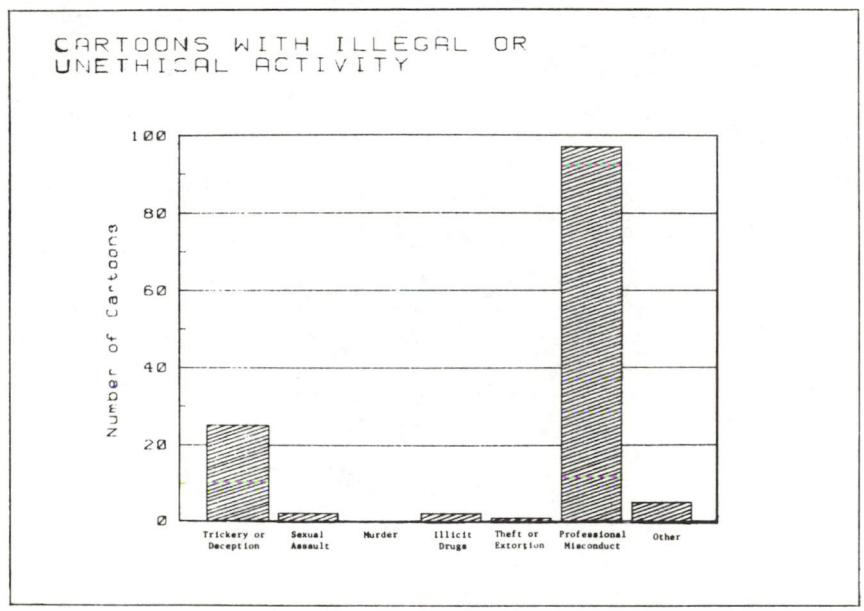

Source: Compiled by the authors.

Of the sexual cartoons that could be classified, 87 percent involved heterosexuality. In addition, 5 percent involved homosexuality, 4 percent involved bestiality, and 4 percent involved group sex activity.

Nudity (partial or complete) was depicted in more than one-third of the health professional cartoons. While the provision of drape cloths, gowns, or smocks is common practice in the medical environment, in very few cases was a patient provided with any covering. While nudity would be regarded as a normal, nonsexual phenomenon in the real medical environment, it was regarded as inherently sexual in the context of the health professional cartoons.

Violent or Morbid Activity

Traditional forms of violence occurred in only a small number of health professional cartoons. Identified were two cases of hitting, kicking, or grabbing; two cases of ripped or pulled clothes; five cases of whippings or bonding; one case of decapitation; and one case involving the consumption of human flesh. No case of shooting or stabbing was found. Quite common,

FIGURE 12.3.

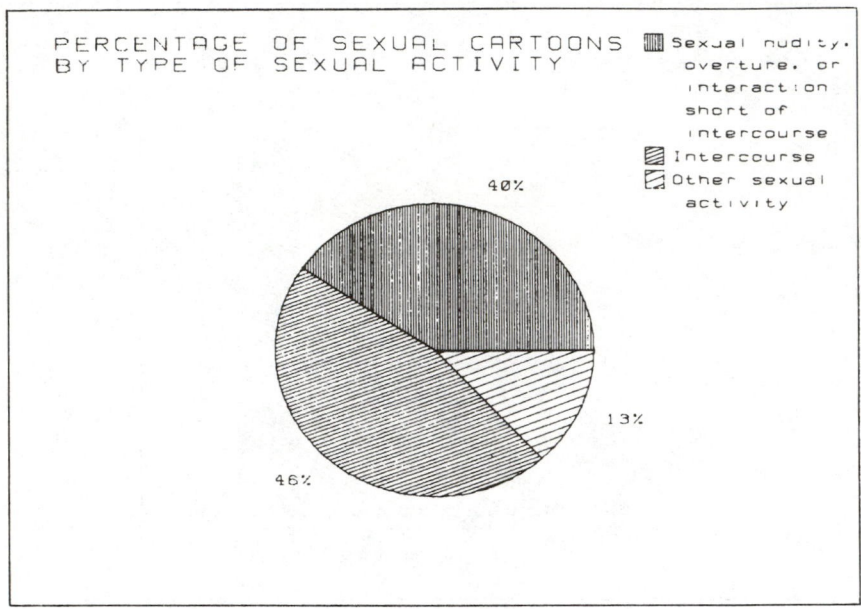

Source: Compiled by the authors.

however, were cartoons that were morbid in nature. During the period under study 26 such cartoons were published (see Figure 12.4).

Setting

Nearly all of the cartoon activity occurred within the conventional health care environment (see Figure 12.5). In 152 of the 187 cartoon cases, the setting was either a hospital, doctor's office, or therapy room. Most of the remaining cases occurred in the waiting room of a health professional's office, a medical studio or lab, or another institutional setting. Fewer than 10 percent of the cartoons occurred in a nonmedical environment.

Characters

The number of characters in most of the cartoons was small: one or two health professionals and either one or two patients, depending on the specific health profession depicted. The specialty of the health professional was easily discernable. If the profession was not evident by means of explicit cues (e.g., couch and notebook, dentist chair, gynecological stirrups),

FIGURE 12.4.

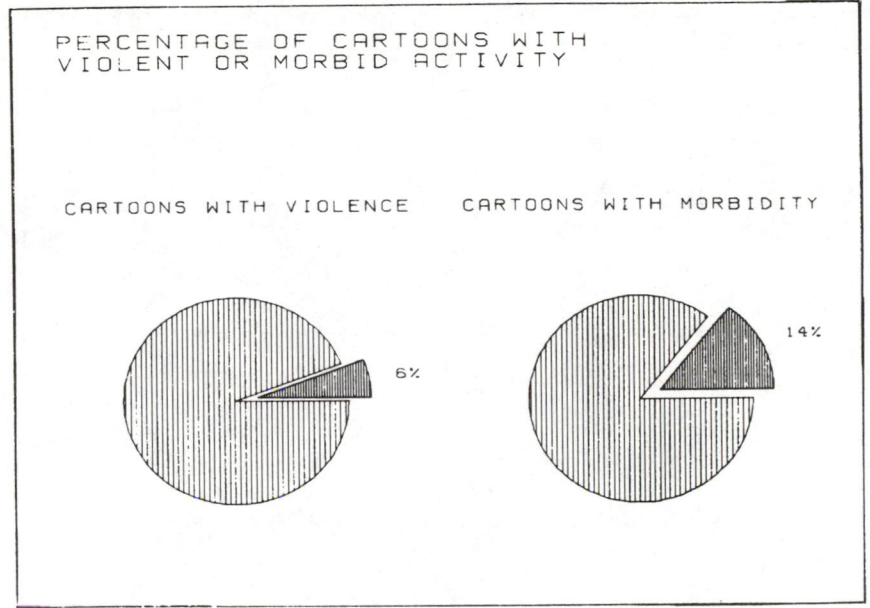

Source: Compiled by the authors.

then this information was provided directly by the display of diplomas, door signs, or reference to the specific profession in the cartoon's caption.

Health Professionals

A spectrum of health professionals was represented in cartoons (see Figure 12.6). Most commonly depicted (37 percent of the cartoons) was the general physician (i.e., no noted specialty). Also found, however, were nurses (16 percent), psychiatrists/psychologists (14 percent), marriage counselors (10 percent), sexologists (10 percent), gynecologists/obstetricians (5 percent), dentists (3 percent), sex therapists (2 percent), social workers (0.5 percent), and other health professionals (12 percent). The "other" category included surgeons, pharmacists, coroners, dermatologists, and proctologists. The sum exceeds 100 percent because occasionally a single cartoon depicted members of more than one health profession.

The 255 health care professionals identified and coded in the 187 cartoons have one general characteristic in common—they are white. There are no clearly depicted racial minority group members cast as health professionals.

FIGURE 12.5.

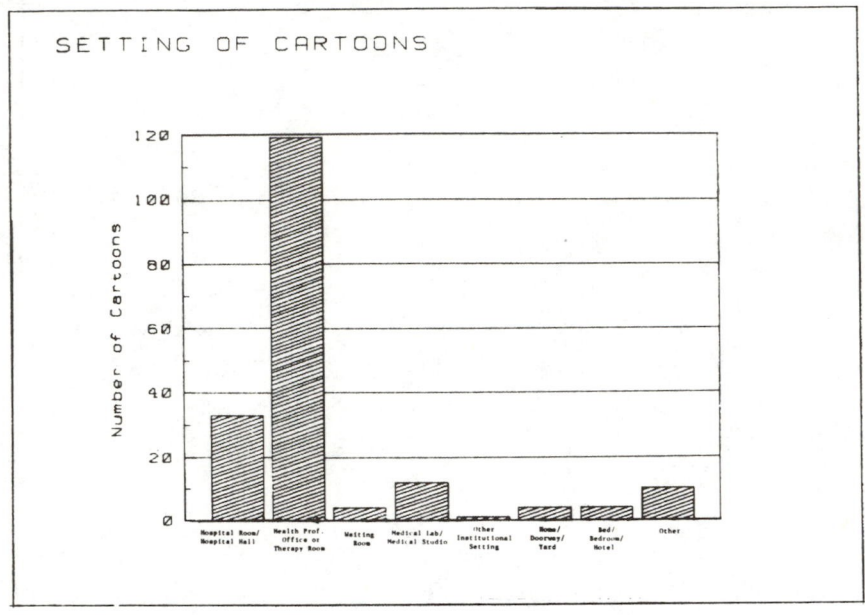

Source: Compiled by the authors.

According to the U.S. Census Bureau (1982), races other than white constituted 14 percent of the total population of practicing physicians in 1981. Similarly, nonwhite dentists, pharmacists, therapists, and other health professionals constituted a substantial portion of their respective fields. In the same year, more than 14 percent of all registered and practical nurses were nonwhite. Yet, minority racial group health professionals were not represented in the cartoons.

Women are both stereotyped and statistically underrepresented in the health professional cartoons. Of the 255 identified health professionals, 52 were women; of these female health professionals, 35 were nurses and 14 were sexologists or assistants to sexologists. In only three instances was a female health professional portrayed as anything other than a nurse or sexologist: one was a social worker, one was a health researcher/administrator, and one was a physician. In this last case, the female doctor was the subject of acute sexual harrassment.

According to statistics published by the American Medical Association (1983), the percentage of female licensed physicians in the United States increased from 7.7 percent in 1970 to 12.8 percent in 1982. Nevertheless, females constituted less than 1 percent of all medical doctors depicted in the cartoons.

FIGURE 12.6.

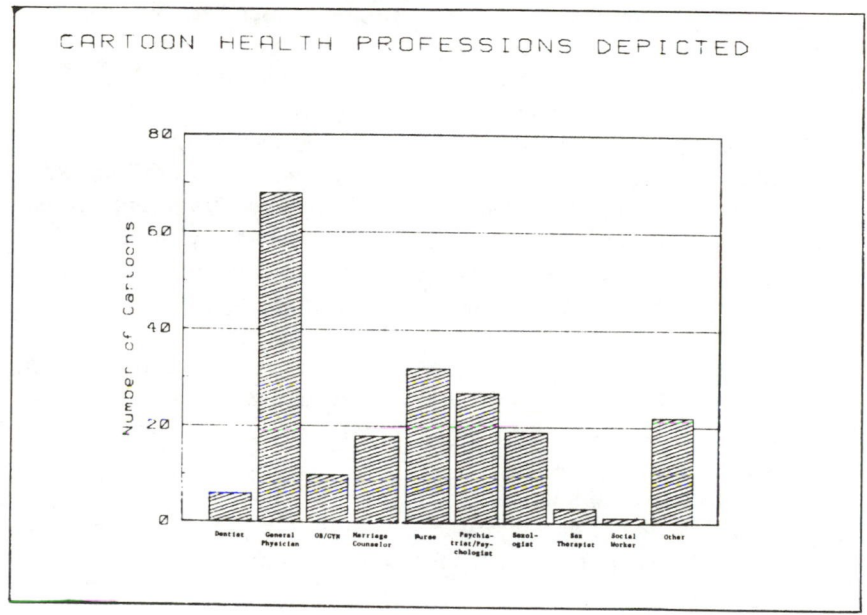

Source: Compiled by the authors.

Clients and Other Characters

In cases in which the sole or principal patient was female, about 80 percent of the cartoons were sexual in nature. Female patients were two and one-half times more likely than male patients to be depicted as partially or completely naked. Of the cartoons with female patients, two-thirds involved some form of misconduct by the (nearly always male) health professional. Almost 40 percent of the time this entailed some form of trickery or deception.

Male patients are somewhat less likely to be cast in a sexual scenario. Less than half of the cases in which the sole or principal patient was male involved activity that was classified as sexual. Of the cartoons with male patients, 40 percent involved some form of misconduct by the (usually male) health professional. Only one-tenth of the time did the misconduct entail trickery or deception. Morbidity was a common motif, appearing in approximately one-fifth of the cartoons involving male patients.

Minorities rarely appeared in any situation in the health professional cartoons. Although in 1980 minorities accounted for 11.1 percent of the total visits to physicians in the United States (U.S. Bureau of the Census 1982, p. 110), in no case was a cartoon patient identifiably portrayed as nonwhite. In the two instances where minority members *were* clearly depicted in a cartoon, they were background characters within a group of ten or more people. In one cartoon, two racial minority group members were included in a group sex scenario involving white children.

Minor-age children and adolescents appeared in 9–11 percent of the cartoons. Included were two infants, 12 children, five adolescents, and four young characters of ambiguous age. Girls and boys were both represented.

Where boys were represented, they were generally the subject of nonsexual humor. With the exception of one case in which two boys witnessed a rape, the only boys found in a sexual setting were in the company of girls.

Where girls were represented, the cartoons were uniformly sexual in nature. The specific themes involved child pregnancy, sexual intercourse, group sex, and child sexual abuse by foster parents. One case involved the devouring of little girls by a wolf.

In nine instances, animals were portrayed as characters. The animals were anthropomorphized in eight cases, and in four of these cases they were the recipients of sexual attention from a human female.

Cartoon Scenarios by Specific Health Profession

Clear stereotypes were manifest in the cartoon scenarios pertaining to each individual health profession. Some of the common stereotypes are described below.

General physicians. The general physician (nearly always male) was normally depicted with a single patient. Male and female patients were represented with approximately the same frequency. Male patients commonly suffered from venereal disease or some other negative consequence of sexual activity. The general physician was frequently cast in a demeaning or derrogatory light in cartoons involving male patients.

In nearly every cartoon involving a female patient, the patient was young, white, attractive, and the subject of some sexual activity, behavior, or innuendo. Over half of these patients were completely or partially naked. The female patient was directly engaged—willingly or unwillingly—in a sexual interaction with her personal physician in roughly half the cartoons. The nature of these interactions ranged from a sexual overture on the part of the female patient to sexual assault by the physician.

Nurses. The nurse was typically portrayed as an initiator or recipient of sexual involvement with patients and/or physicians, as a passive or helpless bystander, or as a negligent caretaker.

Psychiatrists/Psychologists. The psychiatrist/psychologist (always male) was depicted with both male and female patients in approximately equal numbers. About half the cartoons with male patients were sexual. In some of these, homosexuality or a sex change was discussed during therapy. Another common motif involved the verbal disparagement of a patient by a psychiatrist/psychologist.

Almost all cartoons with female patients were sexual. Frequently the psychiatrist/psychologist was the recipient of a direct sexual overture from the patient. In other cases, he was engaged in a reciprocal sexual relationship with the female patient, or he derived sexual gratification from personal confessions of the patient during the course of therapy.

Marriage counselors. The marriage counselor (always male) often became sexually involved in a female spouse—commonly in the presence of her husband.

Sexologist. The sexologist cartoons were mainly a comic-strip series. Typically in these cartoons, either sex histories were collected via interviews or sexual experimentation was conducted on human subjects. (In two cases, a male sexologist was personally involved as part of the sexual experimentation.)

Gynecologists/obstetricians. The gynecologist/obstetrician (always male) generally accosted, seduced, or otherwise engaged in sexual activity with his female patients.

Dentists. The dentist (always male) typically abused local anesthesia or some other pharmaceutical agent to exploit his female clients.

DISCUSSION

The results of this investigation suggest that there is a clear and consistent sociopolitical commentary contained in the sexually explicit magazine's health professional cartoons. The 187 cartoons analyzed communicate several notions regarding health professionals and their patients:

1. Male health professionals are untrustworthy and sexually exploitive.
2. Female patients are often openly responsive to or solicitous of sexual relations with male health professionals.
3. Patients, especially female, are legitimate sexual targets.
4. Women have little place in high-status health professions.
5. Racial minorities are not represented as either health professionals or patients.

Health professionals assume enormous responsibilities. The execution of these responsibilities requires the exercise of wisdom and well-considered judgment. The health professional must be free from influence of stereotyped views or sexual interest. Moreover, the safe and effective delivery of health care services demands the patient's full confidence in the proficiency and commitment of the health professional.

While the debate continues over the nature and extent of the link between mass media imagery and human attitudes and behavior, recent research suggests at least some cause for concern. The specific question here is whether or not the repetition of sexually and racially stereotyped ideas may in some measure help to subvert the effective delivery of health care treatment or the essential trust between patient and health professional.

Within only a 12-year period, millions of people have encountered nearly 200 cartoons that depicted health professionals as self-serving, incompetent, and unrealiable sensualists. It is important for those in the health professions to be aware of the exploitative manner in which their roles have been repeatedly defined.

REFERENCES

The American Medical Association. 1983. *Physician Characteristics and Distribution in the U.S.* Chicago: Survey and Data Resources.

Austin, B. A. and J. W. Myers. 1984. "Hearing-Impaired Viewers of Prime-Time Television." *Journal of Communication* 34:60–71.

Bogardus, E. S. 1945. "Sociology of the Cartoon." *Sociology and Social Research* 30:139–47.

Bryant, J., J. Gula, and D. Zillmann. 1980. "Humor in Communication Textbooks." *Communication Education* 29:125–34.

Cantor, J., and G. G. Sparks. 1984. "Children's Fear Responses to Mass Media: Testing Some Piagetian Predictions." *Journal of Communication* 34:90–103.

Comstock, G., S. Chaffee, N. Katzman, M. McCombs, and D. Roberts. 1978. *Television and Human Behavior.* New York: Columbia University Press.

Eysenck, H. J. and D. K. B. Nias. 1978. *Sex, Violence and the Media.* New York: Harper and Row.

Gerbner, G., L. Gross, M. Jackson-Beeck, S. Jeffries-Fox, and N. Signorielli. 1978. "Cultural Indicators: Violence Profile No. 9." *Journal of Communication* 28:176–207.

Gombrich, E. H. 1980. *Art and Illusion.* Oxford: Phaidon Press Limited.

Harrison, R. P. 1981. *The Sage CommText Series. Vol. 7, The Cartoon, Communication to the Quick.* Beverly Hills: Sage Publications.

Johnson, I. S. 1937. "Cartoons." *Public Opinion Quarterly* 1:21–44.

Reisman, J. A. 1984. *A Content Analysis of Playboy, Penthouse, and Hustler Magazines with Special Attention to the Portrayal of Children, Crime and Violence.* Unpublished manuscript, The American University, Office of Pornography, Sexual Exploitation, and Juvenile Delinquency (cooperative agreement #84-JN-AX-KOO7).

Runco, M. A. and K. Pezdek. 1984. "The Effect of Television and Radio on Children's Creativity." *Human Communication Research* 11:109–20.

Ryan, T. A. and C. B. Schwartz. 1956. "Speed of Perception as a Function of Mode of Representation." *American Journal of Psychology* 69:60–69.

Saenger, G. 1955. "Male and Female Relations in the American Comic Strip." *Public Opinion Quarterly* 19:195–205.

Schaffer, L. F. 1930. *Children's Interpretations of Cartoons*. New York: AMS Press.

Singer, J. L., D. G. Singer, and W. S. Rapaczynski. 1984. "Family Patterns and Television Viewing as Predictors of Children's Beliefs and Aggression." *Journal of Communication* 34:73–89.

Stauffer, J., and R. Frost. 1976. "Male and Female Interest in Sexually-Oriented Magazines." *Journal of Communication* 26:25–30.

U.S., Bureau of the Census. 1982. *Statistical Abstract of the United States: 1982–83* (10 ed.). Washington, D.C.: Government Printing Office.

Zillmann, D. 1983. "Disparagement Humor." In *Handbook of Humor Research. Vol. 1, Basic Issues*, edited by P. E. McGhee and J. H. Goldstein, pp. 85–107. New York: Springer–Verlag.

Zillmann, D., J. Bryant, and J. R. Cantor. 1974. "Brutality of Assault in Political Cartoons Affecting Humor Appreciation." *Journal of Research in Personality* 7:334–45.

Zillmann, D., and J. R. Cantor. 1972. "Directionability of Transitory Dominance As a Communication Variable Affecting Humor Appreciation." *Journal of Personality and Social Psychology* 24:191–98.

13

Institutional Resistance to Self-Study: A Case Report

Nanette K. Gartrell, Silvia Olarte, and Judith L. Herman

Sexual contact between doctor and patient is explicitly forbidden by the Hippocratic oath and by the *Principles of Medical Ethics* of the American Psychiatric Association (APA). Nevertheless, a significant proportion of doctors, including psychiatrists, take advantage of the authority of their position to engage patients in a sexual relationship. Although documentation of the extent of this problem is limited, the best available data indicate that psychiatrist-patient sexual contact occurs, that it is overtly approved by a considerable minority of psychiatrists, and that it is tacitly condoned by the majority [1–4]. Most studies indicate that about 5 percent of psychiatrists have been sexually involved with their patients [1, 3]. As in other cases of sexual exploitation, the vast majority of perpetrators are male, and the majority of victims are female.

In 1982, the Committee on Women of the APA began an investigation into the sexual abuse of patients by psychiatrists. We established four preliminary goals for this investigation: (1) to document the prevalence of psychiatrist-patient sexual abuse, (2) to increase consumer and professional awareness of the extent of the problem and to open public discussion, (3) to improve professional education, reporting methods, and disciplinary procedures, and (4) to begin the work of prevention. This chapter is a chronological account of the efforts by a small group of women psychiatrists to raise consciousness within the American Psychiatric Association about the problem of psychiatrist-patient sexual exploitation.

PHASE ONE: JUNE 1982–MARCH 1983

The committee's investigation began in June 1982, when Dr. Gartrell drafted a letter to the District Branch (DB) women's committees to determine how many cases of psychiatrist-patient sexual abuse were being reported to DB ethics committees (see Figure 13.1). Although the national Committee on Women previously had been freely communicating with the regional DB women's committees, we were told by APA staff that communication with DBs about sexual abuse was not permissible without prior approval of the Council on National Affairs, Joint Reference Committee, and Board of Trustees [5]. The debate among APA staff over this issue lasted for six weeks. It was finally determined that no APA regulation prescribed the manner in which such communication could take place.

In response to Dr. Gartrell's letter, 23 of the 40 women's committees replied. Despite increasing negative publicity and malpractice claims involving psychiatrist-patient sexual abuse, only 55 cases had been reported between 1977 and 1982 to ethics committees. Compared with the 5 percent figure cited in earlier studies, this preliminary information indicated that sexual abuse of patients by psychiatrists was a largely unreported ethical violation.

As a result, the Committee on Women decided in September 1982 to begin a consciousness-raising effort within the APA by conducting a national survey of the entire membership of the APA (approximately 27,000 psychiatrists). A questionnaire would assess psychiatrists' attitudes about sexual contact with patients, the prevalence of psychiatrist-patient sexual contact, and the frequency with which violations were reported. We anticipated that the survey would assist the APA Council on Medical Education in developing ethics curricula for residency training and continuing education programs. We also expected the data to be utilized in establishing more effective APA guidelines for managing reported cases of sexual abuse. Finally, we planned to publicize the results in order to educate consumers about the problem.

According to an APA research staff member, there were "no technical problems to doing such a study." Approval of the survey instrument and project proposal by the APA Council on Research, Joint Reference Committee, and Board of Trustees was needed, as well as funding. We were told that if as little as $1500 were provided by the Women's and Ethics Committees, other costs could be absorbed.[6] The Ethics Committee declined joint sponsorship; however, it called the survey a timely and worthwhile project.[7]

At the conclusion of its September meeting, the Committee on Women informed the Council on National Affairs of the proposed survey. The council acknowledged the severity of the problem but informed us that the APA did not have funds to support the survey. The discrepancy between this response and the APA research staff member's optimism concerning funding suggested that a denial of funding might become one means of communicating disapproval of the project.

FIGURE 13.1. **American Psychiatric Association Organizational Hierarchy**

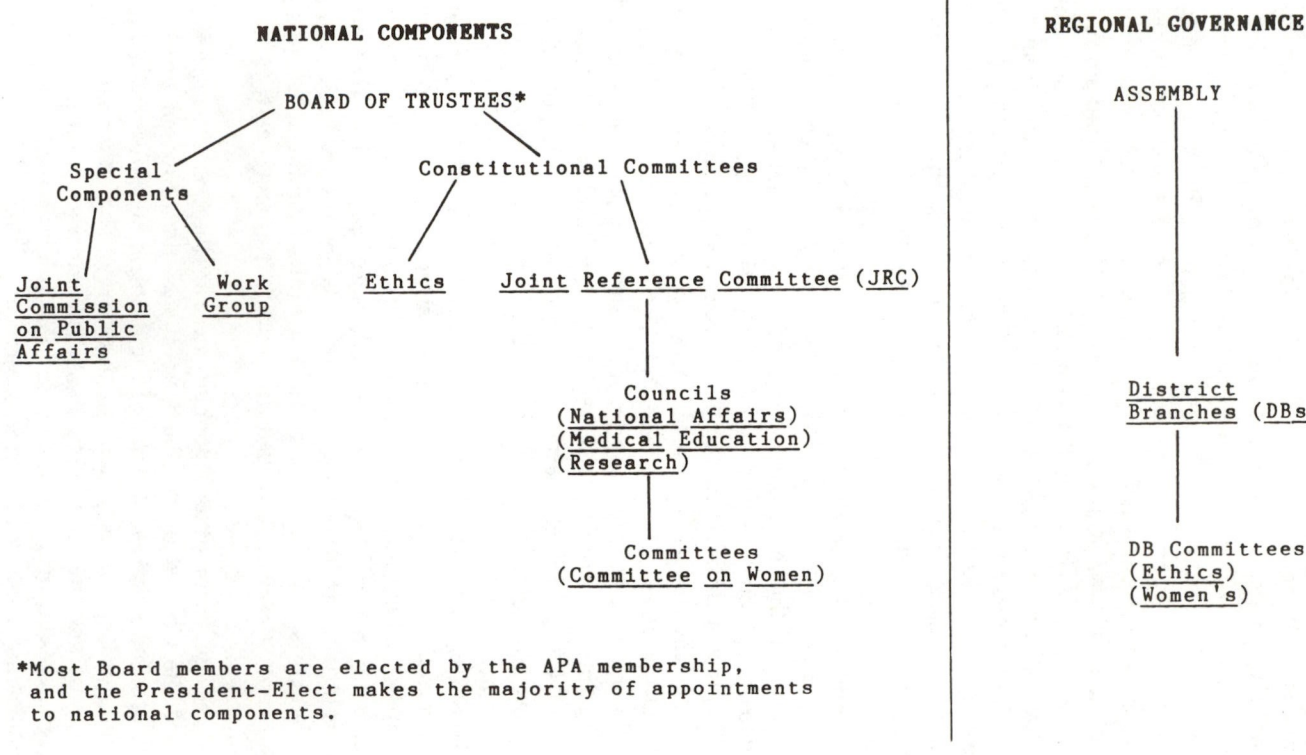

NATIONAL COMPONENTS

BOARD OF TRUSTEES*

Special
Components

Constitutional Committees

Joint
Commission
on Public
Affairs

Work
Group

Ethics

Joint Reference Committee (JRC)

Councils
(National Affairs)
(Medical Education)
(Research)

Committees
(Committee on Women)

REGIONAL GOVERNANCE

ASSEMBLY

District
Branches (DBs)

DB Committees
(Ethics)
(Women's)

*Most Board members are elected by the APA membership,
and the President-Elect makes the majority of appointments
to national components.

Source: Adopted from the May 1985–1986 American Psychiatric Association Directory of Organizational Components and Staff.

During the next four months, a questionnaire was developed. We decided to survey the entire membership because the controversial nature of the study might lower the response rate and because inquiring about unethical and illegal behavior was expected to diminish the likelihood of honest responses. The questionnaire was designed to be anonymous, yet even a large survey might result in a lower prevalence than actually existed because of the dishonesty factor.

In March 1983, the Joint Reference Committee (JRC), one of the committees that needed to approve the study, was informed of the survey proposal. We received no indication of the JRC's response other than a statement in the JRC minutes that the survey would be "reviewed by the councils on national affairs and research prior to circulation to the field"[8].

PHASE TWO: MAY 1983–MAY 1984

During the summer of 1983, we encountered major opposition to the proposed survey. Initially, the opposition from the Council on National Affairs took the form of criticism of the questionnaire. However, after we modified the questionnaire according to the council's recommendations, we were told that some council members were concerned that the survey data could damage the public image of psychiatry.

Objections to the survey then focused on the methodology. We were informed that the survey could not possibly "give an accurate reflection of the sexual acting-out problem"[9]. The issues of a possible low return rate and dishonesty in respondents were raised repeatedly. We explained that even minimal prevalence statistics would be helpful in developing educational programs and more effective disciplinary procedures [1, 3, 10].

When the Committee on Women met with the national affairs council in September, the council again acknowledged the severity of the problem of psychiatrist-patient sexual abuse. However, it was suggested that documentation beyond the limited data in the literature was unnecessary. Instead, the council proposed that we develop preventative educational programs. We informed the council that we had already organized a symposium on sexual abuse of patients by psychiatrists and that education was one focus of our efforts.

In addition, we stated our intention of conducting the survey independently if the APA withheld sponsorship. We were then accused of attempting to blackmail the APA into sponsoring the survey. However, the council voted to refer the questionnaire to the Joint Reference Committee. Because we were not present during the council's final deliberation on our proposal, it is unclear whether this decision was a response to the effectiveness of our presentation or to a concern that the APA could not control publicity surrounding the project if it were done independently.

The Committee on Women also met that September with a representative of the APA's Committee on Professional Liability Insurance. We learned that sexual abuse malpractice claims had increased during the previous ten years. Of the 1800 malpractice claims filed with the APA insurance carrier since 1973, (1) 17 percent were based on sexual abuse cases, (2) sexual abuse claims constituted 10 percent of the dollar loss of the program, (3) in the vast majority, the facts were not in dispute (i.e., the psychiatrist admitted the sexual contact), (4) most of the sexual contacts occurred *during* treatment, and (5) almost all came from female patients who had been sexually involved with male psychiatrists[11].

During October and November 1983, the questionnaire was reviewed by two members of the APA's public affairs staff. Recommended changes in the questionnaire were incorporated. The public affairs staff also began to strategize about enhancing the public image of psychiatry via the survey, suggesting that the extent of sexual contact among other professionals in comparison with psychiatrists be emphasized. In addition, the staff said that any resultant educational programs would reveal psychiatry as sensitive and concerned[12]. Regarding the need for reliable, up-to-date data on prevalence, the staff commented:

> The only hard data we have to deal with are the numbers of psychiatrists who have been sued or prosecuted for such conduct. Needless to say, that's very negative hard data. We would much prefer to say, "A survey of our membership indicates [that] X% have never participated in, and would never consider, such conduct[12].

In October, Dr. Gartrell again wrote to the DB women's committees and asked them to review the questionnaire. Many responded with helpful suggested modifications of the questionnaire, and most supported the idea of the survey despite some suspicions about how the data would be used. Again, the concern was that publicity would damage the public image of psychiatry[13].

However, some responses were alarming. One DB member wrote the following:

> Here in [this state] we're having a minor epidemic. The immediate past president of our District Branch is up for 18 separate counts with [patients]. Two [other] psychiatrists, one each from the two larger psychiatric groups in our state capital, are facing [the] medical examining board . . . on multiple charges with patients[14].

From another DB, a psychiatrist reported on local discussions about the survey:

We did not have any concerns about the questionnaire itself; but we did wonder how many psychiatrists are likely to complete the entire survey in a manner that would make it valid. In talking with some of our colleagues, the men seemed to think it either was a joke or not really worth the effort to complete the questionnaire[15].

The Joint Reference Committee reviewed the questionnaire in October 1983. As a result, we were asked to develop a formal proposal, which we then submitted at the next JRC meeting in February 1984. After considerable discussion, the JRC referred the proposal to the Council on Research, asking "(a) what [were] the advantages or disadvantages of an all-member survey vs. a sample survey; and (b) how could the survey or sample survey be expanded to include physicians in other specialities or professionals in other mental health disciplines . . . in order to put psychiatry in context with a larger group"[16].

We were also informed that the JRC was concerned about ownership of whatever data we collected. Despite our developing the survey instrument without compensation and our understanding that the APA would not contribute any funding, we were informed that the price of APA sponsorship of the project might be exclusive possession of the data[17]. Thus, there would be no guarantee that we would have access to the analyzed data or that results of the survey would ever be released.

We began a national fund-raising campaign among psychiatrists in May 1984. Over the next six months, we raised enough money in private contributions to carry out the project independently if the APA chose not to sponsor it.

Despite concerns that it had been passed a "hot potato" by the JRC, the research council found that the proposed survey was as "methodologically and scientifically sound as could be developed" and that "no further changes were required in the design of the questionnaire"[18]. In response to the specific directives of the JRC, the research council recommended (1) a sample survey rather than a survey of the entire membership, and (2) expansion of the survey to include other health professionals. However, the council *did not* see the usefulness of the questionnaire as an educational device and therefore recommended that the APA develop a mechanism *other than a questionnaire* to achieve the Committee on Women's goals of developing preventative educational programs.

PHASE THREE: JUNE 1984–DECEMBER 1984

Despite our growing pessimism about the prospect of the APA sponsoring the survey, we decided to make a final attempt to convince the JRC of its importance. After listening to our presentation and reviewing the research council's report, the JRC recommended that the board of trustees establish a working group comprising representatives of various committees and councils "to propose an educational program for reducing or eliminating sexual activities between psychiatrists and patients, with consideration of the following:

1. Educating members and patients about the problem, based on current knowledge.
2. Educating members and patients about methods of reporting such incidents and how interests are or are not protected.
3. Reviewing the questionnaire to determine the extent of survey required and to ensure an emphasis on the clinical implications of such incidents as well as educational directions.
4. Recognizing that this it not a problem of psychiatrists only and exploring possibilities of a joint venture with other groups (multiprofessional educational campaign).
5. Including in a national campaign involvement of appropriate District Branch components[19].

The board of trustees agreed, a budget was allocated, and Dr. Olarte was placed in charge of the work group.

In September 1984, the group convened to discuss the need for educational programs and identified target populations. Dr. Olarte organized a workshop for the May 1985 APA annual meeting to acquaint the APA membership with the work group's proposals. When the survey came up for discussion, Drs. Olarte and Herman informed the work group that an independent group of women psychiatrists were prepared to proceed with the project if the APA chose not to sponsor it. Because it was unclear when the work group would meet again, the decision about the survey might have been delayed indefinitely. Therefore, Dr. Herman informed the group that the survey would be withdrawn from APA consideration if a decision was not reached during that meeting. The work group *voted not to utilize the survey* because it was not considered a cost-effective means of educating the membership about psychiatrist-patient sexual abuse. Dr. Herman then told the work group that the survey would be carried out independently and that the data would be made available to the APA and other organizations for the development of educational programs.

During its September meeting, the Committee on Women was informed that the APA was considering eliminating malpractice coverage for sexual abuse cases. The APA's legal counsel informed us that settlements for malpractice suits involving sexual abuse would soon constitute 50 percent of the dollar loss of the APA's insurance program[20]. Despite our recommendation to maintain the coverage to provide victim compensation, the trustees voted to eliminate malpractice coverage for sexual abuse. One member of the APA's insurance staff later commented that the absence of malpractice coverage "should eliminate the lawsuits"[21].

In October, Drs. Gartrell, Herman, and Olarte made final modifications of the questionnaire before distributing it to psychiatrists throughout the United States. Data from the survey are currently being analyzed; the results will be presented at scientific meetings and submitted for publication.

CONCLUSIONS

It was clear from the beginning that sexual abuse of patients by psychiatrists was a politically controversial issue within the APA. As part of a long-term goal to develop preventative educational programs, the Committee on Women chose first to document the prevalence of the problem. The APA responded by requesting a thorough review of the proposed survey instrument and determined by June 1984 that the questionnaire was sound.

The political consequences of any extensive study of sexual abuse of patients by psychiatrists then became the point of discussion. To diffuse the political impact of comprehensive data gathering, several components of the APA acknowledged the severity of the problem while advocating a focus on corrective mechanisms rather than further definition. However, no attempt was made to address the difficulty of educating psychiatrists about a problem whose prevalence and severity could not be documented.

As unwillingness to sponsor scientific inquiry into a controversial problem can be interpreted as a resistance to self-exploration and reflection. Fears about the negative impact of the information gathered—even if it is reflective of unethical behavior on the part of only a minority of psychiatrists—have forced the APA into a position that may suggest to outsiders a posture of protecting those involved.

Institutions that resist serious and timely self-examination and inquiry foster guidance by paternalistic principles. Members will be discouraged from individual and creative thinking, and lack of exposure to information that promotes psychological growth will curtail professional development within the institution. However, if institutions can assist individual members through peer review, not only will members in need of assistance be helped, but creative, inquisitive members will be motivated to work within these institutions to maintain high standards for growth and development.

NOTES

The authors thank Wilma Wake for her helpful comments on this manuscript.
    1. S. H. Kardener, M. Fuller, and I. N. Mensh, "A Survey of Physicians' Attitudes and

Practices Regarding Erotic and Nonerotic Contact with Patients," *American Journal of Psychiatry* 130(1973): 1077-81.

2. H. Grunebaum, C. Nadelson, and C. B. Macht. "Sexual Activity with the Psychiatrist: A District Branch Dilemma." Paper read at the 129th Annual Meeting of the American Psychiatric Association, 1973.

3. Washington Psychiatric Society Survey, 1985.

4. N. Gartrell. "Reporting and Management of Sexual Abuse in the District Branches." American Psychiatric Association Committee on Women survey, January 1983.

5. American Psychiatric Association staff member. Telephone conversation with N. Gartrell, June 1982.

6. American Psychiatric Association. Staff memo, 10 October 1982.

7. American Psychiatric Association Committee on Women. 23-24 September 1982.

8. American Psychiatric Association Joint Reference Committee. Minutes, 13 March 1983.

9. American Psychiatric Association. Liaison letter to N. Gartrell, 29 August 1983.

10. J. C. Holroyd and A. M. Brodsky, "Psychologists' Attitudes and Practices Regarding Erotic and Nonerotic Physical Contact with Patients," *American Psychologist* 32(1977):843-49.

11. American Psychiatric Association Committee on Women. Report, 22-23 September 1983.

12. American Psychiatric Association Joint Commission on Public Affairs, Memo 17 November 1983.

13. American Psychiatrist Association District Branch (A). Letter to N. Gartrell, 6 March 1984.

14. American Psychiatric Association District Branch (B). Letter to N. Gartrell, 18 January 1984.

15. American Psychiatric Association District Branch (C). Letter to N. Gartrell, 3 April 1984.

16. American Psychiatric Association Joint Reference Committee. Report, 24 February 1984.

17. American Psychiatric Association Council on National Affairs. Letter to N. Gartrell, 27 February 1984.

18. American Psychiatric Association Council on Research. Report, 8 May 1984.

19. American Psychiatric Association Joint Reference Committee. Report, 15 June 1984.

20. *News for Women in Psychiatry* 3(November 1984):1.

21. American Psychiatric Association insurance staff member. Telephone conversation with N. Gartrell, 4 March 1985.

PART 5

Treatment Issues

Despite the ability or inability of both professional organizations and society at large to address the problem of sexual abuse of patients, the victims are left to deal with the consequences of the exploitation, consequences that are generally both long term and negative. As previous chapters have recounted, victims of either sex and of all ages are severely impacted by the sexual encounter. In Part 5, we suggest therapeutic approaches to helping victims in their struggle to overcome the effects of abuse and examine the issues raised by the victims' treatment needs. Group work and confrontation with the offending provider offer particular promise as methods to facilitate resolution of conflicts. The response of the intervening health professional deserves special attention, as it may be the most important factor in treating the victim's trauma. We first consider the victims themselves—their symptoms, their reactions, their diagnoses—before presenting several views, with practical applications, of therapeutic intervention. Although several chapters in Part 5 focus on victims of sexual exploitation by therapists, the chapters' insights on treatment efforts are equally applicable to victims of sexual abuse by other health professionals.

In the first two chapters focusing on the psychological problems the exploitation creates for victims, Calvin J. Frederick, discusses post-traumatic stress disorder in the context of child molestation. Based on his analysis of clinical data derived from young boys sexually abused by two physicians, the author's observations link symptomology to the exploitative act. The importance of his guidelines for clinicians is based on the necessity for an accurate diagnosis of post-traumatic stress syndrome if an ineffective and possible detrimental intervention and treatment regime is to be avoided.

In "Sexualized Therapy: Causes and Consequences," Roberta J. Apfel and Bennett Simon first consider why a therapist might engage in a sexual relationship with a patient before turning their attention to the effects of that relationship on the victim. The authors use the catalogue of negative effects of sexual contact with the therapist to discuss the problems of subsequent therapy. Patient issues and therapeutic problems are presented; the consultant or long-term therapist is offered suggestions for the best way of evaluating and understanding the patient's story, avoiding the repetition (in another form) of the previous therapist's counter-transference problems, and determing if, when, and how is it therapeutic for the patient to report and press charges against the previous therapist.

A collaborative effort between an agency that assists victims in processing complaints and an agency providing group and individual follow-up therapy is described in the next two chapters. In Chapter 16, Gary R. Schoener and Jeanette Hofstee Milgrom present a mediation approach based on their experiences with an innovative walk-in counseling center aimed at confronting the sexual exploitation at a level whereby both victim and offender can obtain necessary help. The authors also examine a seldom-addressed issue, that of the need for support of so-called secondary victims, the spouses and other individuals especially close to the victim. Of special interest to administrators are a sample counseling volunteer application and a checklist of safeguards against sexual misconduct.

Complementing the walk-in counseling center's mediation approach is the time-limited treatment group program described by Ellen Thompson Luepker and Carol Retsch-Bogart in Chapter 17. By its time-limited aspect, this group therapy model underscores an expectation of recovery. In addition, victims are given both professional and peer support for the period immediately following the sexual relationship, a time when such support is crucial. Among topics the authors discuss is how group themes such as confidentiality concerns and guilt feelings, are addressed.

In contrast to the time-limited approach is the open-ended approach to group therapy discussed in Chapter 18 by Phyllis A. Kaufman and Elizabeth Harrison. Also led by two therapists, the group sessions have distinct differences from as well as similarities with the shorter-term sessions discussed in the previous chapter. Group dynamics as well as the group process itself provide intervention for the participants; as a new member enters the group, the other members are able to offer support to a fellow victim and to measure their own progress. The authors also highlight the effect that outside events (mediating sessions, publicity, and litigation procedures) can have on the group process. Litigation disrupted the therapeutic process in this group to the point that group sessions terminated after 18 months.

The final chapter, "Dynamics of Treatment Groups for Victims of Therapist Sexual Misconduct," takes our consideration of treatment groups to its final phase. Authors Debra S. Borys, C. Buf Meyer, Roberta L. Falke, and Janet L. Sonne critically evaluate various aspects of the therapist's use of the treatment group modality, including the influence on group sessions of patient problems related to the abuse and the benefits and limitations of the group approach. They also explore in detail the issue of countertransference, an essential consideration for leaders of any treatment group program.

With these final six chapters, our focus is brought back to the individual most impacted by sexual exploitation—the victim. Despite the activity or inactivity of professional and regulatory organizations, the prevailing values and attitudes of socieity, and the treatment efforts of caring health professionals, it is the victim who ultimately bears the burden of the offender's sexually abusive actions.

14

Post-Traumatic Stress Disorder and Child Molestation

Calvin J. Frederick

Historically, the term "private parts" has had special meaning from early childhood. Even before language is mastered, attention is paid to feelings surrounding the genitals. For a child, an invasion of body privacy is apt to elicit a response in sensation and feeling that is beyond the child's level of emotional maturity. Unable to understand and assimilate fully the impact of strong sexual stimulation, the child becomes overwhelmed both psychologically and physically. The loss of personal power or control over one's own being evokes shock, disbelief, and denial. Psychic numbing is accompanied by fear of disclosure which produces diminished verbal responsiveness. Rage and resentment can be expressed only later, with support from others, in a safe environment.

Molestation places the child in a dilemma. Assault on the private areas of the body may evoke fears of mutilation and even death, while gratification may be obtained from pleasing a powerful adult, thereby abating the immobilizing fears. The child's participation and compliance serve to lessen the fear of angering the perpetrator while simultaneously contributing to pleasurable stimulation. Research in this area includes work by Burgess, Groth, and Holmstrom (1978); Finkelhor (1979, 1980); Schoettle (1980); Summit and Kryso (1978); Summit (1983); Burgess, Hartman, McCausland, and Powers (1984); and Sgroi (1982).

THE POST-TRAUMATIC STRESS DISORDER CLASSIFICATION

With the 1980 publication of the diagnostic and statistical manual of the American Psychiatric Association, a broadened understanding of the emotional and mental disturbances that can result from child molestation seems to have developed. Nevertheless, a need exists to provide an accurate clinical and scientific framework for understanding this phenomenon. In this regard, post-traumatic stress disorder (PTSD) has both psychological and legal merit. Prior to the recognition of this diagnostic category, psychic traumas were viewed as neuroses with mental and emotional sequelae related to a physical injury. Victims of crime, especially children, received little attention. However, PTSD recognizes a spectrum of stressors that evoke clear symptoms in both children and adults.

Children are vunerable and often readily available targets for a sexually abusive adult. Although differences do exist between children and adult sexual trauma victims in the manifestation of significant symptoms, basic criteria for PTSD are similar and measureable for diagnostic purposes.

This chapter focuses on information gained from studies of 15 male children molested by two male health professionals and from a sample of other youngsters who were studied as a result of molestation by other perpetrators. Information regarding these 15 young subjects is presented in Table 14.1. The primary diagnosis in all cases is post-traumatic stress disorder.

The 15 boys were sexually molested by two male physicians: 12 (80 percent) were victims of the same perpetrator, and the remaining three boys (20 percent) were victims of the other offender. Each young victim was examined at length by the author. Each of the physicians has been accused of molesting at least one other boy not examined by the author. These 15 cases reveal consistent patterns of molestation with emotional and mental sequelae.

PSYCHOLOGICAL ASSESSMENT

All subjects were examined via psychological tests covering essential areas of mental and emotional functioning. An average of five hours was spent with each victim. In some instances, information was obtained from a significant person in the victim's life, usually a parent.

Results were remarkably consistent with respect to the descriptive accounts of the psychic traumas suffered and the psychological areas affected. A summary of the psychological assessment findings follows:

1. Intellectual functioning: low concentration, gaps in comprehension, faulty abstract thinking ability.
2. Human figure drawings: immature productions, below chronological age, gender identity problems, sexual confusion, insecurity in environment.
3. Free-hand, unstructured drawings: fear of people, difficulty with human contact, lack of trust.
4. Incomplete sentences: difficulty with parental figures, anxiety concerning self-worth, phobias about perpetrator, distrust, marked suspiciousness, anger.

Table 14.1. Age, Primary Diagnosis, and Significant Symptoms Occurring in 15 Male Children Molested by Male Health Professionals

Case	Age	Diagnosis	Mode of Sexual Contact*
1	13	PTSD	FR; FG; MH
2	15	PTSD	FR; FG
3	16	PTSD	MH; SD; PP
4	17	PTSD	MH; PP
5	15	PTSD	HS; GM; PP
6	14	PTSD	MH; FR; FG
7	10	PTSD	MH
8	18	PTSD	MH; SD
9	10	PTSD	MH
10	16	PTSD	SD; MH
11	10	PTSD	MH; SD
12	16	PTSD	MH
13	13	PTSD	FR
14	14	PTSD	MH; FR
15	11	PTSD	MH; FR

Source: Compiled by the author.

*The sexual contact modes refer to the victim as the recipient of the principal acts involved in each case and are defined as follows:

FR Fellatio received
FG Fellatio given
MH Masturbation by hand received
PP Penis to penis frottage
GM Genital massage
SD Sodomy received digitally
HS Hugging sexually

5. Bender Gestalt: inept organization, lack of planning, emotional impulses difficult to control with productions marked by collision tendencies.
6. Thematic apperception: sexual confusion, pervasive sadness, violence, suicide, paranoid thinking, distrust.
7. Reaction index: psychic trauma of severe degree. Reexperiencing unwanted scenes related to trauma, bad dreams, constricted affect, irritability, psychophysiological reactions, tension when perpetrator is recalled, avoidance of anything that symbolizes the trauma, marked phobic reactions, need to act out tensions and frustrations, increased isolation from peers.
8. Clinical interview: feelings of betrayal by trusted authority figures, apprehensiveness toward health professionals, bad dreams and nightmares, expressed thoughts of suicide, doubts about sexual identity, extreme fears that peers would know and view them as weird and gay, doubts about ever being able to be an effective parent, fears that they might molest their own children, anger toward perpetrator with wishes that dire consequences would befall him, fears that perpetrator or an associate would return and harm them.

As a result of this examination process, the primary diagnosis in all cases was post-traumatic stress disorder. As Table 14.2 discloses, other diagnostic entities may appear; nevertheless, the essential and predominant syndrome that fully describes the victim's psychological functioning is PTSD. Initially seen in acute form, PTSD usually becomes chronic without skilled professional intervention sensitive to the problems inherent in sexual trauma.

THE PERPETRATORS

The perpetrators involved in our cases were male, middle-aged physicians whose sexual orientations were essentially homosexual with various perverse elements. Their penchant for male youths as objects of excitement was unmistakable. The physical examination provided the opportunity for the molestations, which took place in office, clinic, or hospital settings. The offenses occurred most frequently late in the afternoon or at night when few adults were nearby.

Youths selected as victims were particularly vulnerable (e.g., they were having difficulty at home or at school, lived in single-parent households, or had divorced or separated parents). The characteristics found in children selected as victims by molesters can be summarized as follows:

1. Sense of vulnerability: an absence of stable parents or parental surrogates in an effective nuclear family unit, as perceived by victim. Subjects often in emotional difficulty; this is apparent to perpetrator.
2. Need for strong identity figure of same sex: absence of valued figure with whom to identify makes relationship with authority figure attractive.

Table 14.2. Psychological Disorders Found in Victims of Child Molestation

Disorder
Post-traumatic stress disorder, acute
Post-traumatic stress disorder, chronic
Simple phobia
Identity disorder
Oppositional disorder
Generalized anxiety disorder
Adjustment disorder with anxious mood
Somatization disorder
Agoraphobia without panic
Adjustment disorder with depressed mood

Source: Compiled by the author.

3. Confusion about personal status: unclear self-concept, doubts about present and future status.
4. Inadequate sexual identity: victim uncertain of own sexual identification.

The chief principles employed to seduce the young victims were coercion and fear. Coercive inducements included the physician's: (1) serving as a father surrogate, (2) emphasizing his position as a doctor who knew what was best for the youngster, (3) assuring early release, especially when the youth was hospitalized, in return for compliance, (4) sanctioning sexual activities of various kinds as a release from tension and ascribing a "normal" quality to such acts, and (5) pressuring the youth to gain favor with the doctor, a controlling authority figure.

Fear-inducing measures were similar to brainwashing procedures and worked with remarkable efficiency. The use of implied or articulated threats for noncompliance served to break any resistances put forth by the youngsters. These include threats to: (1) remove and retain personal clothing, (2) use undesirble and stressful physical treatment techniques, and (3) confine and isolate the victim. In at least one instance, sadistic remarks were made (e.g., "How would you like to have me break [your penis] off [or] cut it off while you are asleep?). All victims spoke of being fearful that their parents would learn of their sexual behavior with the doctor, disbelieve their accounts, view them as sexual perverts, and reject or disown them. Moreover, they were markedly fearful that their peers might find out, regard them as homosexuals, instigate ridicule, or disavow further friendship.

It is significant that perpetrators are often fundamentally religious and highly respected by peers and community members. Marital status is not a conclusive factor; one offender had never been married, while the other was married. However, in our experience, molesters of male children are more likely to be single than molesters of female children. They frequently occupy a position of authority and create a sense of trust and admiration in their victims, along with a pervasive and ongoing fear of the results of noncompliance.

CRITERIA FOR POST-TRAUMATIC STRESS DISORDER

An acknowledged severe stressor. The presence of a stressor that would evoke symptoms of distress in any victim must be evident. Examples of this kind of stressor in the childhood population include experiencing sexual abuse, witnessing or experiencing physical violence that results in serious injury or death, and being kidnapped and living in fear at the hands of the captor.

The replaying or reliving of the stressful event. Indicative of this criterion are such occurences as having intrusive thoughts, experiencing bad dreams about the trauma, and feeling that the stressful situation might develop again.

A psychic numbing in response to the environment. This may be manifested by a decrease in activities previously present or enjoyed. Evidence might include limited ability to express ordinary emotions and loss of interest in former activities.

Newly developed symptoms of distress. Symptoms that were clearly not in evidence prior to the traumatic event appear. Illustrative behavioral signs are: being easily startled, edgy or jumpy; sleeping fitfully; feeling guilty about not attempting to avoid the situation; showing an impairment in concentration and ordinary memory; endeavoring to avoid stimuli that elicit thoughts of the distressing experience; and displaying a heightened responsiveness to stimuli that represent the traumatic disturbance.

SIGNS OF CHILD MOLESTATION

In nearly all cases of child molestation regardless of the age or sex of the child, specific signs are evident. Because the mental health professional does not live with the victim, information about these signs should be sought from the victim's parents or close adult relatives.

1. Need for proximal protection: a trustworthy parent or parental surrogate is often sought to remain or sleep nearby. When this protection is threatened, separation anxiety surfaces.
2. Confused sexual identity: remarks are made about being straight or gay.
3. Fears of being seen nude: avoidance of group bathing appears.
4. Psychophysiological disturbances: stomachaches, headaches, and occasional encopresis or enuresis become evident.
5. Personal discomfiture: victim is fidgety, tense and uncomfortable when molestation is discussed.
6. Withdrawal: victims remain alone and initially resist socializing with others. They are pervasively fearful that peers, in particular, will think negatively about them.
7. Irritability: being easily annoyed and rebellious are commonly observed in victims.
8. Risk-taking behavior: hazardous acts such as riding bicycles dangerously and climbing or jumping from high places often become apparent.
9. Self-destructive thoughts or acts: suicidal thoughts may be overtly expressed.
10. Comments of self-abnegation: lack of self-worth is common.
11. Under-reporting of trauma: withholding of a complete account of the abuse is not unusual, especially information about active participation.
12. Perpetrator harm: fear of retribution by perpetrator for disclosure is likely to haunt victim. This is often followed by a desire for revenge, expressed by a need to inflict harm on perpetrator.

DIAGNOSTIC DILEMMAS

Although all child victims of molestation usually develop PTSD, additional disorders such as an adjustment reaction or a personality disorder may also be present. Because PTSD is frequently viewed as a conduct disturbance, a depression, or an anxiety state, the skilled clinician will detect significant indicators of PTSD and will be alert to diagnostic pitfalls. Clinicians should be particularly observant of the following:

1. Nonverbal clues in demeanor, such as lack of eye contact, avoidance of trauma talk, and movement toward leaving the room, are crucial.
2. Talk about acts of self-destruction, mutilation, or death must be recognized in proper context.
3. Fractious, unruly, high-risk behavior due to tensions and frustrations is seen clinically and reported by significant others.
4. Lack of ease, comfort, and efficiency about activities previously enjoyed, such as sports or school work, suggest psychic numbing rather than depression.
5. Remarks about self-doubt, forlorn bearing, or masked feelings can indicate depressive trends and the presence of phobias.
6. Young victims find it difficult to describe how they feel and may confuse a clinician unfamiliar with children's behavior.
7. The overriding desire to keep the incident a secret should become apparent during interviews or in psychological test responses, especially in the reaction index.
8. If overt symptoms are not revealed in acute form soon after the trauma, problems may move into a more chronic stage in which the disorder becomes covert and not readily perceived.
9. Short-term recovery may be misleading because traumatic effects can be obscured by our projections and hopes that little or no harm was done.

TREATMENT RECOMMENDATIONS

It is of paramount importance to employ appropriate procedures, both general and specific, in order to resolve the effects of the trauma. At the outset, it is necessary to support the victims psychologically and to help them feel they will be understood rather than condemned. Research has not shown that severe or intense exposure to trauma is more damaging than mild or moderate exposure. The problem always lies in how the victim perceived the trauma. It must be emphasized that a victim's prior emotional or mental disturbance is not a necessary precursor for the development of PTSD. Although previous disturbances may contribute to the victim's problem, they are not prerequisites for the occurence of PTSD.

Feelings of hurt, betrayal, resentment, distrust, and ambivalence must be addressed, particularly in teenagers. Illustrative expressions of these feelings by teen-age victims include the following:

> I thought he was a king. I would have done anything he told me to do. He was a person I admired more than anyone in my life. Now look how he let me down and used me. I hate him for it. I wish somebody would do something to hurt him back for what he did. He ought to be locked up and not given any food.

> I was number one. He said we will trust each other and have a real relationship between us. He was like a dad to me. Now I would like to kill him. I want to take a shower and wash away where he touched me. I am afraid to have sex with a girl like I should. I am sorry I let him do it to me. He's fucking sick. . . . I wonder if I am part gay. I feel like I am low-life. He ought to be shot.

These statements represent feelings of teen-age victims who had moved beyond the early stages of disbelief and compliant acquiescence. Younger children find it more difficult to express such feelings.

In dealing with young victims, clinicians need to implement several practices. Youngsters should be accepted as they are. Clinicians need to avoid trying to superimpose any views about what is expected, behaviorally or emotionally. Young subjects must be helped to reestablish and restore feelings of self-worth and personal control; clinicians should encourage them to make decisions that are developmentally appropriate for their age levels. Until they are sensitively prepared, young victims should be permitted to retain protective defenses, such as a wish to defer talking at length about the trauma with an official eager for information needed for prosecution.

Clinicians need to respect victims' feelings so that victims can respect themselves. Allow them to feel whatever they experience. They must be assured that any feeling is permissible. Special attention must be given to depressed and suicidal feelings in order to provide needed intervention. If feelings of frustration or depression are not addressed directly, especially in a person above the age of ten, a real risk of self-destruction may occur. With younger children, indirect methods (such as play with puppets or toys) are used. Training in and an understanding of suicide prevention techniques are essential to competent treatment of older sexual abuse victims.

Clinicians need also consider that it is not uncommon for molested children to repeat or mimic their experiences with yonger children. Soon after the trauma, these victims must be helped to understand that their feelings are not unlike those of others who have undergone similar experiences.

Debilitating fears can be diminished by continuing support and guidance while reworking the disturbing events. People significant to the victim—parents or other caretakers—should augment the therapist's efforts. Young children initially may be permitted to sleep near a comforting parent or caretaker before gradually discontinuing this behavior.

Analogies can be useful to emphasize to victims the importance of realigning their feelings. Medical analogies are easily understood by children. However, victims must be guided at a pace they can tolerate. In young children, play therapy may assist in recreating distressing scenes; visual imagery can be employed with postpubescent victims. Referrals should be made to professionals with expertise in this area. The victim should be skillfully moved through areas of painful experiences to avoid debilitating emotions occuring years later.

Experience and sensitivity are vital to prepare the victim for healing the damage caused by the abuse. There is little doubt that PTSD may lie hidden for years before surfacing in surprisingly egregious and debilitating ways. Charges that youngsters are embellishing, exaggerating, or manufacturing their experiences of molestation have not been substantiated in genuine cases of severe PTSD. Symptoms of this disturbance cannot be manufactured and are visibly painful. Young victims can scarcely talk about their traumas, much less exaggerate or contrive various aspects of them.

Sexually molested children are at serious risk of developing significant emotional and mental problems, including PTSD. Yet misdiagnoses and inadequate or ineffective treatment procedures are not uncommon. Each young victim has a right to professional, incident-specific treatment. Family members entering collateral treatment can provide information to assist the clinician in confirming the diagnosis. Thereby, they enable themselves to understand the child's and their own perceptions of the trauma.

In the absence of effective psychological intervention, the prognosis for child victims of sexual abuse is guarded at best. With the inauguration of appropriate incident-specific treatment, the outcome can be positive and of inestimable value to the reconstruction of young lives.

REFERENCES

American Psychiatric Association. 1980. *Diagnostic and Statistical Manual of Mental Disorders*. 3d ed. Washington, D. C.: American Psychiatric Association.

Burgess, A. W., A. N. Groth, L. L. Holmstrom, and S. Sgroi. 1978. *Sexual Assault of Children and Adolescents*. Lexington, Mass.: Lexington Books.

Burgess, A. W., C. R. Hartman, M. P. McCausland, and P. Powers. 1984. "Response Patterns in Children and Adolescents Exploited through Sex Rings and Pornography." *American Journal of Psychiatry* 141:656–62.

Finkelhor, D. 1980. "Risk Factors in the Sexual Victimization of Children." *Child Abuse and Neglect* 4:265–73.

Finkelhor, D. 1979. *Sexually Victimized Children*. New York: Free Press.

Schoettle, U. C. 1980. "Treatment of the Child Pornography Patient." *American Journal of Psychiatry* 137:1109–10.

Sgroi, S. M. 1982. *Handbook of Clinical Intervention in Child Sexual Abuse*. Lexington, Mass: Lexington Books.

Summit, R. C. 1983. "The Child Sexual Abuse Accommodation Syndrome." *Child Abuse and Neglect* 7:177–93.

Summit, R. C. and J. Kryso. 1978. "Sexual Abuse of Children: A Clinical Spectrum." *American Journal of Orthopsychiatry* 48:237–51.

15

Sexualized Therapy:
Causes and Consequences

Roberta J. Apfel and Bennett Simon

Overt sexual contact between patient and therapist is a disturbing strain of pathology in the psychotherapeutic process. In this review, we have utilized our own experiences in consultation, supervision, and therapy. We have also talked with other psychoanalysts about their experiences in analyzing and/or supervising cases involving previous sexual contact. We have no first- or second-hand information on the personal therapy of therapists who seduced patients; we suspect there are few cases in which these therapists seek treatment.

Although our analysis aims at objectivity and scientific examination, this is not a value-free or morally neutral discussion. The two stances we take are not compatible: (1) the clinical stance of what is most effective in psychotherapy for patients, and (2) the stance of moral indignation toward therapists sexually involved with patients. Rehabilitation and prevention for therapists and patients are thus potentially frustrating ventures for us all.

CAUSES OF PATIENT-THERAPIST SEXUAL CONTACT

Sexual involvement between therapist and patient may not even involve the genitals, although the range of activities is as broad as sexual behavior in other relationships. The genital phase of an individual's development begins in puberty and integrates phallic, anal, and oral components. One predominant group of male therapists who initiate sex with patients are people who have achieved some measure of genital integration in their lives. However,

---

This chapter is adapted from R. J. Apfel and B. Simon, "Patient Therapist Sexual Contact: I. Psychodynamic Perspective on the Causes and Results" and "II. Problems of Subsequent Psychotherapy," *Psychotherapy and Psychosomatics* 43(1985)57–68.

they are perhaps unknowingly experiencing deintegration or regression from the genital phase because of stresses in their lives (e.g., the issues of aging of self and spouse, death and sickness or parents, incestuous and competitive feelings toward adolescent children, professional disappointments in career aspirations, and failures to analyze successfully the impact of these expectable life events). Actual genital inadequacy—impotence or inept sexual technique—characterizes the mid-life therapist having sexual contacts with patients. The patient is seduced into sexual activities that may be flattering, tender, and exciting, but scarcely give the patient much genital pleasure.

One goal of psychotherapy and analysis is for the patient to develop a broadened view of imaginative possiblities and problem-solving solutions to conflicts. We believe it is nourishing to the patient's ego to expand on fantasies and associations in the safety of a therapeutic relationship, with actual physical distance between therapist and patient. However, some therapists directly gratify a patient's instinctual wish. The therapist frequently rationalizes the sex as part of special guidance the patient needs, but the patient singled out for such treatment is not what one would consider a non-narcissistic choice.

Undoubtedly, there are several dynamic constellations underlying the therapist's behavior, and we do not propose that any one accounts for the sexual encounter. However, one discernable configuration is the operation of a rescue fantasy. Freud argued that rescue fantasies typically are part of a parental complex. We surmise that several male therapists who seduce female patients desire to "rescue" sexually the women from a terrible fate, marriage, or problem. Thus, the therapist is likely to be acting out (and reenacting) his own childhood Oepidal fantasy, with the female patient being the suffering mother whom he rescues (or seduces away from) the wicked father.

One common type of sexual contact between patient and therapist that has come to our attention involves the middle-aged male therapist caught in a nexus of personal and professional dissatisfactions, often unacknowledged. He is covertly and sometimes overtly depressed. His marriage is in difficulty, he is likely to be experiencing sexual problems and dissatisfaction, and he does not feel particularly successful in the rearing of his children. He also is beset by doubts either about his own professional competence or about the efficacy of his practice of psychotherapy and psychoanalysis. His basic commitments and relationships are largely ambivalent. His aspirations for generativity (a term used by Erikson to describe the developmental tasks of adulthood and associated with the virtue of caring) have been disappointed and frustrated by external reality and inner ambivalence. He may often rationalize sexual relations with patients as a sign of caring.

Both patients and therapists may attribute benefit to the patient from the sexual relationship. However, the same benefit may well have accrued from therapeutic strategies without the physical contact. For example, a few women patients in subsequent therapies credit the sexual therapist with having helped to foster self-esteem, especially via support of intellectual/academic achievements. They feel grateful and say they could not have "made it" without the special care of that therapist's approach.

However, there are some fallacies in this reasoning. The specialness of the patient has the effect of attributing more to the therapist, making him seem more special and stroking his narcissism. It detracts from the patient's sense of self-worth in that the patient senses that the achievements are totally dependent on the therapist. We believe that the relative good that results in such cases may be more a tribute to the capacities of these patients to make the best out of bad situations than to the clinical shrewdness of the therapists.

For therapists, the technique and theory they espouse are closely wedded to their temperament and unconscious needs. A relationship between one's personality and one's mode of practicing psychotherapy is not to be decried, but rather to be the topic for continuous self-scrutiny, both by individuals and by communities of psychotherapists. By having sex with patients, therapists declare that there is no need for them to sublimate and channel personal needs and motives, no need to examine and to integrate their personalities with the accumulated practice and experience of other therapists. What is needed, both in spirit and in practical institutional arrangements, are ways in which the individual therapist can express dissent, air new discoveries, offer and devise new techniques, and express individuality. Simultaneously, there must be ways for these dissenting ideas to be argued, to be tested, and to receive consensual understanding.

When the necessary nourishment is not available from peers and colleagues, therapists practice in isolation and feel abandoned and ignored. Then, outlandish behavior can be a way for therapists to demand that the community take notice: even if the recognition is disapproval, it may feel better than apathy. Sexual intimacy with patients has the aspect of such outlandish behavior, a cry for help often followed by a defiant or passive refusal to accept therapy or supervision. Part of nurturing is policing, a function that has been inadequately performed by professional organizations. It is far easier to provide a scientific or social forum than to apprehend and punish offenders. Yet corrupt activities become quickly known within the general community, and the concommitant loss of pride discredits the entire professional organization.

We have all witnessed the way in which the so-called "sexual revolution" has been accompanied by sexual therapies. Ironically, the defenders of sex with patients are looking for greater freedom from narcissistic bondage and justify the practice as a way to help share and permit growth. In our experience, exactly the opposite occurs; the trade-off is failed generativity—there is truly an inhibition of growth for both participants and degeneration for the human community.

CONSEQUENCES OF THERAPIST-PATIENT SEXUAL CONTACT

In our experience, as well as in studies reported in the literature, the effects on the patient of therapist-patient sex range from instances of the patient's having more or less buffered the ill-effects of the relationship to instances of psychosis and suicide. Within this range of outcomes, recurrent psychodynamic themes emerge.

Ambivalence toward therapist and therapy. Ambivalent feelings may be expressed in the patient's trouble finding a therapist, frequent changes of therapist and therapeutic modality, and major delays or avoidance in seeking needed therapy. It is not uncommon to hear that a patient has seen several therapists within a two-month period following a sexual relationship with a therapist. Normally any one of the therapists would have been acceptable, but at this vulnerable time, each therapist was seen as having committed an error serious enough to invite mistrust. Exaggerated and continuing allegiance to the former therapist often compounds the difficulty in finding a new therapist.

Questioning of reality and sanity. Patients who are not ordinarily psychotic may experience a split between their view of the actual sexual relationship and their view of the rationalization and deception involved. The patient's sense of reality is particularly unstable if the offending therapist has provided elaborate therapeutic justifications for the relationship rather than honestly admitting to more ordinary motives for sex.

Replay of pathogenic childhood situations. Childhood experiences may be repeated, reinforced, and even escalated by a therapy that should have been aimed at correcting these traumas. If the patient as a child was sexually abused by a family member, the therapist may repeat the role of abuser. The secrecy demanded by the offending therapist often causes the guilty sense of complicity with parental seductiveness to resurface.

Bondage to a therapist. Bondage may result from the acutal physical contact and surrender of independent judgment that accompanies a sexual relationship. Bondage is often a two-way situation: the therapist may be as much a slave of the patient as the patient of the therapist. The only possible termination is abrupt withdrawal of one party, leaving the other feeling wounded and betrayed.

Persistence or worsening of original symptoms. The symptoms that brought the patient to therapy, such as sexual dysfunction, may continue.

There may be illusory gains; the patient may enjoy sex, but only with the therapist. Discussion of other symptoms (e.g., inadequate work performance, chaotic relationships, or inappropriate partner choices) may be circumvented. As mentioned earlier, some women feel that the therapist with whom they had a sexual relationship actually helped them in academic or vocational achievement. Close scrutiny, both of some published accounts and of patients we know, suggests that they continue to belittle their own achievements by ascribing their successes to the therapist.

Constricted intimacy with men. Already troubled marriages become more so, and we have seen instances of reactive sexual difficulties in spouses or worsening of existing difficulties. Even more than other extramarital affairs, the patient-therapist liaison can make the spouse or potential partner seem inadequate and beyond redemption. Masters and Johnson made the similar observation that in cases of a sexual liaison with a therapist accomplishing an orgasmic return, this ability did not necessarily transfer to the spouse or partner.[1] The offending therapist rarely acknowledges that the patient's acting out of hostility may be fostered, a hostility that had been interfering with intimacy.

Rage and desire for revenge. Feelings of rage may be crystallized, particularly at the time of the breakup in the sexual relationship, and may be directed toward all people of the therapist's gender. The patient's angrily ending the relationship is typically precipitated by the realization either that the therapist has other sexual partners or that the therapist has no intention of making a life-long commitment to the patient. In some instances, the intensity of murderous rage may evoke primitive, psychotic defenses on the part of the patient in order to spare the therapist.

Excesses of guilt and shame. Patients sexually involved with their therapists universally feel guilt and blame. One important aspect of these feelings is the patient's conviction that he or she failed to satisfy the needs of the therapist. This sense of failure, combined with guilt and shame over complicity, further impairs the shaky self-esteem that originally brought the patients to therapy. Masochistic character traits and the tendency to self-blame are thereby reinforced, rather than modified.

Somewhat to our surprise, we came to realize that a particular aspect of the patient's shame had to do with various infantile sexual activities engaged in and initiated by the therapist. In our case material, coitus was the exception; nursing, fondling, and oral sex was the rule—often performed in a manner more humiliating than gratifying. These patients went to great lengths to protect the original therapist by not revealing details of these activities to subsequent therapists.

Stifled imagination. Because the sexual contact is rarely playful and diverse and is instead ritualized and repetitive, there is a concreteness and immediacy to the nature of the activities. The sexual activity seems literally to limit the range of topics that patient and therapist could discuss.

Creation of a crisis situation. The ending to the sexual contact is often without a therapeutic termination and referral, leaving the patient stranded in crisis and severely disorganized. The reverberations of such traumatic endings will be felt for many years, particularly at the time of termination of subsequent therapy. The time of abrupt termination, however, is critical to revelation of the sexual relationship and presents an opportunity for consultative intervention.

CONSULTATION AND EVALUATION

If the therapy has been terminated abruptly, the patient comes seeking consultation in a state of mistrust, confusion, and great need. The consultant may be skeptical of the patient's story or horrified by the revelation of misconduct by a colleague. Faced with a patient in turmoil who is unwilling or unable to reveal the relationship, the consultant may be unsure of how to uncover the shameful secret. Generally, the combination of the patient's state and the array of details presented leaves little room for doubt about the truthfulness of the account. In our experience, stories of bizarre sexual practices with the previous therapist confirm the tale, rather than weaken its credibility. We doubt there exists a condition of an isolated delusion about patient-therapist sex without other evidence of psychotic thinking or behavior being present.

The consultant must listen with interest and objectivity. Frank questioning and honest curiosity about details of the account encourage the patient to speak. The consultant's role is to help the patient believe and integrate the reality of the experience, rather than to question the account or to establish its veracity.

Although contacting the previous therapist generally is valuable professional practice, in situations of therapist-patient sexual interaction the patient may have strenuous objections to or painfully ambivalent feelings about such contact. The consultant also may feel ambivalent and must acknowledge these feelings and defer a decision on contact with the previous therapist until the patient's feelings have been explored and a working relationship developed.

In choosing a mode of treatment, the consultant should not automatically reject the previous therapist's mode of therapy (e.g., individual psychotherapy) if that mode is warranted. The value of a support group of patients with similar experiences has been demonstrated as one validating experience.[2] Long-term group therapy, with its diffused transference relationship, also may be beneficial. In addition, the possible value of an interruption or postponement of therapy should be considered. This is not the same as dismissal or adandonment, which are antitherapeutic and can deepen the patient's despair.

A similar open-mindedness should accompany the selection of a new therapist by the consultant, and the consultant should continue some supervising interest in the subsequent therapy. The gender of the new therapist may be important to the patient. In our experience, women patients who had participated in a sexual relationship with a male therapist generally sought a female therapist. The discussion of the new therapist's gender may be an important first step in clarifying some issues that were acted out but not analyzed in the previous therapy. Subsequent therapies are workable with therapists of either gender.[3]

The consultant indicates trustworthiness to the patient by straightforward discussion of fees, hours, and availability. These will be recurrent issues in long-term therapy, and patients will be forever sensitive to real or imagined lapses on the part of the therapist. Occasionally, a patient may need hospitalization; this too must be discussed honestly.

There are patients who, having been treated once in a "special" way, continuously both wish for and dread any other form of special treatment. The main form of special treatment that therapists and patients are at risk for colluding about is to exempt the patient (and the therapist) from confronting long-term, painful feelings. As the subsequent therapists, we have become angry and frustrated with patients, and we are particularly aware of the dangers of unanalyzed countertransference hate. Some patients are impressively skilled and experienced at inducing in the therapist all the conflicting feelings that they as patients wish to disclaim. In order to persist in analyzing these conflitcs, the next therapist must resist the temptation either to rescue or withdraw. Unfortunately, the sexual relationship with the previous therapist makes the subsequent analysis more difficult.

Termination of therapy is almost certain to be difficult and prolonged. Consultation and supervision are especially useful at this time. Dread of abandonment, fears of not being able to function independently, fears for the well-being of the therapist, rage at the therapist, and many other individual feelings may emerge. For some patients, the second termination highlights the degree to which they may have preserved the illusion of a continuing relationship with the first therapist.

A serious question is whether or not and under what circumstances it can be therapeutically beneficial for the patent to press charges against the offending therapist. The question is a complex one, and the therapist can err by colluding with the patient to avoid even discussing the possibility or by urging such action in a coercive manner. The potential benefits for the patient include the opportunity to turn passivity into activity in a socially constructive manner. Patients frequently are concerned, and often with good reason, about the previous therapist's repeating sexual offenses with other patients.[4,5] Reporting may thus be an expression of genuine altruistic motives and hence of considerable value in enhancing the patient's self-esteem. To pose the question and examine it with the patient is to keep alive and in focus major characterological issues dealing with the real world. The one stance that is clearly unacceptable and antitherapeutic is ignoring the question altogether.

We cannot offer any formula for how therapists should deal with the issue of reporting, except to suggest that they address it in a manner that will best facilitate thorough analysis of how the patients cope with painful realities. The obligation to analyze patients' behaviors in this area may run counter to therapists' professional obligations to report unethical behavior.[6,7] We concur with Stone's recommendation that a consultant other than the treating therapist handle issues of reporting and of possible litigation.[8] If the consultation concluded with referral to long-term therapy, the original consultant might be the best individual to deal with the patient on professional and legal matters. For the therapist to be involved beyond the usual therapy situation risks the repetition of an aspect of the earlier sexual relationship, that is, the engaging in an activity allegedly for the patient's benefit but beyond the usual degree of professional involvement. It may, however, be necessary at times for the therapist to testify in a hearing or to submit a letter of opinion to an examining board. Decisions about the therapist's role should be discussed over the course of therapy, as both feelings and circumstances may change.

Pressing charges carries its own risks. It can be painful, arduous, humiliating, expensive, and inconclusive. Furthermore, litigation is slow and may keep alive, with full intensity, the ambivalent relationship with the previous therapist. In addition, neither therapist nor patient should minimize the importance of the amount of money that the patient spent on the previous therapy and might spend on litigation. In some cases, the patient is left without resources to continue needed therapy. Pressuring the former therapist (either through legal action or through professional societies) to reimburse the patient may be not only a moral issue, but an absolute necessity.

Finally, we offer a suggestion to all new therapists. Probably the best mix of attitudes includes a large measure of respect for the power of good psychotherapy, a fair bit of curiosity about how patients and therapists become involved in sexual situations, a sprinkling (no more) of competitive wishes to demonstrate one's professional superiority, a concern and a balanced respect for the patient, and a measure of regard for the basic dignity of the profession.

NOTES

1. W. H. Masters and V. E. Johnson, *Human Sexual Inadequacy* (Boston: Little Brown, 1970).

2. G. Schoener, J. Milgrom, and J. Gonsiorek, "Responding Therapeutically to Clients Who Have Been Sexually Involved with Their Psychotherapists," Unpublished manuscript, Walk-In Counseling Center, Inc., 1981.

3. K. M. Mogul, "Overview: The Sex of the Therapist," *American Journal of Psychiatry* 139 (1982):1–11.

4. H. Kardener, "Sex and the Physician-Patient Relationship," *American Journal of Psychiatry* 131 (1974): 1134–36.

5. *Roy V. Hartogs,* 81 Misc.2d 350, 366 N.Y.S.2d 297 (1975), 85 Misc.2d 891, 381 N.Y.S.2d 587 (1976).

6. American Psychiatric Association, "The Principals of Medical Ethics with Annotations Especially Applicable to Psychiatry." *American Journal of Psychiatry* 130 (1973): 1058–64.

7. American Psychological Association. "Ethical Standards of Psychologists." *APA Monitor* (March 1977): 22–23.

8. A. A. Stone, "Sexual Misconduct by Psychiatrists: The Ethical and Clinical Dilemma of Confidentiality." *American Journal of Psychiatry* 140 (1983): 195–97.

16

A Walk-In Counseling Center Approach to Therapist Sexual Misconduct

Gary R. Schoener and Jeanette Hofstee Milgrom

Founded in 1969 as a volunteer organization, the Walk-In Counseling Center (WICC) in Minneapolis provides easily accessible walk-in, short-term therapy without any fee to individuals, couples, and families. In addition to short-term therapy and referral, WICC also offers consultation and training services to other community groups and programs. Over the years, it has become a place where both lay persons and professionals can seek consultations.

In 1974, the first therapist sexual misconduct case was brought to the attention of the center's staff. After it became known that the center would assist victims of sexual involvement with therapists, patients began contacting the center for assistance. A therapy/support group for women who were struggling with this issue was developed and later taken over by the Minneapolis Family and Children's Service; the two agencies now enjoy a collaborative relationship. WICC focuses on processing complaints, and Family and Children's Service focuses on providing group and individual follow-up therapy. Based on WICC's ten years of experience, this chapter discusses the initial meeting with the victim, therapeutic responses to victims, mediation through a processing session, the aftermath, secondary victims, and the therapist as offender.

INITIAL MEETING WITH VICTIMS

Our approach to working with victims follows some basic rules:

1. Be open to the experience of the clients. If and when the patient is willing to discuss the sexual encounters, explore the specifics of the involvement. Do not make any assumptions about the sexual behaviors or verbal advances. Sexual encounters

with therapists cover a wide range of behaviors, including kissing, breast or genital fondling (with or without orgasm), oral sex, and vaginal and anal sex, with either party playing various roles. Therapists may experiment sexually with patients, engaging in sexual acts atypical for them in other contexts.

2. Be open to the reaction of the client to the experience. Patients have ambivalent feelings about their sexual experiences with a past therapist. Do not make assumptions about how the sexual involvement affected the patient, and avoid expectations of patient consistency from one session to the next. Allow the feelings to unfold, and do not force a resolution of mixed or confusing feelings. Try to give reassurance and permission to talk about the positive and negative feelings that may be present.

3. Examine the nature of the relationship carefully. Did the patient experience the relationship as a love affair, perhaps with meetings outside of the therapy sessions and promises of an ongoing affair or marriage, or was the sex introduced as a therapeutic technique? When and how did the romantic talk or sexualizing of the relationship begin? How did it develop? Words and fantasies are important as guideposts. Seductiveness by the therapists, even if not acted upon, can be destructive and confusing. What boundaries or rules were broken, and when did the relationship start moving away from the traditional patient-therapist relationship?

4. Explore how the patient feels about seeing you. Most patients are understandably cautious, fearful, or ambivalent about reentering therapy. They feel betrayed by the previous therapist and distrustful of therapists in general. State clearly that you do not become sexually involved with patients, and be clear about the limits you place on touching. Emphasize to patients their power in the therapy relationship to: (1) question if they do not agree or feel comfortable, (2) request a cotherapist or consultant, or (3) request a referral to another therapist.

5. Focus initial intervention on crisis issues. First, is the patient suicidal? Second, what real-life issues are facing the patient, including issues related to complaints that have been filed and planned confrontations with the therapist? Third, assist the patient in dealing with emotional pain, grief, anger, and feelings of victimization. Any exploration of personality dynamics of the patient can occur later.

THERAPEUTIC RESPONSES TO VICTIMS

Therapists need to explore the patient's experience to determine what issues need resolution. Some pateints have had brief "affairs" with past therapists, have resolved most of their feelings, and have come to the counseling center for assistance in reporting the exploitation. However, when sex has been ongoing or when there has been substantial entanglement with the therapist, the previous therapeutic relationship may be the primary problem. Patients may still be involved in the relationship when they seek counseling.

Patient's other problems also need evaluation. The patient may be in a crisis or struggling with a significant depression that requires attention. In most instances, patients have several problems their past therapy did not resolve and life stresses that need intervention. Even if this is not the case, it is important to help prevent patients from becoming so involved in dealing with the sexual exploitation that their lives become dysfunctional. Most of our patients have been able to put the exploitation in context, focus on their other problems, and perhaps even joke about their past therapy.

The therapist can assist the victim in exploring different avenues of complaint. Patient responses vary from not having even considered filing a complaint, to assuming that the therapist will do so, to asking specific assistance in filing. Thus, it is important to be well informed on various complaint options. In virtually all our cases in which a complaint was made, the patient or a person close to the patient reported that filing the complaint was beneficial to the patient's resolution of the exploitation.

Support groups can be helpful. While groups for victims of sexual exploitation are rare, some therapists have assembled small support groups. In the absence of such groups, a women's support or therapy group may be of assistance. Consumer advocacy groups may also provide helpful support or validation.

Consider a processing session with the former therapist and the patient. Although attorneys or licensing boards may discourage this, we have found that a properly facilitated session with the patient and former therapist can help restore the patient's reality-testing and provide useful ventilation of feelings. Some patients prefer to confront the therapist themselves. In several instances, they have done this over the telephone and taped the conversation for later processing.

MEDIATION THROUGH A PROCESSING SESSION

In some patient-therapist sexual situations, we have been able to facilitate a meeting between both parties to process what happened between them. Usually this is not possible when litigation or a complaint procedure is in progress. A session usually involves the patient, the therapist, a WICC staff member, and at least one of the following parties: the therapist's clinical or administrative supervisor, the patient's current therapist, and a colleague of the therapist. In rare instances, the patient may not wish to participate; then the meeting may involve just the staff, the therapist, and the supervisor.

Obtain the client's reaction to possible sites for the meeting. In the majority of cases, we hold meetings at our center, which tends to be neutral for all parties and which reinforces our role as the facilitator of the meeting. It is important when organizing the session, usually via telephone calls, and again when beginning the session to explain its purpose and to assure all parties that it can be terminated if necessary.

Our typical processing session is scheduled for one and one-half to two hours. In most cases, we ask the patient to recount memories of several events and try to establish a clear understanding of the patient's version of events. We then ask the therapist to comment, question, and add to this understanding. It has been our experience that patients and therapists, when interviewed together in this nonadversarial process, tell remarkably similar stories in most instances. We avoid following any rigid formula and try to "flow" with the sessions. However, the basic rules we follow are:

1. Make certain that the client is emotionally stable enough to handle the encounter.
2. Terminate the session if it gets out of control.
3. Carefully describe the purpose of the session to everyone.
4. Ask the patient and then the therapist to recount the history of their relationship, including:
   a. how they met;
   b. original presenting complaint/therapeutic contract;
   c. course of therapy;
   d. how the patient-therapist boundary broke down, including:
      (1) the breaking or changing rules for the patient,
      (2) the patient's assuming "special" status,
      (3) the attraction—sexual or emotional,
      (4) the seduction or eroticizing of the therapy,
      (5) the general physical contact and sexual touching;
   e. feelings, fantasies;
   f. termination or lack thereof;
   g. residual feelings.
5. Use terms like "your memory" or "your perceptions" to underline the tenuousness of each party's memories of the events.
6. Attempt to formulate a summary description of what happened.

THE AFTERMATH

At the end of each processing session, we emphasize that each party involved needs to allow time for their feelings to sort themselves out. Our staff typically sets up a follow-up contact with the patient. If the therapist is employed by an agency or clinic, an appropriate person there usually provides follow-up information. If agency disciplinary action is to be undertaken, we arrange for feedback both to ourselves and to the client about what action was taken. We usually recommend further evaluation of the therapist to assist in making subsequent decisions regarding discipline, therapy for the therapist, and future supervision.

Clinics and agencies often request feedback concerning administrative safeguards to prevent future problems of therapist sexual misconduct. From our experience, three suggestions for prevention have emerged:

1. Careful checking of background references before hiring. Our center obtains a broad release from volunteer applicants; this encourages references to speak candidly.

2. Well-publicized complaint procedure and an organizational stance that encourages patient feedback.
3. An atmosphere that encourages peer and supervisory feedback. In most instances, other staff members suspected that something was unusual about a particular patient relationship.

When a staff member resigns or is terminated due to sexual misconduct, we have on several occasions facilitated meetings with clinic or agency personnel to address the matter. Such meetings have helped clear the air, have reduced staff guilt about the situation, and have clarified what can be done to reduce the likelihood of repeat occurance. This has also set the stage for examining organizational and systems issues that may have contributed to the loss of control by the therapist or to the failure to uncover the situation or intervene earlier.

SECONDARY VICTIMS

For those who work with patients sexually exploited by a previous therapist, it is important to remember that those people close to the patient (spouses, children, friends, etc.) are also affected. These secondary victims may need your services for understanding, support, and resources.

Some victims are married or involved in an intimate relationship. They may tell their partners about the sexual contact either while it is still going on or after it has ended; they even may not tell at all. It is our observation that the patient can best decide whether or not to tell the partner. Some women do not reveal the sex with the therapist because they believe that the partner will ask for a divorce, sue the therapist, or threaten to harm the therapist. Others do tell their partners and receive a range of responses. The husband already may have suspected it or be totally surprised; he may be angry, hurt, devastated, or may tell his wife never to mention it again; he may blame his wife or be supportive and join her in filing a complaint or a lawsuit. It may be helpful to the patient and the partner to explore the ramifications and effect on their relationship of the sexual exploitation by the therapist.

If the patient chooses not to tell the partner, there may also be consequences. Patients who want subsequent therapy or who want to attend a support group may have difficulty explaining their whereabouts to their partners and justifying fees paid for these services. Patients in small, rural communities may have to travel great distances if they want to obtain services and not have their partners hear about it.

Many women clients have reported having shared the essence of the sexual exploitation with their adolescent children. The women felt a need to tell their children why they were depressed, preoccupied, or anxious. They usually received supportive responses from their children. However, adolescent children have in some cases been reluctant to support a lawsuit for fear the family's name might end up in the newspaper. It appears that regardless of whether the patient shares any information with the children, they are affected by the patient's emotional or physical unavailability.

Some sexually exploited patients, especially young adults, have shared the information about the exploitation with their parents. Some parents feel that in some way they are responsible for the exploitation. Especially when the patient was exploited at an early age, there is a tendency for parents to blame themselves.

Our experience indicates that friends, roommates, and co-workers are the people with whom the patient is most likely to talk about the sexual involvement. They are also the most likely to give the patient feedback, pointing out the exploitation and urging the patient to leave the situation. We have received telephone calls from friends, roommates, and co-workers asking for assistance regarding their anonymous friend. In some cases, it is appropriate to give these persons permission to set limits on how much supportive responsibility they are willing to assume. The limit may include discouraging lengthy, frequent or late-night telephone calls from the distressed friend.

Although employers are not secondary victims in the sense of the previously described individuals, it is clear that they often are affected, whether they are aware of it or not, by temporarily reduced work performance on the part of the exploited patient and sometimes on the part of the patient's spouse or close relative or friend. Many patients have told us that they shared the essence of what they were going through with an employer and received a positive and supportive response (this is probably because those who anticipated a negative response had the good judgement not to let their bosses in on the matter). Clearly, patients with a less secure job are at greater risk of being fired for work interruptions or poor performance than those with good job security. It is therefore important to be available to patients during hours other than the patient's working hours.

THE THERAPIST AS OFFENDER

Finally, our work with victims provides some interesting observations on the offending therapists. Although patient attractiveness or certain personality characteristics are cited by several authors as classic descriptions that can be applied to most victims in patient-therapist sexual relationships (Belote 1974; D'Addario 1977; Marmor 1976), this has not been the case in the population of victims we have seen. Many patients we have interviewed do not fit cultural norms for attractiveness, nor do they fall into any narrow range of personality style. In fact, in terms of history (e.g., whether they have been a victim of incest or abuse) and diagnosis, they are not distinguishable from other patients. Their only common denominator is that they sought help from a counselor or therapist.

Rather than victim characteristics, we believe that the characteristics of the therapist are the major factors in determining whether a sexual involvement will develop. The vast majority of situations we have dealt with involve therapists who have been sexually involved with several patients, whereas it is comparatively rare for any patient to have been involved sexually with more than one therapist. Holroyd and Brodsky's (1977) data indicated that therapists who had intercourse with patients reported in most instances (80 percent) that they had intercourse with more than one patient. In fact, the best single predictor as to whether a patient and therapist might become sexually involved in a given community is the name of the therapist. Many therapists who become sexually involved with one patient will do so with others.

VICTIM ADVOCACY RESOURCES

We suggest the following sources for victim assistance:

1. Local chapter of the Mental Health Association. While they traditionally have not focused on patients in outpatient therapy, many Mental Health Association chapters either have dealt with abuse issues or might be willing to do so.
2. Association of Psychologically Abused Patients. The address is Box 9682, Ft. Worth, Texas 76107.
3. National Committee for Preventing Psychotherapy Abuse. The address is 175 W. 93rd St., New York, New York 10025.
4. **Stop** Abuse by Counselors. The main address is 5651 S. 144th, Tukwila, Washington 98168.
5. Consumers Against Psychotherapy Abuse (CAPA). The organization's address is Box 3966, Berkeley, CA 94703.

REFERENCES

Belote, Betsy. 1974. "Sexual Intimacy between Female Clients and Male Psychotherapists: Masochistic Sabotage." Ph.D. dissertation, California School of Professional Psychology.

D'Addario, Linda. 1977. "Sexual Relationships between Female Clients and Male Therapists." Ph.D. dissertation, California School of Professional Psychology.

Holroyd, Jean, and Annette Brodsky. 1977. "Psychologists' Attitudes and Practices Regarding Erotic and Nonerotic Physical Contact with Patients." *American Psychologist* 32:843–49.

Marmor, Judd. 1976. "Some Psychodynamic Aspects of the Seduction of Patients in Psychotherapy." *American Journal of Psychoanalysis* 36:319–23.

APPENDIX A: SELECTED ITEMS FROM THE SUPERVISOR/COUNSELOR VOLUNTEER APPLICATION OF THE WALK-IN COUNSELING CENTER

1. All past and present licensure and certification is requested, and then applicants must answer:

   Has your license or certification ever been limited, suspended, or revoked in any jurisdiction, or have you ever surrendered your license or certification or been placed on probation? NO _____ YES _____ N.A. (Never licensed) _____ If YES, attach an explanation to the end of this form.

   Have you ever had a malpractice suit or charges of unprofessional conduct brought against you? NO _____ YES _____ If YES, attach an explanation to the end of this form.

2. All training and clinically relevant experience is requested, and applicants must answer:

   Have you ever been asked to resign or been terminated by a training program or employer? NO _____ YES _____ If YES, attach an explanation to the end of this form.

3. Past supervisors are contacted by telephone and, in addition to being asked about skills, abilities, limitations of the applicant in a setting like ours, are asked about any questions they have about the applicant's professional judgment and ethics and any reservations they might have about the applicant's work. We read them the "statement of applicant" to indicate that providing us with such information should not leave them liable:

STATEMENT OF APPLICANT

All information submitted by me in this application is true to the best of my knowledge. I understand that any significant misstatement in, or omission from, this application may be cause for denial of appointment as a volunteer or cause for dismissal from the volunteer staff.

By applying for appointment to the volunteer staff of WICC, I acknowledge that I have the responsibility to read the "Ethical Guidelines at Walk-In Counseling Center" and other WICC rules and regulations. I agree to act in accordance with these ethical guidelines and any other rules or regulations adopted by WICC.

I authorize the Walk-In Counseling Center, its staff, and their representatives to consult with persons or institutions with which I have been associated and with others, including past and present employers, who may have information bearing on my professional competence, character, and ethical qualifications. I release from liability all representatives of WICC for their acts performed in good faith and without malice in connection with evaluating my application and my credentials and qualifications, and I release from any liability all individuals and organizations who provide information to WICC in good faith and without malice concerning my professional competence, ethics, character, and other qualifications.

I understand and agree that I will notify WICC of any changes in my job or training status, licensure, censure, or sanction by professional bodies, or any other information relating to my ability to perform as a volunteer at WICC.

_____   _____
Name (Please Print or Type)   Date

_____
Signature

Since we began using this pledge, approximately 500 applicants have signed it. We have had no refusals. Some of the benefits have been:

- People have commented that they feel this gives a clear message about the high standards we try to maintain.
- Past supervisors who act as references report feeling more comfortable about commenting on the applicant, especially as regards his/her deficiencies.
- University training programs that have recently tightened up on information they are willing to give out will accept this release as sufficient to permit disclosure, thus saving everyone time and expense.
- Some clinics have begun using it to screen job applicants for employment as professionals.

Furthermore, because we contact licensure boards and supervisors directly, we suspect that we are far more likely to learn of past problems or concerns.

APPENDIX B: CHECKLIST OF ADMINISTRATIVE SAFEGUARDS

STAFF SELECTION AND HIRING:
Does you job application explicitly ask about: YES   NO

Past terminations/resignations?
Past ethics complaints?
Past lawsuits, whether adjucated or not?
Past licensure complaints?
When dealing with licensed or certified practitioners, do you directly contact licensure boards concerning areas of competency, existence of complaints, and whether the license is in force without limitations:
Boards in this state?
Boards in states where previously employed?
Do you check via direct conversation (not letter, or in addition to letter) with past supervisors to ask about:
General professional strengths and weaknesses?
Any concerns or past complaints that might relate to special problems, vulnerabilities, or the need for tight supervision in some circumstances?

STAFF POLICIES:
Do you have a written policy forbidding:
sexual involvement or other unprofessional conduct with clients?
sexual involvement with ex-clients?
Do you have written policy for handling complaints of unprofessional conduct?
Do you have a peer review system/process?
Do you have a professional standards review committee or ethics committee that reviews concerns or complaints?

STAFF SUPERVISION AND CONTINUING EDUCATION:
Do you have agency inservices or staff discussions on the issues of eroticism in psychotherapy at least once a year?
Do you have regular clinical supervision?
Does your program have an atmosphere that encourages nonpunitive confrontation and constructive questioning among staff?

	YES	NO

Does your agency offer readily available alternatives when therapeutic relationships become sexualized to the point that they are dysfunctional: Referral in-house or to another program?

Use of a cotherapist or consultant in the sessions?

Is it general staff practice to evaluate carefully past treatment, with thorough assessment of clients' complaints and negative impressions of past therapists?

CLIENTS

Do you hand out a sheet of information or have staff read to new clients standardized information that:

Actively seeks to solicit feedback and complaints about the service?

Gives clients a specific vehicle for making a complaint known (e.g., procedure, contact person)?

Do you survey your client population periodically to obtain consumer satisfaction or outcome data and follow-up on negative feedback?

Are all complaints processed as complaints and taken seriously—not just seen as "transference" or some other therapeutic event?

Are complaining clients and the therapists in question given a chance to confront each other with a mediator present?

After you have decided on action relative to a complaint, are the complaining client(s) always given feedback as to outcome?

MISCELLANEOUS:

Are therapists' doors locked?

Is there review of long-term treatment or treatment that exceeds usual length of treatment; and/or situations in which clients phone the therapist a great deal?

17

Time-Limited Treatment Groups for Patients Sexually Exploited by Psychotherapists

Ellen Thompson Luepker and Carol Retsch-Bogart

In recent years, public attention increasingly has focused on sexual exploitation of patients by psychotherapists. This unethical conduct occurs despite explicit prohibition by professional mental health organizations and the community's reasonable expectation that therapists will put their patients' needs and interests ahead of their own.

Although patients who have been sexually involved with therapists suffer a range of negative reactions, until recently they have been ignored by the therapeutic community. This chapter describes group treatment services developed and provided for these patients. The authors hope to encourage further understanding of the experiences and needs of these patients through their presentation of a practical model for treatment.

Our discussion is based on the development and experiences of seven treatment groups for 27 women who were victims of sexual exploitation by various psychotherapists, all of whom were men. The women participated in various levels of sexual activity, and several of them required psychiatric hospitalization at some time after the onset of sexual activity. Although we lack data to make a definite comparison, our own and our colleagues' unequivocal impression is that this population's characteristics are representative of our general agency client population. This reinforces observations that sexually exploited patients have no characteristics that distinguish them from patients who are not exploited. An exception is this population's high percentage (40 percent) of psychiatric hospitalizations, which appears greater than that found in the agency's total client population.

In response to the needs of victims of sexually exploitative therapists, the Family and Children's Service, in cooperation with the Walk-In Counseling Center (WICC) of Minneapolis, offers time-limited treatment

Initial data for this chapter were presented at the annual meeting of the American Orthopsychiatric Association, San Francisco, California, March 1982.

groups. Treatment was offered in addition to advocacy services, provided by WICC, which gave information and assistance in pursuing ethical and licensure complaints. Groups used a brief therapy format with the following goals:

1. To provide an opportunity to discuss and clarify in confidence feelings and reactions associated with the sexual involvement.
2. To provide information about appropriate psychotherapy and its availability.
3. To educate the patient in being a more effective mental health services consumer.
4. To assist the patient in identifying and utilizing alternative responses to the exploitation.

Each of the seven groups lasted from two to 12 sessions, with three to five members and two group leaders per group. The shorter groups were those with fewer members, although group length also varied as a function of patients' needs. The weekly group sessions lasted one and one-half hours each.

INTAKE INTERVIEWS

In their previous therapy, the patients had experienced undesirable involvement with their therapists, had lacked boundaries, had not known what to expect in treatment, and had felt compelled to secrecy. Thus, we believed that creating a predictable, open, group structure was crucial to establishing a useful therapeutic relationship.

Both group leaders were present for the intake interviews. This established a relationship with both therapists from the beginning. During intake interviews, we obtained information about the patients' reasons for seeking help, their current life situations (including specific problems, support systems, and areas of strength), pertinent family history, their relationships and sexual involvement with the therapist, and other treatment history. We provided information about the group's purpose and goals. We also shared our expectations of group members: that they arrive on time, that the group conclude at the appointed time, and that members attend regularly. It was stressed that what was said in the group would remain confidential and that patient contacts with other group members between meetings would be shared with the group to facilitate group processing. Another important message was that the group members would be encouraged, but not forced, to share their feelings during meetings. The leaders explained the usefulness of collaboration with WICC staff when the patient was active in both agencies and requested the patient's permission to talk with WICC staff about the patient's confidential situation. Fees were scheduled on a sliding scale, based on the patient's ability to pay.

PRESENTING PROBLEMS AT INTAKE

At the time of intake, many of the patients were having trouble getting along with other people and had low self-esteem. The discomfort about their involvement with their former therapists and the wish to feel better were the primary reasons for patient participation in the groups. Nearly all patients expressed shame and guilt about the relationship with the therapist. Each woman felt responsible for what had happened, believing it had been her fault and that she had seduced the therapist. Some victims felt angry and betrayed, and several were angry because they now needed additional therapy to help them resolve their past experiences with therapy. But although there was anger and sadness over help they never received, most victims felt they had received something worthwhile from their former therapists.

Several women had filed or were considering filing complaints or lawsuits and were afraid of possible retaliation. Some were afraid of hurting the therapist in his personal or professional life. Many of the women who had hoped for an enduring special relationship or marriage with their therapists were filled with feelings of sadness, disappointment, rejection, jealousy, and desire for renewed contact. Many of the victims expressed frustration with themselves for their "poor judgment" and "naiveté." They considered themselves "dumb," even though they knew they had been needy and vulnerable at the time of the previous therapy. Some group members reported feeling emotionally numb, others had a fear of their feelings resurfacing. Several expressed confusion at not knowing how they really felt.

Nearly every patient explicitly expressed an intense need for confidentiality. Their trust in therapy was minimal, which we acknowledged as understandable and adaptive. Most had received little support from family, friends, and peers and reported a sense of isolation. Often well-meaning people had suggested that they "leave the past to the past" and "sweep this experience under the rug." This had left them with little opportunity to talk about their feelings.

Patients reported other problems that existed before had been exacerbated by the exploitative therapy, resulting in major interruptions in their developmental growth. All victims questioned their reality testing and lacked a clear sense of what was appropriate in therapy.

GOALS AT INTAKE

Victims had the following goals entering the group:
1. To meet other women who had been exploited by therapists and to share their experiences.

2. To receive support from others in a safe and confidential atmosphere.
3. To talk about their many mixed feelings.
4. To discuss various aspects of their own experiences to gain some perspective, and to work through the experiences.
5. To feel less ashamed and guilty and more acceptable as a person.
6. To become more trusting of self, more independent, and more assertive.
7. To learn what is and what is not appropriate behavior in therapy.
8. To acquire support while filing lawsuits or making complaints to ethics boards.
9. To discuss other areas of life that had been affected by their sexual involvement, including their relationships with men or with friends, peers, and families; to discuss their sexuality; and to consider their future life directions.

OBSERVATIONS OF THERAPISTS' ROLES AT INTAKE

Victims later revealed that it had been crucial at intake for them to feel believed by their new therapists. Members also said they found it helpful to be told that patients usually have a range of feelings regarding patient-therapist sexual intimacy. Group leaders needed to remain aware that their expressions, manners, or behaviors might block the victims' abilities to express their feelings fully and freely.

GROUP THEMES

Concerns about Confidentiality

All victims felt it imperative that what they said would be kept in strict confidence. Although this is necessary in any treatment group, fears of retaliation by the previous therapist and intense guilt about the involvement heightened the need for assurance of privacy. Some group members were involved in litigation and, for legal reasons, were obliged not to discuss their involvement. In one group, a member prepared a written contract pledging confidentiality for everyone to sign. In the other groups, the agreement was verbal.

Initial Cohesion

Group members expressed relief when they realized that they were not alone in their feelings. Knowing that rapid group cohesion provides a false sense of security, the group leaders proceeded cautiously. They informed members that although they were experiencing a sense of closeness and relief, these feelings should not be mistaken for the deeper sense of trust that develops only over time.

Countertransference Issues

We define countertransference in the broadest sense and include all of the therapist's feelings toward the patient. The countertransference that the group leaders experienced initially was a desire to be a better therapist than the one who exploited the patient. They imagined that they would do everything right and that group members would eventually see them as models of the helpful therapist. Sometimes this countertransference fantasy was promoted by the victims themselves, who wanted us to undo the disaster of the previous therapy.

The leader's fantasies soon eroded, however, as it became clear that what group members really wanted was to be able to talk freely and comfortably with a therapist who would not be angry, shaming, or seductive. It was also clear that group members wanted to see the leaders as occasionally imperfect and to have the opportunity to point this out. The following example illustrates this need as well as the therapist's temptation to be overly accommodating in a desire to compensate for the victim's past pain.

> Anne, 33, arrived at the agency for her intake interview feeling furious at the group-leaders. She stated emphatically that while she was interested in being in the group, she refused to pay for further therapy relating to the damage that was caused by her first therapy. Anne was trying to hold the leaders responsible for what previously had happened and to punish her prior therapist through punishing them. The leaders were empathic with Anne's feelings and were tempted to waive her fee. Nonetheless, they adhered to the agency policy that clients pay what they are able to pay. While they could appreciate her feelings, they could not make up for the hurts she had experienced elsewhere. Although Anne was furious with their decision, she did decide to join the group and pay the required fee. Following completion of her group experience, Anne continued in individual therapy.

Another countertransference issue involved the group leaders' anger and discomfort as they listened to the group members recount their experiences. The leaders' overidentification with these patients sometimes became an obstacle to facilitating further discussion. The leaders found it helpful to have regular consultation as well as to talk together after each group session. This minimized the likelihood that their own feelings would become inadvertent obstacles to the group.

Still another countertransference issue that threatened to become a barrier to effective work was the leaders' own initial fears of harassment or accusations of slander. This fear helped them understand the victims' similar fears. It was sobering to learn from WICC staff that these fears were realistic, as some patients had actually been threatened by their therapists when they had pursued complaints to licensing boards.

Grief Work

Each of the group members had experienced a profound loss as a result of sexual exploitation by the former therapist. In most cases, the therapist had suggested that this sexual involvement would help solve their problems. For many, the therapist's sexual advances raised their needs to believe that they indeed were lovable, interesting, and desireable. For some, there had been a greater degree of sexual response than in other relationships. Therefore, when the involvement ended, there was not only the loss of hope that therapy would be helpful, but also a loss of enhanced self-esteem and sexual pleasure. In addition, the involvement with the therapist had distracted those patients from establishing and working on satisfying relationships with others. When cut off from their therapists, many realized how isolated they had become.

Because of these losses, grief issues were a common group theme. The patients needed to conclude the old relationships in order to begin new ones with other people. The following case example illustrates one woman's mourning process and how this process facilitated a more effective and satisfying relationship with her children.

> Marilyn had been referred for counseling for help with her marital problems. Her husband was an alcoholic, and she hoped to obtain information and guidance about problems connected with alcoholism. Her counselor told her that she could be a "better wife, mother, employee, and friend" if she cooperated in some sexual fondling with him. She agreed because she believed him. As a result, she became distracted from the problems in her relationship with her husband. When she began to distrust the helpfulness of this approach, questioned the counselor, and finally threatened to speak with others on the staff about their behavior in therapy, the counselor accused her of "playing one of her crazy games."
>
> At first Marilyn appeared to be in an initial stage of mourning. She seemed disbelieving as she described the events surrounding therapy and her subsequent divorce. She wondered if the loss of her marriage was related to her therapy. As she realized the seriousness of her situation, she decided to turn to WICC for advocacy services. She wished to make a complaint against the counselor and his agency, and later she decided to file a formal charge of unethical conduct.
>
> After her first group ended, Marilyn decided to join a second group because she was feeling anxious about the upcoming litigation. In this second group, she described feelings of pervasive anxiety and anger. She

was tearful as she spoke of feeling responsible for her divorce and her children's loss of their father. She went on to describe her difficulties in setting limits for her teenage children, and she related this to her guilt. The group helped Marilyn to express her feelings at her own pace. Gradually, she became able to set limits for her children, thereby gaining more control in her relationship with them. This, in turn, helped her feel more successful.

As part of the grieving, it was as important for group members to talk about their affectionate feelings toward their former therapists as it was to express their anger and distrust.

Betrayal by Professionals Associated with the Therapist

All of the women in the groups reported a sense of betrayal by other agency personnel with whom the former therapist was associated or by those who had originally referred them. Several group members wondered why other agency personnel associated with the former counselor were not aware of what had gone on and why they had not attempted to stop the exploitation. Others who had complained to referring physicians or counselors felt their concerns were discounted. As a result of therapy in the group, one woman decided to make an appointment with her referring counselor to tell her how she felt about the dismissal of her concerns about an exploitative therapist.

The Group as Mirror for Other Relationships

By examining the group interaction in the "here and now", members could see how their difficulties within the group were like those in their families, friendships, and work settings.[1] The following example illustrates how here and now observations helped to highlight conflicts and dilemmas that group members faced in both past and current relationships.

> Martha spoke elatedly of how much better she was feeling in contrast with the previous meeting, when she had shared desperate and suicidal feelings. Her comments in the preceding session had alarmed all the group members. No one believed that she had recovered so quickly, yet all participants remained silent. In the subsequent session, Jane expressed anger that the group leaders had not confronted Martha more directly with her unbelievable recovery. She had felt hesitant to express her own disbelief in Martha's sudden change, and blamed the group leaders from whom she "took her leads" for her own silence. If they remained mute, so should she. Martha, on the other hand, wondered why no one had challenged her and instead had kept their distance. In fact, she was aware that she had not felt as well as she had claimed.
>
> Jane began to examine her own silence and talked about her family's style of denying serious events. For example, when her sister

had returned home from the hospital after a suicide attempt, the parents spoke of her having had the flu. In her relationship with her former therapist, she had also tried to pretend that his fondling was not really happening. The group noted that Jane's feelings and perceptions were accurate and helpful to them. So why should she be reluctant to share them? Jane then revealed her fear that being perceptive might lead to abandonment by significant others. She noted that her own family did not like her to be critical or to say what she thought. Awareness of her fear of speaking out resulted in Jane's taking risks to share her perceptions in the group and elsewhere.

Reality Testing

Jane's example illustrates a dominant theme in all of the groups: a distrust of one's own reality testing. While most of the women had a sense that something was wrong in the relationship with the therapist, they had distrusted their doubts. Some also distrusted their decisions not to pursue complaint options available through legal or professional organization channels. A major function of the group, using the here and now approach, was to encourage sharing of feelings and to support trust in one's feelings and unique judgments.

Guilt

A major need among group participants was to talk about guilt feelings and about their feelings of responsibility in initiating sexual relationships with their therapists. Several had felt attracted to their therapists and believed these feelings had encouraged or caused the sexual involvement. Some victims had felt initially relieved that the sexual relationship diverted them from talking about the problems that they were afraid to face. Group members asked for help in talking about their guilt feelings and experienced some relief in knowing that others also had felt guilt.

Need for Education

Another major need expressed by all of the group members was to clarify what is appropriate and ethical treatment. The group leaders were often asked to repeat that it is not appropriate for therapists to act out sexual feelings, even though the therapists as well as the patient may have such feelings. It was difficult for these women to comprehend that sexual contact is inappropriate even when invited by the patient. Group members referred frequently to an article by Schoener et al.,[2] that spells out the therapist's responsibility, as though needing repeated assurance that it is the therapist's responsibility to set limits for acting on feelings.

Confusion regarding what constitutes therapy was also expressed. Specifically, there was confusion about whether therapy is supposed to be an actual reenactment of earlier family experience; this was especially true for women who had been told by their therapists that the sexual relationship would help them work through their earlier child-parent relationships. These patients needed to learn that effective therapy cannot literally reenact earlier relationships, but rather should clarify and sometimes solve the problems by helping them express in words their important thoughts and feelings.

The group leaders had an opportunity to model the use of boundaries within the therapeutic relationship. For example:

> In the final minutes of the last session, Denise spontaneously invited all of the group members to her home for a party to be held in the near future. The group members were interested and pleased by the invitation. However, the leaders were uncomfortable, feeling that the boundaries of the therapeutic relationship would become blurred in such a social setting. One of the leaders stated that although she appreciated the invitation, she considered it inappropriate to socialize with patients. She said she would, however, be pleased to meet with group members again in the agency, should they wish to have another group meeting. The group members were satisfied by this answer and decided to request a follow-up meeting a few months later.

OUTCOME

As a result of group treatment, the patients experienced the following outcomes: relief in having a confidential opportunity to share their experiences with others, relief in discovering some universality in experiences and feelings, benefit from education on how to become an effective mental health services consumer, and benefit from the opportunity to mourn. These experiences allowed them to form new and more satisfying relationships. Group members also learned to trust their feelings and use them as tools in relationships with others. Problems for which the victims originally had sought help could once again be addressed. As one woman said, "The problems for which I originally sought help have been 'on hold' all these years. As a result of work in the group, I can now move forward." This sense of becoming "unstuck" was experienced by nearly everyone.

DISPOSITION AT TERMINATION

Many of the group members chose to continue in other types of groups in order to work further on problems. One member, who had been struggling with issues surrounding her sexuality, joined an educational discussion group on sexuality. Several women felt renewed interest in defining career goals and arranged to obtain career counseling. One member, who had experienced low self-esteem since childhood due to a severe learning disability, gained enough confidence to obtain psychological testing and consultation. Alcohol dependency problems prompted another member to obtain an evaluation and recommendation regarding chemical dependency treatment. Other members continued in Alcoholics Anonymous, and several joined Al-Anon groups. One woman decided to participate in another group for patients sexually exploited by therapists because her anger toward therapists and anxiety about upcoming litigation became overwhelming. Several participants were referred back to WICC for consultation and support regarding the decision to confront their therapists or to seek legal action.

CONCLUSIONS

The brief therapy groups were experienced as critical stepping stones in the recovery process. At the onset of the groups, many of the victims were angry and distrustful of therapists and felt cynical about the therapeutic process. The gradual trust-building between group leaders and group members, the growing relief from shame and isolation, and the use of clear and respectful boundaries in the group helped to restore members' faith in the possible value of therapy. This corrective experience also helped them to re-identify the problems that originally had led them to seek therapy years earlier. Many realized that their problems had been "on hold" for years and became ready to finally move on in their lives.

Our patients represent a group that is often ignored by the professional community. Because of our favorable results, we recommend that such services be made available elsewhere. If this is not feasible, educational materials that describe appropriate treatment and resources for clients who have concerns about their treatment should be made available to the public as a preventive measure.

NOTES

1. I. Yalom, *The Theory and Practice of Group Psychotherapy* (New York: Basic Books, 1975), pp. 121–40.

2. G. Schoener, J. Milgrom, and J. Gonsiorek, "Responding Therapeutically to Clients Who Have Been Sexually Involved with Their Psychotherapists." Unpublished monograph, 1983.

18

Open-Ended Group Therapy for Victims of Therapist Sexual Misconduct

Phyllis A. Kaufman and Elizabeth Harrison

Patients reporting seduction and sexual intimacy with former therapists have been so consistently disbelieved and blamed by many traditional psychotherapists that they have tended to retreat into self-blame and isolation with their secret. The authors, a psychiatrist and a social worker, have found the victims of such therapist abuse to be severely traumatized and left with sequelae similar to that observed in victims of incest and rape (Burgess and Holmstrom 1979).

Recognizing that a growing population in their caseloads of women who had been involved in a sexual relationship with a former therapist had remarkably similar presenting symptoms, the authors decided to unite these patients into a treatment group. The women all seemed to fit the diagnostic category of post-traumatic distress disorder, either acute or delayed. The authors felt that group methods would be the most effective approach to the treatment of post-traumatic stress disorder and that these women, who previously were being seen individually, would be strengthened by the support from one another and by the sharing of a common traumatic past. The two therapists together leading the group would provide more therapeutic availability, as well as an arena for dealing with splitting, which they expected would occur when the group members projected their rage at the offending therapists in the group setting. Two therapists can also provide role model assertiveness and comfort with confrontaton—needs that were expected to arise in the group.

GROUP DESCRIPTION

The initial group was formed of women drawn from both therapists' caseloads. Intake was open, and new members would be invited. The group members who joined later were either self-referred or referred by other therapists or by various women's organizations. Newspaper and television publicity stimulated several self-referrals. All intakes were screened in individual interviews prior to being invited into the group. Incumbent group members were told in advance when a new member would be joining them. Group size was limited to ten and fluctuated between four and eight members. The group met for 18 months.

Criteria for new members included a history of sexual intimacy with a former therapist, physician, counselor, or clergyman and an ability to withstand the confrontations of the group process. No victims who were suicide risks were admitted to the group. Some group members supplemented group sessions with individual treatment. Others participated only in group sessions and requested individual sessions from either of the group leaders as needed. All group members were women.

GROUP GOALS

The common goal for all participants was to resolve conflict and to reduce pain and suffering resulting from the victimization. The direction of treatment varied with the individual and her situation. In this sense, there were individual and immediate goals as well as group goals. For example, an individual goal might be to maintain the strength to function during the stress of testifying in a licensing board hearing. A goal shared by several participants was to invite the offending therapist to join them in confrontation sessions with the group leaders.

More general group goals included:

1. Rebuilding trust in the psychotherapeutic process within a safer therapeutic milieu.
2. Understanding and resolving unresolved transference.
3. Reducing isolation through sharing of similar experiences and responses to the victimization.
4. Building and enhancing self-esteem through empathic identification with a support network that extends beyond the group session time and through therapist role-modeling and self-disclosing (Williams 1976).
5. Alleviating guilt and self-blame through victim education about therapist responsibility, ethics, and the concept of transference and countertransference.
6. Supporting self-validation and responsible action-taking. This might include participating in a mediation session with the offending therapist, requesting restitution for therapy costs, reporting to a licensing board, and bringing a civil action for damages.

GROUP ISSUES

Trust. Issues of trust were pervasive and understandably exaggerated in this group for whom trust had previously been so violated. Relationships with the group therapists, group members, physicians, and even friends ranged from suspicion and lack of trust to idealism and excessive gullibility.

Dependency. Related to trust were issues of dependency. These included a fear of needing the therapist and the group as well as an excessive dependency on the therapists and group (wanting to be taken care of, requesting support beyond group hours, making daily telephone calls with numerous requests for advice and help).

Self-esteem. Self-blame, guilt, and self-doubt were massive as a result of the trauma. Day-to-day functioning was affected, causing further erosion of self-esteem.

Sexuality. Sexual functioning was disturbed by the trauma, raising questions for the victims about the ability to perform sexually or to love again. This, in turn, raised additional questions and doubts about sexual identity and sexual preference.

Abandonment and loss. Grief work was needed to resolve the intense feelings of abandonment following the loss of the loved, trusted therapist. Anticipation of future abandonment interfered with the ability to concentrate on new objects, to trust, and to fantasize and dream about future events.

Validation of anger. Victims of sexual abuse at the hands of their therapists have reason to be angry. They have been cheated, abandoned, sexually exploited, and psychologically damaged. Nevertheless, victims often direct anger toward themselves or feel helpless and hopeless when anger toward the offender would be the more appropriate response.

THE GROUP PROCESS

A gradual evolution from alienation and isolation to a growing trust in others and in self is one way to view the group process. It is a process of self and group validation, reducing guilt and self-blame and enhancing personal identity and self-esteem. The group process is characterized by support, education, and a growing sense of righteous anger.

Because the group was open ended with new members joining at any time, the group process was enhanced by a series of individual treatment processes supportive of new members as they entered. They were welcomed by empathic survivors who understood and were eager to convince them that the loss they had experienced was a wrong done to them. The struggle of the newer members allowed the other participants to see the progress that they had made and to recognize themselves in the women just beginning the group sessions.

The stages of the group treatment process were as follows:

1. *Acceptance into the group* occurred when the patient was in an acute state of depression, post-traumatic shock, and low self-esteem. Guilt, self-blame, and even self-destructive ideation were usually evident and were confronted by other group members. A strong attachment to the offending therapist was evident, no matter how long ago the abuse had occurred.

2. *Group cohesion* was enhanced by the sharing of similarities of experience, which released the secrets that had kept the victim isolated and stimulated the discovery that no one was alone in experience or reaction. The occasional discovery that another woman in the group had been victimized by the same offending therapist also worked as a unifying force.

3. *Sympathy and anger for the other* emerged as group participants listened to the details of other victimizations. This was enhanced by support from group leaders and by education about the responsibilities of therapists to be ethical and aware of transference and countertransference. Insight into why they could experience sympathy and anger for another person but not for themselves advance group members to the next stage of the process.

4. *Self-righteous anger* for oneself and the victimization emerged and promoted a letting go of the attachment to the offending therapist.

5. *Grief reactions*, characterized by sadness, ambivalence, rage, and frequent shifts among these states, were evidence of the gradual letting go of the former therapist and were precipitated by the experience of appropriate self-righteous anger.

6. *Anxiety and neediness* usually increased after the first experience of rage, which often resulted in fears of abandonment, rejection, or loss.

7. *Frustration* by the therapists and the group was evoked as the patients realized that increased needs would not be met and many requests would be denied. The intensity of the frustration and disappointment led to the next step in the process.

8. *Anger and disappointment* directed at the therapists and group members followed frustration. Confrontation of this anger in the group initiated the most difficult stage in the process. Some participants could not tolerate the frustration and resulting angry feelings. Anticipating rejection, they left the group. The stronger and emotionally healthier members continued, emerging more comfortable with the assertive expression of appropriate anger. Patients were encouraged to express anger in the group in order to experience a safe, nonrejecting milieu for expression.

9. *Appropriate and adaptive use of anger,* self-directed toward action, self-preservation, and change, emerged and took the form of future planning. This included improved vocational planning, planned confrontation sessions with offending therapists using the group therapists as mediators, requests to offending therapists for restitution of treatment expenses, and plans for exploring litigation possibilities.

10. *Termination* included reviewing and consolidating one's progress in the group and saying goodbye to group members. Individual treatment addressing other issues continued for some group participants.

IMPACTING EVENTS

The event having most positive impact on the group process was the mediation sessions between a cooperating former therapist and patient. This offered the patient the opportunity to confront the offending therapist with her feelings about the violation of trust and its impact on her and to hear the therapist take full responsibility for the abuse. This is significant for patients, as they blame themselves less after the therapist's admission. The session also offers the patient an opportunity to ask for financial restitution. The mediation session appears to be healing for both patient and the offending therapist, and it is often successful in avoiding the expense and stress of litigation when the offending therapist is cooperative.

The group process was also impacted by publicity, which became a problem for the group. As anticipated, the need for such a group was viewed with suspicion from some mental health colleagues and was sought-after news for the media. Although the publicity brought forward numerous victims, there was increased anxiety among group members that their identities would be discovered. The group leaders were increasingly aware of their growing isolation in the therapeutic community as colleauges became more curious and suspicious. Who was attending group sessions and what the therapists knew about them were open to speculation.

Detrimental to any therapeutic process, group or individual, is litigation. The victim's trust is violated or expected to be violated once a therapist and therapeutic records are subpoenaed and the legal process of discovery begins. Litigation is a major stressor in itself and disrupts and complicates any treatment process. It was this factor that had the greatest negative impact on the group sessions and eventually led to their termination. The impact of litigation continues long after therapy ends. Continued reasearch and experience is needed in the area of combining psychotherapy and litigation, as the patient involved in litigation is probably most in need of the therapist's support.

REFERENCES

Burgess, A. W., and L. L. Holmstrom. 1979. *Rape: Crisis and Recovery.* Bowie, MD: Brady Co.

Williams, E. F. 1976. *Notes of a Feminist Therapist.* New York: Praeger.

19

Dynamics of Treatment Groups for Victims of Therapist Sexual Misconduct

Debra S. Borys, C. Buf Meyer, Roberta L. Falke, and Janet L. Sonne

The increased professional and public attention over the past ten years to the topic of sexual intimacy between psychotherapists and their patients has resulted in greater acknowledgement of the scope and seriousness of the problem. A recent task force study sponsored by the California State Psychological Association estimated that 6 percent of psychotherapists have been sexually intimate with one or more of their clients (Bouhoutsos et al. 1983). Of the clients involved, 90 percent suffered adverse effects, often severe. In response to this problem, the Post Therapy Support Program (PTSP) was established in 1982 at the University of California at Los Angeles Psychology Clinic. The program provides group and individual therapy to people who have been sexually involved with their therapists.

This chapter describes our observations based on two time-limited treatment groups and over 25 interviews conducted with individuals who have been sexually intimate with their therapists. Many of the individuals entering the groups showed symptoms of post-traumatic stress disorder. Overall, most of the patients felt desperate, alone, embarrassed, and vulnerable. Because many of the group members were acutely distressed in this way, the groups were designed to be primarily supportive, rather than uncovering.

The therapists with whom the group members, all women, had been involved include marriage and family counselors, psychologists, psychiatrists, social workers, and paraprofessionals. The demographics of these clinicians differed in two ways from what previous research had led us to expect. First, three of the women had been involved with female therapists, whereas an overwhelming majority of the cases reported in the literature involve male therapists and female clients (Holroyd 1983). Second, several of the

This chapter is adapted from J. Sonne, C. Meyer, D. Borys, and V. Marshall, "Reactions to Sexual Intimacy in Therapy," *American Journal of Orthopsychiatry* 55 (1985): 183–89.

offending practitioners were in their 30s and 40s, considerably younger than the average age reported in the literature (Bouhoutsos et al. 1983; D'Addario 1977; Taylor and Wagner 1976).

IMPACT OF PATIENT PROBLEM AREAS ON GROUP SESSIONS

Based on our observations, the clinical population appeared to be characterized by difficulties in several major areas, including mistrust of self and others, difficulties with interpersonal boundaries, low self-esteem, and difficulties with anger management. These difficulties became manifest in the patients' lives and in the group sessions. Our discussion focuses on the impact these problem areas had on the group process.

Mistrust of Self and Others

Not surprisingly, our patients displayed a great deal of mistrust toward the group leaders and their fellow group members. The therapists were challenged regarding their level of training, their competence, and their motiviations for leading the group. They were accused of trying to meet their own neeeds (i.e., research or training) at the expense of group members. At times, members directly voiced their desire to equalize the balance of power between themselves and the group leaders. Some resented having to take a screening test and asked the therapists if they were willing to do the same to prove their "fitness" for leading the group. Leaders of one group were asked to sign confidentiality contracts that group members had completed in the initial meeting. On the rare occasions when the therapists made psychodynamic interpretations, some of the women became very angry. They claimed the therapists were self-servingly trying to discount the patients' perceptions, much as their previous therapists had done. It was very important to these group members that the therapists agree with their perceptions. This seemed to reflect both their understandable mistrust of therapists and their desire to have their own perceptions confirmed by an authority figure.

Mistrust of fellow group members was also evidenced in several ways. Participants were hesitant to share their feelings toward other group members. Several individuals complained that the participants were too polite with each other, while others were afraid to be honest because some members were viewed as too fragile. One of the groups was characterized by poor attendance and chronic tardiness; this may have both reflected and perpetuated a lack of group cohesiveness and trust. Not surprisingly, the issue of trust within the group came up most forcefully around the matter of touching among participants. Offering physical comfort, such as holding hands while a member was crying, was experienced as very threatening by some patients.

Difficulties with Interpersonal Boundaries

Group members had difficulty setting appropriate boundaries in their relationships within and outside of the therapy group. While desiring nurturance from others, some members feared that emotional involvement in a relationship might mean losing their own identity and objectivity, as had happened in their previous therapy relationship. For example, one member feared she might slip into a caretaker role in the group at the expense of having her own needs met. Other members questioned whether they could be both independent and intimate. Some of the women felt guilty when they assertively set limits in outside relationships or in the group, while others described how they hated themselves for giving in to others' demands.

Group members at times tested the limits of their relationship with group leaders. They requested longer sessions and asked the therapists to make more personal disclosures. One of the groups invited the therapists to dinner with them and appeared disappointed when the invitation was declined. In a later session, however, they expressed relief that the therapists had set limits on social contacts.

Low Self-Esteem

The two groups differed in the extent of self-blame expressed, with such feelings more prominent in the first group. The second focused much of their anger outward, as evidenced by group pressure for all members to feel angry at their former therapists. This marked externalization of anger appeared to keep members of the second group from acknowledging their feelings of self-blame and exploring their own contributions to the sexualized therapy.

Many of the women were afraid of being independent. In the first group, members were relatively inactive and dependent on the therapists for structuring sessions. For example, they expressed disappointment when unfinished issues from previous weeks were not brought up again, but they did not want to take responsibility for reintroducing these topics. Similarly, they wanted to exchange telephone numbers with other group members, but looked to the therapists to organize this effort. Being smaller and more cohesive, the second group was more active and more independent of the therapists.

Certain behaviors in group sessions seemed to be attempts to regain the sense of "specialness" members had experienced with their previous therapists. For example, some members would draw attention to any individual contact they had made with the group therapists, fellow group members, or other members of the program staff. Other members seemed to mourn their lost sense of specialness, with some women disparaging the group because it didn't have the same "magic" as their previous therapy.

Difficulties with Anger Management

The two groups differed markedly in the way their members managed anger. Members of the first group had difficulty expressing anger, whether directed towards the former therapist, the present group leaders, other group members, or significant others. The second group was characterized by more overt anger expression. The one woman in this group who continued to feel positively toward her former therapist was repeatedly encouraged by group members to identify unacknowledged anger.

Anger toward the group therapists, other group members, and significant others seemed to be expressed in a passive, nonverbal manner (e.g., grimacing or ignoring others' comments). On those occasions when it was voiced openly, it was typically presented in an intellectualized or sarcastic fashion. As another means of gaining distance from such feelings, some of the patients would wait until the following session to reveal they had been angry in the previous group meeting.

BENEFITS AND LIMITATIONS OF THE GROUP APPROACH

In light of the complexity and sensitivity of the issues involved in treating patients who have been sexually involved with their therapists, it is difficult to imagine a flawless intervention. The group therapy approach appeared to offer several benefits to the participants, but also had some significant limitations. Opportunities and constraints are inherent in a group approach.

Most of the women in our groups stated that they benefited from their participation. They felt they had received support and were less isolated. Moreover, the patients reported that their disturbing thoughts, fantasies, and dreams about the sexualized therapy experience had dissipated significantly by the end of the group.

Feelings of self-blame were also reduced. Most participants entered the group feeling intense self-blame, inappropriately assuming full responsibility for the sexualized therapy relationship (even for the therapist's actions). As the clients shared their stories with one another, they saw that they did not blame each other and consequently felt less guilty themselves.

As feelings of self-blame and guilt diminished, expression of anger toward the former therapists became more prominent. While the women struggled with ways of dealing with this anger, they gradually learned more appropriate and assertive means for expressing themselves. Several group members reported that this new-found assertiveness extended to relationships with parents and partners.

Although the benefits of the group therapy were significant, limitations were also apparent. The progression from confusion and self-blame to appropriate anger expression was gradual. As a result, most members were not ready to explore realistically their own role in the sexualized therapy relationship until near the end of the time-limited groups. At that point, insufficient time remained for exploring this issue in depth.

Members frequently complained about having insufficient time in the group sessions. The women felt that the group discussions raised important issued that could be only partially explored. A few of the members appeared to expect the group therapists to meet all of their needs within each session. This expectation seemed to stem from the patients' engaging in an idealizing transference and having difficulty recognizing the realistic boundaries of the therapeutic context. Those patients who were concurrently engaged in individual treatment found the more focused therapy time in that modality invaluable in exploring the emotional reactions stimulated by group discussions. Furthermore, it was our impression that the patients who were in both group and individual therapy were less distressed from week to week.

The nature of the group and the presenting problems of the members heavily influenced the working orientation of the therapists. The consensus of the program staff was that most of the patients entered the groups too distressed and vulnerable to engage in uncovering therapy. Group members were also understandably suspicious of therapists and unlikely to give the group leaders' interpretations much credibility, especially in the beginning. Consequently, we did not interpret unconscious feelings or behavior unless a client expressed curiosity about them. Similarly, the group therapists tended to be active and did not encourage the development of transference. Initially, the women's perceptions of their previous therapists tended to be distorted by a strong positive transference; they struggled to integrate these positive feelings with their recognition of the therapist's inappropriate behavior. Consequently, we encouraged objective perceptions of the group therapists to help participants recognize the fallibility of authority figures and to regain trust in their own perceptions.

COUNTERTRANSFERENCE

An important aspect of our work was regular discussion among co-therapists and other program staff regarding the group therapists' reactions and perceptions of the group. As a result, we recognized a range of common countertransference reactions.

As noted by Ulanov (1979), the therapist is likely to feel angry at a previous therapist who had sex with the patient. The more the subsequent therapist identifies with the patient, the greater the outrage is likely to be. Thus, a therapist who has experienced victimization or is of the same gender as the patient may find such anger through identification a particular problem. Such reactions arise in work with other victimized populations (e.g., incest and rape victims) as well.

Other aspects of the patient's previous therapy experience may anger the subsequent therapist. The misuse of the profession by a colleague may be resented. The unethical behavior of the previous therapists may seem to tarnish the profession, thereby reflecting poorly on the new therapist. As a result, the new clinician's credibility is likely to be diminished in the eyes of the patient. This mistrust, along with the intense rage typically presented by these patients, makes the establishment of a therapeutic alliance difficult. All of these factors greatly complicate the work of the subsequent therapist. During therapy sessions, anger over these matters can easily foster both overt and subtle devaluation of the previous clinician. Devaluation of the offending practitioner by the subsequent therapist may encourage maladaptive splitting, rather than the integration of the patient's positive and negative feelings toward the previous clinician.

It is not uncommon to want to be "perfect" for patients who have been mistreated by a previous therapist. This impulse has a number of possible roots. The subsequent therapist may identify with the previous clinician and/or the types of feelings acted upon. Such identification can lead to a sense of shared responsibility or guilt for the sexual misconduct. The new therapist may compensate for this guilt by striving to be perfect. In an attempt to be as different as possible from the offending therapist, a clinician may neglect to recognize and manage appropriately sexual feelings toward clients. In addition to using reaction formation, subsequent therapists may protect themselves from the threat of misconduct by projecting the danger onto the unethical colleauge (Ulanov 1979).

In an attempt to be the ideal therapist, some clinicians become extremely self-conscious, thus impeding their empathy and observational skills. Others become overly indulgent and forego interpretations or limit-setting that might displease the patient. However, these patients do not need another over-involved clinician; they need to learn the appropriate limits of the therapeutic relationship and work through their reactions to these limits.

There is a real strain on the countertransference of clinicians working with this population because of the magnitude of the patient's transference. Its intensity most likely results from the patient's overinvolvement with the previous therapist. The transference is characterized by its rapid development, stronger than usual needs for the therapist's approval, and simultaneous outrage, jealousy, and mistrust of the clinician's power and position. An ill-prepared therapist may try to minimize or deflect the patient's projections of anger and dependency, rather than identifying them for the patient and encouraging their exploration. The intense rage and dependency of these patients can at times resemble aspects of the transference of borderline personalities. Familiarity with the management of countertransference in the treatment of borderline patients (Briggs 1979; Gutheil 1985; Kernberg 1975) can therefore help with the challenges that arise in working with this population.

CONCLUSIONS

One step toward reducing the occurrence of sexual intimacy in therapy is to learn more about the circumstances under which it occurs. We need to obtain more empirical data on the clients involved. In addition, we need further investigation of whether these clients share any personality dynamics. We found some commonalities among our clients, but empirical study is needed to investigate whether our observations are generalizable to the population as a whole. What is the best treatment for such individuals? We believe that a combination of group and individual therapy is optimal, but we have no objective data to support this hypothesis. Additionally, while we successfully employed a supportive approach, the utility of psychodynamic and behavioral approaches (e.g., assertion training) merits investigation.

REFERENCES

The authors express their gratitude for the contributions provided by the staff of the UCLA Post Therapy Support Program and for the support of the UCLA Psychology Clinic.

Bouhoutsos, J., J. C. Holroyd, H. Lerman, H. Forer, and M. Greenberg. 1983. "Sexual Intimacy between Psychotherapists and Patients." *Professional Psychology* (14): 185.

Briggs, D. 1979. "The Trainee and the Borderline Client: Countertransference Pitfalls." *Clinical Social Work Journal* (6): 133–46.

D'Addario, L. 1977. "Sexual Relationships between Female Clients and Male Therapists." Ph. D. dissertation, California School of Professional Psychology.

Gutheil, T. G. 1985. "Medicolegal Pitfalls in the Treatment of Borderline Patients." *American Journal of Psychiatry* (142): 9–14.

Holroyd, J. C. 1983. "Erotic Contact As an Instance of Sex-Biased Therapy." In *Bias in Psychotherapy,* edited by J. Murray and P. R. Abramson. New York: Praeger.

Kernberg, O. 1975. "Transference and Countertransference in the Treatment of Borderline Patients." *Journal of the National Association of Private Psychiatric Hospitals* (7):14–24.

Taylor, B. J., and N. W. Wagner. 1976. "Sex between Therapists and Clients: A Review and Analysis." *Professional Psychology* (7): 593–601.

Ulanov, A. B. 1979. "Follow-up Treatment in Cases of Patient-Therapist Sex." *Journal of the American Academy of Psychoanalysis* (7): 101–10.

Index

abandonment: dread of, 149; and loss, 175

administrative safequards, checklist of, 161–162

aggression, feelings of, 81

ambivalence, toward therapist and therapy, 146

American Psychiatric Association (APA), 95, Committee on Women, 120, 123; debates of sexual abuse issue, 121

anesthetized patients, sexual abuse of 61–65; aftermath, 65; civil suits, 63–64, community response to, 61–62; consequences to anesthesiologist, 63; official response to, 63; patient response, 64–65

anger, 31, 39, 47, 81, 181; validation, 175

anger management, difficulties with, 181

animals, in sexually explicit cartoons, 116

assault and battery, 13

assertion training, 184

assertive action, 82

behavior: ethical, 6; standards of, 18

betrayal, 31, 78; by doctor, 89; professionals associated with the therapist, 169

Board of Trustees, 121

bondage, to a therapist, 146

budget allocation, 126

California State Psychological Association, 178

cardiologist, sexual exploitation case, 28, 37–41

cartoon content analysis coding instrument (CCACI), 109

cartoon, sexual exploitation, 107; characters, 112; content analysis, 108–109, clients and other characters, 115; of health professionals, 113; illegal or unethical activity, 109; results of contents analysis, 117; setting, 112; sexual activity, 110; violent or morbid activity, 111

cartoon scenarios by specific health profession, 116

case disposition procedures, 22

child-adult sexual activity, 1

childhood experiences, replaying, 146

child molestation, 133–141; signs of, 138

children, sexual abuse of, 1, 99–106

civil lawsuit, 12–13, 56; corroborative evidence, 57; first step in, 57; in sexual abuse of anesthetized patients, 63–64

codes of ethics, 11, 19

coercion, 137

Committee on Women, 126

community, goals of, 105

community response, to sexual abuse of anesthetized patients, 61–62

community and social standards, 12

complaint, processing a, 15–18

complaint filing, 19–20

confidentiality, victims, 166

consultation, therapist-patient sexual contact, 148–150

consumer education, 21

continuing education, 21

Council on National Affairs, 121, 123

Council on Research, 121

countertransference, 167, 182–184

credibility, treatment issues, 46–48

criminal action, 13

criminal justice system, response of to patient sexual abuse, 90

crisis situation, creation of, 148

denial, of abuse incident, 77, 133

dentists, cartoon scenarios, 117

dependency, 175

disbelief, 31, 61, 133
disclosure: fear of, 133; molestations, 30–31; sexual abuse, 76; stress and, 77, 88
dissatisfaction, professional, 144
distress, newly developed symptoms of, 138
District Branch (DB) women's committees, 120, 124

education, need for, 170
employer action, 13
Ethical Principles of Psychologists, 6, 11
ethical standards, 11; review of, 22
evaluation, therapist-patient sexual contact, 148–150
evidence, obtaining, 69–70

false accusation, 82
fantasies, in therpeutic relationship, 144
fear, 137
flashback symptoms, 83

general physicians, cartoon scenarios, 116
generativity, 144; failed, 146
genital inadequacy, 144
grief, 31
grief work, 168–169, 175
group cohesion, 166
group sessions, impact of patient problem areas on, 179
group therapy: benefits, 181–182; limitations, 182; long term, 148
guardian-ward relationship, 11
guilt, 170, 181; excesses of, 147
gynecological examinations, sexual exploitations in, 7; coping with examination, 75; ending examination, 76; physiological response, 76
gynecologists/obstetricians, cartoon scenarios, 117
gynecologist-patient sexual abuse: abusive incident, 75; case history, 66–68; case investigation, 69–71; decisions after incident, 76; evaluation of victims, 74–83; medical board decision and community response, 79; medical board's view, 66–73; patients' background, 74; patients' reactions, 79–82; settlement negotiations, 71

health professionals: guidelines for, 18–20; roles of in sexual exploitation cases, 5–23; selection of for key roles, 22
helping professionals, response of to patient sexual abuse, 90

imagination, stifled, 147
immoral behavior, 11
impaired professionals, resources for, 22
impotence, 144
incest, 1
incest victims, 94
informed consent, 11
insurance coverage, as factor in malpractice litigation, 58
internal examinations, sexually abusive, 66
interpersonal awareness, 103
interpersonal boundaries, difficulties with, 180
intervention, goals of, 105
interview, sexual abuse victim, 56
intimacy: constricted, 147; irreversibility, 10; levels of, 8; in nonpsychotherapeutic settings, 7; varying standards, 10; vulnerabilities, 10; in professional setting, 7–12
intimacy vs. sex, 10

Joint Reference Committee (JRC), psychiatrist-patient sexual abuse study, 121–123, 125
justice vs. care, 103

legal process, 47–48

legal standards, 11; review of, 22
license revocation, 12, 72, 79
licensing, regulation of on national
    level, 48
licensure actions, advantages, 14
litigation, 177
long-term measures, 20–23

magazines, sexual exploitation in, 107;
    content analysis, 108–109
malpractice claims, sexual abuse, 124
malpractice coverage for sexual abuse
    cases, elimination of, 126–127
malpractice litigation, sexual abuse:
    interviewing victim, 56; in-
    vestigating cases, 57; jury selec-
    tion, 59; negotiation, 57–58;
    overview of cases, 49; special
    issues, 58–59; trial, 58
marriage counselors, cartoon scenarios,
    117
Maryland State Board of Examiners of
    Psychologists, licensing board
    case, 15
mediation, patient-therapist sexual
    situations, 154–155, 177; basic
    rule, 155
medical community, official response
    of to patient sexual abuse, 91
medical profession, goals of, 105
mistrust, of self and others, 179–180
molestation, 133; aftermath, 36; dis-
    closure of, 30–31; earlier in-
    cidents, 32; filing charges, 33;
    hospital reaction, 32; pretrial
    maneuvers, 33; reporting of,
    31–33; response to disclosure, 31;
    trial, 34
moral conflicts, of sex with children,
    100, 104; conventional orienta-
    tion, 104; egocentric orientation,
    104; individual orientation, 105
morality, issue of, 102
morality of justice and morality of
    care, conflict between, 103–104
mourning, 47

negotatiation, in civil case, 57

notice of claim, 49, 57
nurses, cartoon scenarios, 116

Oedipal fantasy, 144
official response, to sexual abuse of
    anesthetized patients, 63
open-ended group therapy, 173; goals,
    174; group description, 173; group pro-
    cess, 175; impacting events, 177;
    issues, 175; treatment process,
    176
outrage, 61

panic attacks, 47
patient response, to sexual abuse of
    anesthetized patients, 64–65
patients: assistance to, 19; sexual
    attraction to, 20
pediatrician, sexual exploitation cases,
    27, 29–36
pediatrician pedophile, 99–106; moral
    analysis, 102–105; responsibility,
    105–106
pedophilia, classic characteristics
    of, 101
pedophiles, 99; sexual desires, 106
perpetrators, child molestations,
    136–137
physical contact, 7
Post Therapy Support Program
    (PTSP), 178
post-traumatic stress disorder (PTSD):
    classification, 133–134; criteria
    for, 137–138; diagnostic dilem-
    mas, 139; psychological assess-
    ment, 134–136; treatment recom-
    mendations, 139
powerlessness, 133; feeling of, 77, 78;
    strategies to neutralize, 78
preventive educational programs, 125
preventive measures, 20–23
prior bad acts, as evidence, 51
professional association review, 13
professional education, 20
proof, 56
psychiatrist-patient sexual contact, 120;
    survey to assess, 121

psychiatrist-patient sexual exploitation, 120; investigation phase I, 120–123; investigation phase II, 123–125; investigation phase III, 125–127

psychiatrists/psychologists, cartoon scenarios, 117

psychiatry, public image of, 124

psychic numbing in response to environment, 138

psychological diagnosis, 47

psychotherapist-patient sexual exploitation, time-limited treatment groups, 163–172

psychotherapy, 93

public disclosure, of case findings, 21

rage, 133, 147

rape, 1

rape crisis center, 84–91

reality testing, 146, 170

redress, options for, 12–14; malpractice litigation, 56; sexual misconduct, 19

Reisman Model for Child Cartoon Analysis, 109

rescue fantasy, 144

research, need for additional, 23

resentment, 133

retraining program, 72

role models, 21

sadness, 47

sanity, questioning of, 146

self-blame, 80, 181, 182

self-esteem, 145, 149–150, 175; low, 180

self-interest and responsibility, conflict between, 103

self-study, institutional resistance to, 120–127

self-worth, 59

settlement negotiations, sexual abuse case, 71–73

sexologist, cartoon scenarios, 117

sex rings, 99

sexual abuse: anesthetized patient, 61–65; gynecologic patient, 66–73; need for legislation on, 48

sexual abuse case: background, 45–46; questions for the profession, 48

sexual assault: long-term impact of, 89; victim reaction during, 87–88; victim reaction following, 88–89

sexual exploitation, defined, 1; reasons for, 2

sexual feelings, 96; expression of, 95; understanding, 94

sexual harassment, 11

sexual intimacy, 145; as form of therapeutic intervention, 7, 11; therapist/patient, 5–6. See also intimacy sexual involvement, patient disclosure of, 6

sexuality, 175

sexual misconduct, 1; group therapy, 173–184; license revocations, 5; prevention, 155–156 (see also therapist) sexual misconduct

sexual victimizations (see rape)

shame, excesses of, 147

shock, 31, 133

Southern California Psychiatric Society meeting, 95

state licensing board review, 14

statute of limitations, sexual abuse cases, 58

statutory rape, 13

stereotyping, 6

stress, 77

stressful event, reliving of, 137

Task Force on Sexual Exploitation by Counselors and Therapists, 2

therapist: as offender, 157–158; selection of new, 149

therapist-patient sexual contact: causes of, 143–146; consequences of, 146–148

therapist-patient sexual exploitation, secondary victims, 156–157

therapist sexual misconduct, 173; open-ended group therapy, 173–177; treatment groups, dynamics of, 178–184

time-limited treatment groups, 163–172; disposition at termination, 171–172; goals at intake, 165–166; group themes, 166; intake interviews, 164; as mirror for other relationships, 169; observations of therapists' roles at intake, 166; outcome, 171; problems at intake, 165
treatment groups, dynamics of, 178
treatment issues, 129–131
trust, 175; building, 56; loss of, 59; violation of, 177
transference love, 59

unequal power relationship, 11, 78
unethical behavior, 183; reporting, 149–150
unprofessional conduct, 11

victim(s), 85–86; finding other, 57; as first line of investigation, 102; goals of, 105; reaction immediately following assault, 88; reactions during assault, 87–88; secondary, 156–157
victim assistance, sources for, 158
victimizations, 86–87; patients backgrounds, 74

walk-in-counseling: aftermath, 155; initial meeting with victims, 152; mediation through processing session, 154; therapeutic response to victim, 153–154
Walk-In Counseling Center (WICC), 152–155, 163; supervisor/-counselor volunteer application of, 159–160
witnesses, sexual abuse cases, 57
Woman Against Medical Oppression, 62
Women Against Rape, 84
workshops on patient-therapist sexual relationships: dealing with the problem, 94; definding the problem, 93; questionnaire responses, 94–95

List of Contributors

Roberta J. Apfel, M.D., M.P.H.
Assistant Professor of Psychiatry, Harvard Medical School at Beth Israel Hospital, Boston.

Marylin Beck, Esq.
Attorney, Wynn and Wynn, P.C., Taunton, Massachusetts

Debra S. Borys, M.A.
Ph.D. Candidate in Clinical Psychology, University of California at Los Angeles

Marjorie Braude, M.D.
Senior Attending Staff, Westwood Hospital, Los Angeles

Ann Wolbert Burgess, R.N., D.N.Sc.
van Ameringen Professor of Psychiatric Nursing, University of Pennsylvania School of Nursing, Philadelphia

Daniel Burnstein, J.D.
Attorney, Williams, Jackson, and Spero, Boston

Marieanne Lindeqvist Clark, M.S.
Editor, Department of Health and Hospitals, Boston

B. Joyce Dale
Executive Director, Delaware County Women Against Rape, Media, Pennsylvania

Barry S. Elman
Analyst, U.S. Environmental Protection Agency, Washington, D.C.

Roberta L. Falke, M.A.
Ph.D. Candidate in Clinical Psychology, University of California at Los Angeles

Barbara Hull Foster, J.D.
Assistant Attorney General, State of Maryland, Baltimore

Calvin J. Frederick, Ph.D.
Professor, Department of Psychiatry and Biobehavioral Sciences, University of California at Los Angeles

Nanette K. Gartrell, M.D.
Assistant Professor of Psychiatry, Harvard Medical School, Boston

Elizabeth Harrison, M.D.
Clinical Faculty, School of Medicine, University of California at Davis

Carol R. Hartman, R.N., D.N.Sc.
Associate Professor and Coordinator of Graduate Program in Psychiatric Mental Health Nursing, Boston College, Boston

Judith L. Herman, M.D.
Assistant Clinical Professor of Psychiatry, Harvard Medical School, Boston

Phyllis A. Kaufman, M.S.W., A.C.S.W.
Clinical Faculty, School of Medicine, University of California at Davis

Lori Long, Esq.
Attorney, Goodwin, Procter, and Hoar, Boston

Ellen Thompson Luepker, M.S.W.
Clinical Social Worker and Group Treatment Supervisor, Minneapolis Family and Children's Service, Minneapolis

Audrey W. Mertz, M.D., M.P.H.
Assistant Clinical Professor of Psychiatry, Department of Psychiatry, School of Medicine, University of California at Davis

C. Buf Meyer, M.A.
Ph.D. Candidate in Clinical Psychology, University of California at Los Angeles

Jeanette Hofstee Milgrom, M.S.W.
Director of Consultation and Training, Walk-In Counseling Center, Minneapolis

Carolyn Moore Newberger, Ed.D.
Research Director, Family Development Study, Children's Hospital, Boston

Eli H. Newberger, M.D.
Director, Family Development Study, Children's Hospital, Boston

Frederic E. Oder, M.D.
Medical Director, Inpatient Psychiatric Unit, Beverly Hospital, Beverly, Massachusetts

Silvia Olarte, M.D.
Associate Clinical Professor of Psychiatry, New York Medical College, Valhalla

S. Michael Plaut, Ph.D.
Associate Professor of Psychiatry and Pediatrics, University of Maryland School of Medicine, Baltimore

Deborah F. Reisman
Staff Child Advocate, The House of Ruth's Shelter for Battered Women and Their Children, Washington, D.C.

Judith A. Reisman, Ph.D.
President and Executive Director, The Institute for Media Education, Arlington, Virginia

Carol Retsch-Bogart, M.S.W.
Clinical Social Worker, Minneapolis Family and Children's Service, Minneapolis

Gary R. Schoener, Licensed Psychologist
Executive Director, Walk-In Counseling Center, Minneapolis

Bennett Simon, M.D.
Associate Clinical Professor of Psychiatry, Harvard Medical School at Beth Israel Hospital, Boston

Janet L. Sonne, Ph.D.
Staff Psychologist, Loma Linda University Medical Center, Loma Linda, California

Karen B. Woelfel
Editorial Assistant, Department of Health and Hospitals, Boston

DATE DUE

GAYLORD			PRINTED IN U.S.A.